Researching and Writing
Across the Curriculum

Researching and Writing
Across the Curriculum

Christine A. Hult
Utah State University

✦ ✦ ✦

Allyn and Bacon

Boston ✦ London ✦ Toronto ✦ Sydney ✦ Tokyo ✦ Singapore

Copyright © 1996 by Allyn & Bacon
A Simon & Schuster Company
Needham Heights, Mass. 02194

Vice President and Editor in Chief, Humanities: Joseph Opiela
Editorial Assistant: Susannah Davidson
Marketing Manager: Lisa Kimball
Production Editor: Catherine Hetmansky
Editorial-Production Service: Ruttle, Shaw & Wetherill, Inc.
Text Designer: Denise Hoffman
Composition Buyer: Linda Cox
Manufacturing Buyer: Aloka Rathnam
Cover Administrator: Suzanne Harbison

Library of Congress Cataloging-in-Publication Data

Hult, Christine A.
    Research and writing across the curriculum/Christine A. Hult.
        p.   cm.
    Includes bibliographical references and index.
    ISBN 0-205-16838-8
    1. Report writing. 2. Research. 3. Library resources.
I. Title
LB2369.H84 1995
808.02–dc20   95-10390
                                               CIP

Printed in the United States of America
10 9 8 7 6 5 4 3 2 1   99 98 97 96 95

Contents

✦ ✦ ✦

PART TWO   MODEL RESEARCH PROJECTS

✦ CHAPTER 6   Writing a Review Paper in Science and Technology   179

✦ CHAPTER 7   Writing a Research Paper in Social Science   229

Preface

✦ ✦ ✦

Researching and Writing Across the Curriculum is an interdisciplinary research text that introduces you to research processes used in the sciences and technology, the social sciences, the humanities, and business. By reading this book you will gain experience in posing and solving problems common to an academic discipline, learning both primary research strategies and library research strategies. A comprehensive list of library resources is included to provide you with access to the important tools used by researchers.

Also included, as examples, are model student reports and research papers from various disciplines to show you how your peers have solved research problems similar to your own. The exercises are designed to guide you through research processes and to teach the important supporting skills of summarizing, synthesizing, and critiquing source materials. Complete listings of citations show you how to document your sources within each discipline. In addition, this textbook stresses principles of research presentation and documentation common to all disciplines.

Many students feel a bit inadequate when thinking about college-level research. Students often find they are introduced to various disciplines piecemeal. Students may be justifiably confused about the larger issue of research—its nature and use in the humanities, social sciences, sciences, and business. Furthermore, they may be confused about the relationships among academic disciplines. By providing students with an introduction to college writing, reading, thinking, and research, this book will show students important relationships among disciplines.

Many of the research guides now on the market fail to provide the broad introduction to research that students need. Traditional research texts are often focused very narrowly on the library "term paper." They discuss formal considerations at length, from the form of notecards and bibliography cards to the form of a completed term paper. But they do not explore the entire research process, which is an integral part of any successful research project. In contrast, *Researching and Writing* explains and fosters intellectual inquiry; compares research in the humanities with that in the sciences, social sciences, and business; and provides students with logical practice in research methodology.

Researching and Writing is divided into two main sections. Part One, "Research Methods," contains five chapters of general information about research methods and resources in the academic disciplines. In this part, students are first introduced to college research in general, and then to library resources (both general and discipline-specific), library research methods, and primary research methods. Next, students receive explicit instruction in the planning, writing, and presentation of research papers in any field.

Part Two, "Model Research Projects," offers specific guidance in writing research papers for science and technology, social science, humanities, and business. Exercises in Part Two are designed to help students conduct their own research projects in a systematic and organized fashion.

Researching and Writing is both a comprehensive guide to research processes and an easy-to-use, complete reference tool designed to be used throughout students' academic career and into their professional life. As with all research, my own work on this book has been a challenging process of discovery. I am grateful to the many researchers and theorists in the field of composition and rhetoric on whose work this book is built. Although I have cited in chapter notes only those authors whose ideas directly contributed to my own, many others contributed their ideas indirectly through journals, conferences, and textbooks. Teachers I have studied under and worked with, students who have patiently tried my ideas, and friends and family who have supported me along the way have all helped in the genesis of this book.

Finally, I am grateful to the editors and production team at Allyn & Bacon for their personal, professional attention, and to the reviewers of this edition of my manuscript.

TO THE INSTRUCTOR:

Instructors will find *Researching and Writing* flexible enough to use as a primary textbook in a research/writing course or as a supplementary textbook and reference guide in a writing course that covers research. In most courses, students would first read and work several exercises from Part One as a general introduction to college research. Then, depending on the time constraints of the course, instructors would allow students to select one chapter in Part Two as their research chapter (for example, a business major might choose to write a business report and an engineering major might choose to write a scientific or technical review paper). Alternatively, teachers of an entire course devoted to research writing could assign two or three short research papers based on the research projects outlined in Part Two. Whatever the actual assignments, students will find the information in Part Two invaluable in subsequent courses requiring research paper projects.

1

♦ ♦ ♦

College Research

INTRODUCTION

As a college student, regardless of your major, you are probably taking courses in the sciences, such as geology or chemistry; in the social sciences, such as sociology or political science; and in the humanities, such as philosophy or English literature. You may also be taking "applied" courses in home economics, agriculture, or business. Each of these academic disciplines seeks understanding and knowledge in traditional ways; each shares with all other academic disciplines basic research processes. In this book, we explore the nature of college work in an effort to understand both the general processes of research and the particular research tools used in the disciplines. Exploring these important relationships among disciplines will help you to interpret and use the research methods and established ways of proceeding employed by researchers.

RESEARCH IN THE DISCIPLINES

What is research? Broadly defined, it is systematic inquiry designed to further our knowledge and understanding of a subject. Using this definition, nearly everything you do in college is "research." You seek to discover information about people, objects, and nature; to revise the information you discover in light of new information that comes to your attention; and to interpret your experience and communicate that interpretation to others. This is how learning proceeds both for all of us as individuals and for human beings together as we search for knowledge and understanding of our world.

People are interpretive animals. In our interaction with the world, we seek to represent internally to ourselves what we have experienced externally. We generally assume that the universe is an orderly, reasonable, meaningful place, and that, if we but look, we will be able to discern that order. However, we may also be confronted with problematical experiences in the world. At such times, since we are inquiring animals, we seek to discover the cause or a reasonable explanation for that problematical experience, that is, we "research" the subject to discover its meaning. In the accompanying cartoon, the character is confronted with a problematical experience. As he relaxes under the shady tree, he is rudely awakened from his reverie.

In searching his own internal representation of the world, the character finds a "solution" to the problem. The humor of the cartoon is the result of its parody of Archimedes, who shouted "Eureka" when he discovered a new principle of physics, and of Newton, who deduced the principle of gravity from a falling apple. We recognize the circular reasoning the character has used in solving the problem. Because we are familiar with the orderly procedures people use to solve problems, procedures that this character has not used, we understand that his response is ludicrous.

This same issue, concerning the falling apple, could be researched by a scientist, perhaps a physicist, who might ask, "Why does the apple fall?" "How fast does it fall?" "How long will it take to reach the ground?" Such questions involve broad issues about the nature of the physical universe and the "laws" that govern it. The physicist observes natural phenomena within reasonable limits and then develops a systematic body of principles to account for or predict other similar events

FIGURE 1-1

Reprinted by permission of Johnny Hart and Creators Syndicate, Inc.

in the universe. For example, physicists have deduced the following principle: Any object at a distance from the earth will be acted upon by gravity, which is the force of mutual attraction among all bodies, proportional to the product of the masses of the bodies divided by the square of the distance between them.

A social scientist, perhaps an economist, researching the falling-apple issue might focus on the need for a reliable food source in a society, asking such questions as: "How do people provide for their basic need for food?" "What laws of supply and demand operate on the production and distribution of food?" An economist also seeks to define the broad issues of how people in society structure their economic relationships. The economist develops a systematic body of ideas to be used in accounting for other similar economic systems or events. Responding to the falling-apple issue, the economist might make the following statement: "The increasingly prevalent view by consumers that food is a public good and that all citizens should be assured of an adequate and nutritious food supply, plus the fear of prolonged food shortages together have led to a growing demand for change in the agricultural economic policy of this nation."

A humanist, perhaps a historian, researching this issue would attempt to explain and explore the human experience of the character in the cartoon by asking such questions as: "What is the significance of the event to this character and to others of his historical period?" "How does this event relate to other similar events?" The historian would account for, reconstruct, and narrate all the events related to this character's so-called discovery that apples cure hunger, relating the discovery to other more general cultural events. Then the historian might postulate the following explanation: The invention of agriculture was a significant historical event, often called the Neolithic Revolution. Occurring between 8000 and 3000 B.C., the Neolithic Revolution involved a change from the gathering society (in which humans gathered wild grasses) to the agricultural society (in which humans prepared the soil and sowed seeds for harvesting).

In these examples, it is clear that researchers in different disciplines ask different questions about the same subject. What distinguishes them is the perspective that the researcher in each field has.

THE IMPORTANCE OF RESEARCH

Researching, that is, exploring a problem systematically, is a crucial skill for an educated person. In college, you gain habits of mind that will serve you in every endeavor. Learning to research promotes careful, critical, systematic thinking. Learning to write promotes the effective communication of the ideas and insights gained in the research. Researching and research writing necessarily go together, with each building on and promoting the other.

Researching is different in kind from much of the work you did in high school and even from much of what you are probably doing in your introductory college courses. When you are first introduced to a new subject, you spend a great deal of time memorizing facts. However, once you move beyond that initial phase, you spend much of your time both in and out of the classroom discussing and examining the bases for current beliefs and claims in an academic discipline, claims that may seem questionable. This type of intellectual activity occurs in *addition to* and goes beyond the simple recall of material. College teachers are not concerned with simply imparting information; their main objective is to present and examine the basis on which the information or claim rests. Students and teachers together search out the justification for an accepted belief or claim. This search is research, because only such inquiry, not rote memorization, advances knowledge and understanding in an academic discipline.

As an example, suppose your roommate says to you, "Everybody knows that liberals are bleeding hearts who are soft on criminals." As with all claims, you would have to maintain reservations regarding this statement until you had reasons for believing it. To search out or research those reasons, you might begin by systematically exploring the basis or grounds for the claim. The "everybody knows" part of the statement implies that your roommate considers the claim to be common knowledge. But is it? Your roommate would need a pretty large research sample to justify the claim that "everybody knows. . . ." At the outset, then, you could reasonably discount the claim as unwarranted simply because it is overgeneralized.

What about the basis for equating liberalism with a softness on criminals? Perhaps your roommate is basing the equation on an assumption that being liberal means having a hyperactive social conscience. But perhaps your roommate is unaware that, as you find out from looking it up in the library, liberalism is a political and social philosophy that advocates individual freedom and the protection of civil liberties. A person may be liberal, you discover, and still advocate a strong system of criminal justice or even favor capital punishment. Consequently, the grounds on which your roommate made the claim are tenuous. As a rational person, once you have investigated—that is, researched—the particular grounds, you would have to reject the claim.

Similarly, much of the work you will be doing in college, and much of the work researchers do, involves looking into a particular claim. A second kind of research involves the exploration of a problem or event to arrive at a claim or hypothesis. Whether you are investigating a claim or hypothesis made by someone else or exploring a problematical experience you have encountered to arrive at a hypothesis yourself, the research process will be much the same.

✦ EXERCISE

Briefly describe a research project that you did in the past. What exactly did it involve? How did you feel about the project's success? What did you learn from it?

The General Process of Research

Many accounts of the process of research have been written by scientists, artists, and philosophers. Researchers generally agree about the outlines of the process regardless of the discipline. The process often begins with a troubled feeling about something observed or experienced followed by a conscious probing for a solution to the problem, a time of subconscious activity, an intuition about the solution, and finally a systematic testing to verify the solution. This process may be described in a number of ways but may generally be divided into four stages: preparation, incubation, illumination, and verification.[1] These stages are discussed in order, but during a research project, each stage does not necessarily neatly follow the next. Quite probably the researcher moves back and forth freely among the stages and may even skip a stage for a time, but generally these four stages are present in most research projects.

Preparation

The preparation stage of the research process involves the first awareness in researchers that a problem or a question exists that needs systematic inquiry. Researchers formulate the problem and begin to explore it. As they attempt to articulate the exact dimensions and parameters of a particular problem, they use language or symbols of their discipline that can be more easily manipulated than unarticulated thoughts or the data itself. By stating the problem in a number of ways, looking at it from various angles, trying to define its distinctive characteristics, and attempting possible solutions, researchers come to define for themselves the subtleties of the problem. Preparation is generally systematic, but it may also include the researchers' prior experiences and the intuitions they have developed over time.

Incubation

The incubation stage usually follows the preparation stage and includes a period of intense subconscious activity that is hard to describe or define. Because it is so indistinct, people tend to discount it as unimportant, but the experience of many researchers shows that it is crucial to allow an idea to brew and simmer in the subconscious if a creative solution is to be reached. Perhaps you have had the experience of trying and failing to recall the name of a book you recently read. You tell your conversation partner, "Go ahead. It'll come to me." A few minutes later, when you are not consciously trying to recall the name but have gone on to other matters in your conversation, you announce, *"The Scarlet Letter,"* out of the blue. This is an example of the way your subconscious mind continues to work on a problem while your conscious mind has gone on to another activity.

We need to allow ourselves sufficient time for incubating. If you have ever watched a chicken egg in an incubator, you will have a sense of how this works. The egg rests in warmth and quiet; you see no action whatsoever, but you know that beneath that shell tremendous activity is going on. The first peck on the shell from the chick about to hatch comes as a surprise. This is analogous to the next stage of the process, illumination. You cannot really control the incubation of a problem, but you can prepare adequately and then give yourself enough time for subconscious activity.

Illumination

In the illumination stage, as with the hatching chick, there is an imaginative breakthrough. The idea begins to surface out of its concealing shell, perhaps a little at a time. Or the researcher leaps to a hypothesis, a possible solution to the problem, that seems intuitively to fit. Isaac Newton discovered the law of universal gravitation as he watched an apple fall, and Archimedes deduced his principle of the displacement of water while in the bathtub. The illumination of a hypothesis can come suddenly or gradually, after laborious effort or after an ordinary event that triggers the researcher's thinking along new lines. We must remember, though, that the hypothesis comes only after the researcher has investigated the problem thoroughly. The egg must be prepared, fertilized, warmed, and cared for. The solution to a complex problem will come only after much conscious study and preparation in conjunction with subconscious intuition. Sometimes the solution will not be so much a breakthrough as it will be a clearer understanding of the problem itself.

Verification

Once a researcher has arrived at a hypothesis, he or she must systematically test it to discern whether it adequately accounts for all occurrences. Sometimes, this testing requirement necessitates a formal laboratory research experiment; in other cases, only an informal check against the researcher's own experience is necessary. In the sciences, the verification stage tends to be highly rigorous, involved, and lengthy. One should also be prepared at the verification stage to discover that the original hypothesis will not work. Although we are often reluctant to make mistakes, without a willingness to err we would never be led to make an original contribution. Research often progresses as a series of increasingly intelligent mistakes through which the researcher ultimately is led to a reasonable and workable solution. Sometimes hypothesis testing goes on for years and, for a particularly promising hypothesis, is performed by the research community in general. To be judged as sound, or verified, such a hypothesis must survive the critical scrutiny of the whole research community.

A Physician Uses the Research Process

In the following essay, Charles Nicolle, a physician and scientist of the early twentieth century, describes the research process he used to discover the mechanism that transmitted the disease typhus.[2] As you read the essay, pay particular attention to the research process Nicolle outlines.

The Mechanism of the Transmission of Typhus

Charles Nicolle

It is in this way that the mode of transmission of exanthematic typhus was revealed to me. Take all those who for many years frequented the Moslem hospital of Tunis, I could daily observe typhus patients bedded next to patients suffering from the most diverse complaints. Like those before me, I was the daily and unhappy witness of the strange fact that this lack of segregation, although inexcusable in the case of so contagious a disease, was nevertheless not followed by infection. Those next to the bed of a typhus patient did not contract the disease, while, almost daily, during epidemic outbreaks, I would diagnose contagion in the *douars* (the Arab quarters of the town), and amongst hospital staff dealing with the reception of patients. Doctors and nurses became contaminated in the country in Tunis, but never in the hospital wards. One day, just like any other, immersed no doubt in the puzzle of the process of contagion in typhus, in any case not thinking of it consciously (of this I am quite sure), I entered the doors of the hospital, when a body at the bottom of the passage arrested my attention.

It was a customary spectacle to see poor natives, suffering from typhus, delirious and febrile as they were, gain the landing and collapse on the last steps. As always I strode over the prostrate body. It was at this very moment that the light struck me. When, a moment later, I entered the hospital, I had solved the problem. I knew beyond all possible doubt that this was it. This prostrate body and the door in front of which he had fallen, had suddenly shown me the barrier by which typhus had been arrested. For it to have been arrested, and, contagious as it was in entire regions of the country and in Tunis, for it to have remained harmless once the patient had passed the Reception Office, the agent of infection must have been arrested at this point. Now, what passed through this point? The patient had already been stripped of his clothing and of his underwear; he had been shaved and washed. It was therefore something outside himself, something that he carried on himself, in his underwear, or on his skin, which caused the infection. This could be nothing but a louse. Indeed, it was a louse. The fact that I had ignored this point, that all those who had been observing typhus from the beginnings of history (for it belongs to the most ancient ages of humanity) had failed to notice the incontrovertible and immediately fruitful solution of the method of transmission, had suddenly been revealed to me. I feel somewhat embarrassed about thus putting myself into the picture. If I do so, nevertheless it is because I believe what happened to me is a very edifying and clear example, such as I have failed to find in the case of others. I developed my observation with less timidity. At the time it still had many shortcomings. These, too, appear instructive to me.

If this solution had come home to me with an intuition so sharp that it was almost foreign to me, or at least to my mind, my reason nevertheless told me that it required an experimental demonstration.

Typhus is too serious a disease for experiments on human subjects. Fortunately, however, I knew of the sensitivity of monkeys. Experiments were therefore possible. Had this not been the case I should have published my discoveries without delay, since it was of such immediate benefit to everybody. However, because I could support the discovery with a demonstration, I guarded my secret for some weeks even from those close to me, and made the necessary attempts to verify it. This work neither excited nor surprised me, and was brought to its conclusion within two months.

In the course of this very brief period I experienced what many other discoverers must undoubtedly have experienced also, viz. strange sentiments of the pointlessness of any demonstration, of complete detachment of the mind, and of wearisome boredom. The evidence was so strong, that it was impossible for me to take any interest in the experiments. Had it been of no concern to anybody but myself, I well believe that I should not have pursued this course. It was because of vanity and self-love that I continued. Other thoughts occupied me as well. I confess a failing. It did not arrest my research work. The latter, as I have recounted, led easily and without a single day's delay to the confirmation of the truth, which I had known ever since that revealing event, of which I have spoken. ✦

Nicolle's struggle to discover a solution to the problem of typhus transmission illustrates a research process. Nicolle worked on the problem of typhus transmission both consciously and subconsciously; his "Eureka" experience came unexpectedly and forcefully. Nicolle was awarded the Nobel Prize for medicine in 1928 for his discovery and for the experiments that conclusively confirmed that typhus was indeed transmitted by parasites.

✦ QUESTIONS FOR DISCUSSION

1. What stages of the research process outlined in this chapter are revealed in Nicolle's description?
2. What incongruity led Nicolle to research the question of typhus transmission?
3. What experience triggered the solution to the problem?
4. What procedures did Nicolle use to verify his hypothesis?
5. You may have noticed that Nicolle grew bored at points during his research. What kept him going?

✦ EXERCISES

1. The four research stages discussed in this chapter come from words we often associate with different contexts. For example, we use the term *preparation* in connection with preparing dinner or preparing for a test. First, briefly describe a situation (other than research) commonly associated with each term. Then list any similarities between the connotation of each word in your situation and the particular research stage.

   A. To prepare:

   B. To incubate:

   C. To illuminate:

   D. To verify:

2. Think of an activity with which you are familiar, such as a sport (football or tennis), a hobby (cooking or gardening), or an art (painting or dancing). In one paragraph, describe the process

you use when participating in the activity and relate the process to the research stages discussed in this chapter (preparation, incubation, illumination, and verification).

THE INQUIRY PROCESS IN SCIENCE AND TECHNOLOGY

In the Western world, the sciences hold an authoritative position and are a dominant force in our lives. The sciences have been enormously successful at formulating and testing theories related to phenomena in the natural and physical world. These theories have been used to solve physical and biological problems in medicine, industry, and agriculture. Generally, the sciences have been divided into life sciences (such as biology and botany), physical sciences (such as physics and chemistry), and earth sciences (such as geology and geography). Scientific insights and methods have also been carried over to fields of applied science and technology, such as computer science and engineering.

The Importance of Observation in the Sciences

As discussed earlier in this chapter, the motivation or impetus for much research is an observed event or experience that challenges our existing ideas and promotes inquiry. In the context of existing theories, such an event is incongruous and thus sparks in the researcher's mind a question or problem to be investigated. The researcher must be prepared to recognize the inconsistency and to see its importance. He or she must be familiar with current theories and concepts about the natural and physical world. In general, the aim of scientific work is to improve the relationship between our ideas (theories and concepts about the world) and our actual experiences (observations of the world).

An example of a scientist using educated observation is described by Rene Taton in his book *Reason and Chance in Scientific Discovery*.[3] In 1928, Sir Alexander Fleming, an English biologist, was studying mutation in some colonies of *Staphylococcus* bacteria. He noticed that one of his cultures had been contaminated by a microorganism from the air outside. But instead of neglecting this seemingly inconsequential event, Fleming went on to observe the contaminated plate in detail and noticed a surprising phenomenon: the colonies of bacteria that had been attacked by microscopic fungi had become transparent in a large region around the contamination. From this observation, Fleming hypothesized that the effect could be due to an antibacterial substance secreted by the foreign microorganism and then spread into the culture. Fortunately for us, Fleming decided to study the phenomenon at length to discover the properties of this secretion (which turned out to be a variety of the fungus *Penicillium,* from which we now make the antibiotic, penicillin) on cultures of *Staphylococcus* bacteria. Fleming designed experiments that tested his hypothesis concerning the effects of *Penicillium* on bacteria, and eight months later, he published his research findings in the *British Journal of Experimental Pathology.* Fleming's research is another example of the research process: first there was prepared observation, then a struggle with the problem and the formulation of a hypothesis, and finally the verification of that hypothesis using experiments.

The Importance of Formulating and Testing Hypotheses

On the basis of a scientist's prior knowledge and preparation, he or she formulates a hypothesis to account for the observed phenomenon that presents a problem. Arriving at a hypothesis takes much effort on the part of the researcher. Brainstorming for possible hypotheses is an important component of research, because the researcher can creatively make conjectures based on prior experience. The researcher may have to test several possible hypotheses before deciding which one seems to account for the observed phenomenon. Fleming, for example, hypothesized that the clear circle he observed around the bacteria resulted from the contaminating microorganism in the culture. In the sciences, there are systematic ways of testing a hypothesis once it is formulated. Fleming used such a procedure to verify his hypothesis. he demonstrated through scientific experiments that *Penicillium* was effective against bacteria.

The following outline describes the systematic way, or *scientific method,* by which scientists customarily proceed:

1. The scientist formulates a question and develops a hypothesis that might shed light on the question posed.
2. On the basis of the hypothesis, the scientist predicts what should be observed under specified conditions and circumstances.
3. The scientist makes the necessary observations, generally using carefully designed, controlled experiments.
4. The scientist either accepts or rejects the hypothesis depending on whether or not the actual observations correspond with the predicted observations.

Using the scientific method, a researcher is able to integrate new data into existing theories about the natural and physical world. In step 2 above, the researcher draws on accepted scientific ideas and theories to predict an outcome for the experiment. Fleming, for example, predicted that his experiments would show the antibacterial action of *Penicillium* when used on certain bacteria, and he confirmed his hypothesis through careful laboratory experiments.

Neither Fleming nor the scientific community of his day recognized the profound implications of his research for the field of medicine. The antibiotic, *Penicillium,* was a difficult-to-handle, impure, and unstable substance, which at the time made it seem impractical for widespread application. Subsequent discoveries and refinements of antibiotics, however, proved that penicillin would revolutionize modern medicine.

Ordinarily, the individual researcher uses currently held scientific theories and ideas to incorporate new data into the mainstream of current scientific belief. Research advances are the cumulative result of researchers working on various problems in various parts of the world; a synthesis of existing data is used to create new ideas and theories. Taton notes that many of the immense scientific discoveries of the twentieth century have been the collective work of teams of specialists from various schools working with more and more nearly perfect technical resources.[4] Although the role of the individual researcher is important, he or she is but a cog in the wheel of the scientific community in general.

Critical Scientific Research

Much of the research conducted by scientists is an attempt to incorporate new data into existing theories, but another type of scientific research, critical scientific research, attempts to challenge currently held beliefs and theories in an effort to improve them. Critical scientific research investigates the adequacy, or the sufficiency, of theories about the natural and physical world. In this context, the question asked is, "How well do current theories actually explain the natural and physical world as we know and observe it?"

A particular field of science may operate for years under certain theoretical assumptions. For example, Newtonian physics, based on the theories of Isaac Newton, dominated the scientific world for some time, and thousands of scientists conducted regular experiments based on Newton's theories. But because physicists encountered numerous phenomena that were incompatible with Newton's laws of physics, new theories became necessary. The physicist Albert Einstein challenged the agreed-upon Newtonian physics by presenting an alternative system that accounted for more of the observed data. Most physicists have now adopted Einstein's more comprehensive theories or have gone on to develop and adopt new theories.

This process of challenging and replacing scientific theories is one way scientific fields advance their knowledge and understanding of the natural or physical world. In this way, scientific thought progresses both by regular scientific observation and experimentation, using widely accepted theories and beliefs, and by critical scientific research that challenges those widely held theories and suggests new ones.

The Importance of Replicability and Scientific Debate

Scientists who have created and tested a hypothesis must then report their findings to other scientists, as Fleming did by publishing his experiments in the British journal. The goals of publishing one's findings include having other scientists accept the hypothesis as correct, communicating knowledge, and stimulating further research and discussion. A report of the research must necessarily include a careful, accurate description of the problem, the hypothesis, and the method (experimental design) used to test the hypothesis, in addition to the researcher's experimental findings and conclusions.

Other scientists then test the validity and reliability of the findings by attempting to repeat the experiment described by the researcher. A carefully designed and executed scientific experiment should be accurately described in writing so that other scientists using a similar experimental process can replicate it. The community of scientists as a whole then critiques the new research, deciding collectively whether or not it is good, sound research. To do this, other scientists will test the experiment's validity (Did it measure what the researcher said it would measure?), its reliability (Can it be repeated or replicated with similar results by other scientists?), and its importance (How does this experiment fit into a larger theoretical framework and what does it mean for our currently held assumptions and beliefs?). The forums of science—the professional organizations and journals, universities, scientific societies, and research laboratories—combine to resolve scientific issues to the benefit of all scientists.

✦ QUESTIONS FOR DISCUSSION

1. What is the general goal of inquiry in the sciences?
2. What often sparks a scientist's interest and motivates research?

3. How does observation contribute to scientific inquiry?
4. What is "critical scientific research"? How do its goals differ from those of science in general?
5. What is meant by replicability and why is it important in science?

THE INQUIRY PROCESS IN SOCIAL SCIENCE

Social sciences such as psychology, anthropology, political science, sociology, economics, and education have as their overall goal the systematic study of human behavior and human societies. The social sciences developed much later than the natural and physical sciences and so are comparatively young disciplines. Because social sciences followed the enormously successful and influential natural and physical sciences, they understandably adopted much of the scientific method—its goals, procedures, and standards. The field of sociology, for example, has been called the science of social organization; psychology has been called the science of the mind. Many social scientists today study people using the scientific method: they develop hypotheses and design and conduct controlled experiments to test those hypotheses.

A notorious example of a controlled social science experiment was conducted by Stanley Milgram, a Yale psychologist, during the 1960s.[5] Milgram sought to determine to what extent ordinary individuals would obey the orders of an authority figure. Through his experiment, he wished to probe the psychological processes that allowed the Germans to carry out mass human exterminations during World War II. Using simulated shock experiments, which were admittedly controversial, Milgram showed that an alarming proportion of adults (65 percent of those tested) were willing to inflict severe and, as far as they knew, permanent damage on strangers simply because they were instructed to do so by an authority figure, in this case the experimenter. The conclusions Milgram draws from this experiment are frightening:

> This is, perhaps, the most fundamental lesson of our study: ordinary people, simply doing their jobs, and without any particular hostility on their part, can become agents in a terrible destructive process. Moreover, even when the destructive effects of their work become patently clear, and they are asked to carry out actions incompatible with fundamental standards of morality, relatively few people have the resources needed to resist authority. A variety of inhibitions against disobeying authority come into play and successfully keep the person in his place.[6]

The research process used by Milgram closely follows that of other scientific research. His research began with a starting question: How could Hitler have succeeded in marshaling so much support from those who were called on to carry out his inhuman orders? After sufficient preparation, Milgram set out to determine the extent to which ordinary individuals would obey immoral orders. The psychologists were surprised by their results, which showed a large percentage of normal people obeying immoral orders from an authority figure. From the results, Milgram was able to verify that, indeed, there was something in human nature that could explain the behavior of so many Germans during World War II. The people who followed orders to annihilate others were not brutal, sadistic monsters, he stated, but rather normal people who acted out of a sense of duty and obligation to their country and their leader.

The Importance of Observing Human Behavior

A great number of the experiments created by social scientists are designed to observe human behavior. Because the goal of any science is the systematic, objective study of phenomena, the social sciences had to observe those aspects of humans that were observable. The only objectively observable part of humanity is behavior. We cannot observe human emotions or consciousness directly, but we can observe the behavior that results from feelings and thoughts in human consciousness. The social sciences, consequently, have focused heavily on behavior and thus have been called the behavioral sciences. The Milgram experiment is an example of a behavioral-science experiment. Milgram observed how his subjects behaved in a carefully controlled experimental setting to arrive at his conclusions about why people act as they do.

The Importance of Understanding Human Consciousness

Many people, both within and outside the social sciences, have felt that this objectification of observable human behavior produces a false picture of human beings. The real "inside" of a person may be missed when only the behavior manifested on the outside is observed. Human beings are conscious beings; we have thoughts, feelings, and intuitions that are private and never seen by others. Some in the social sciences argue that because we cannot observe consciousness directly, it is not a proper subject for scientific study at all. Others take the position that it is not only appropriate to study human consciousness but also essential, because consciousness is what makes us uniquely human. Modern social scientists have developed methods of exploring human consciousness that are admittedly subjective but nevertheless reveal important information about how people think and feel. Such methods include case studies of individuals, clinical evaluation, psychoanalysis, and hypnosis.

Social scientists also study the interaction among people in societies. A social scientist attempting to discover social rules and conventions is somewhat analogous to a natural scientist attempting to discover laws of nature. The social rules and conventions adopted by a particular society are important for understanding human behavior within that society. For example, a Polynesian native accustomed to using shells as money would have a rude awakening in an American marketplace where, by convention, slips of paper are used to trade for goods and services. The slip of paper we accept as a dollar bill has meaning for us only within our particular set of social conventions. Much of the work done in social sciences attempts to describe and define the social laws, rules, and conventions by which people operate within societies.

An example of a social scientist whose work has been important in the twentieth century is the Austrian psychologist Sigmund Freud, who sought to describe and predict the complex operation of the human subconscious mind. Freud also sought to apply his theories of individuals to the operation of human beings in societies. In one of his last books, *Civilization and Its Discontents,* he expressed his views on the broad question of the human being's place in the world.[7] Freud posed the question, Why is it hard for humankind to be happy in civilization? Through his years of preparation and study, Freud was able to posit the hypothesis that unhappiness is due to the inevitable conflict between the demands of instincts (aggression and ego gratification) and the restrictions of civilized society:

> If civilization imposes such great sacrifices not only on man's sexuality but on his aggressivity, we can understand better why it is hard for him to be happy in that civilization. In fact, primitive man was better off in knowing no restrictions of instinct. To counterbalance this, his prospects of enjoying this happiness for any length of time were very slender. Civilized man has exchanged a portion of his possibilities of happiness for a portion of security.[8]

Freud's sociological theories have been as influential as his psychological theories. Verification of this particular hypothesis—that instinct and society conflict—was achieved through Freud's extensive citation of examples taken from psychological case studies and from primitive and modern societies (including the Soviet Union and the United States). Through these examples, Freud showed that human instincts are in conflict with society's constraints.

As discussed at the opening of this section on the social sciences, researchers attempt to describe and predict human behavior and human relationships in society. Barzun and Graff, in their text *The Modern Researcher*, observe that "the works of social science that have made the strongest mark on the modern mind have been those that combined description with enumeration and imparted the results with imaginative power."[9] The work of Freud is a classic example of the way good social science research combines an understanding of individual human behavior and consciousness with an understanding of how people are organized and influenced by the societies in which they live and operate.

Objectivity versus Subjectivity

In the sciences, researchers attempt to remove their own particular preferences, desires, and hopes from the experimental process as much as possible. Scientific researchers are looking for "objective" truth. However, because each researcher as observer necessarily brings background preparation, knowledge, and experience to the situation, it is seldom possible to remove the researcher from the research altogether. But what about the social sciences? Can they be as objective as the natural sciences in their search for knowledge and understanding? Many would charge that subjectivity and values are inescapable and necessary parts of social science research. The social scientist studies people, social systems, and social conventions. As a person, the researcher is necessarily a part of the system being studied. Perhaps this is not altogether a bad thing. A social scientist's own beliefs, attitudes, and values can contribute to his or her understanding of what is being observed, even though he or she can, to a certain degree, demonstrate detachment from a situation and function as a relatively impartial observer. But the question of objectivity and subjectivity in the social sciences is not easily resolved, because it is not always possible to know exactly what subjective influences are affecting "objective" research. The issue of subjectivity versus objectivity is the cause of much ferment and continual debate within the social science fields as these young disciplines seek to define for themselves an appropriate method, whether it is modeled after the scientific method or something quite different.

✦ QUESTIONS FOR DISCUSSION

1. What is the general goal of inquiry in the social sciences?
2. Why are social sciences often called "behavioral sciences"?

3. What is meant by the understanding of human consciousness?

4. What is the relationship between objectivity and subjectivity in the social sciences?

THE INQUIRY PROCESS IN THE HUMANITIES

The humanities, such as classical and modern languages and literature, history, and philosophy, have as an overall goal the exploration and explanation of the human experience. Some would include the fine arts (music, art, dance, and drama) in the humanities, but others view the arts as a separate category. (We will not discuss the performance of fine arts in this book, but we will touch on the interpretation of fine arts.) In most disciplines in the humanities, written texts are extremely important, particularly in history, philosophy, and literature. Historians attempt a systematic documentation and analysis of past events related to a particular people, country, or period. Philosophers endeavor to examine coherent, logical systems of human ideas. Literary authors and artists attempt to capture for others their own lived, human experiences and their own understanding of the world. The humanities involve inquiry into consciousness, values, ideas, and ideals as they seek to describe how experience shapes our understanding of the world.

Let's take an example to show how the sciences, social sciences, and humanities all contribute to an understanding of our world. The Mississippi River has played an important role in American history. A scientist—perhaps a biologist—would study the river's wildlife, fish, surrounding vegetation, and ecology in an attempt to objectively describe the river itself. A social scientist—perhaps a sociologist—might study the river's contribution to a riverfront society and that society's dependence on the river for transportation of goods and services. A historian, who often bridges the gap between the social sciences and the humanities, might report on the importance of the Mississippi and other American waterways to our westward expansion and the development of America. A humanist—for example, a novelist—might write about the actual experiences people had on or near the Mississippi. Mark Twain, for instance, wrote his autobiographical novel *Life on the Mississippi* to share with his readers what he had *felt* as a youth learning the trade of riverboat pilot on a Mississippi steamboat. Without such a work of imaginative literature, we would have a hard time understanding what it was really like to be a youth on the river during Twain's time. Such a work of literature contributes to our understanding by putting us in a different time and place from our own, thus broadening our horizons in a manner that is somewhat different from either the natural or social sciences. The sciences attempt to give us the outside, external knowledge of a phenomenon, whereas the humanistic disciplines attempt to give us the inside, internal knowledge of a phenomenon.[10] Both make important contributions to our understanding of the world.

The Importance of Texts in the Humanities

Written texts in the humanities are generally of three types: (1) creative writing (literature, poetry, and drama), (2) interpretive writing (literary and art criticism), and (3) theoretical writing (historical and social theories of literature and art).

Creative writing produces numerous literary texts that provide us with an aesthetic experience and capture new insights into humanity. Creative writing is comparable to other creative, artistic endeavors in that it often has this twofold objective: the aesthetically pleasing (or emotionally moving) and the imaginative reenactment of human experience. We ask a work of art to move us and to mean something to us, to show us a way of looking at ourselves and the world that we may not otherwise have seen.

As we receive creative art and literature as an audience, interpretive questions arise, such as: What sort of work is it? How are we to respond to it? Much of the writing connected with the humanities is interpretive, because the audience tries to understand both the meaning and the significance of a particular creative work. Often, an interpretive critic attempts to disclose the particular intention of the artist: the novelist's attitude toward the heroine, for example, or the intended aesthetic impact of a dance. Interpretive critics research their claims by using the evidence found in the work itself to support the hypothesis, that is, the particular "reading" of the text or work of art.

The third kind of humanistic writing is theoretical. For the theorist, creative art and literature are important insofar as they exemplify more general social and historical principles. The theorist, for example, looks for connections between a particular work of art and its social and historical context or for relationships among different artistic media, such as fresco painting and architecture in medieval Europe. Theorists provide links between our understanding of art and literature and other subjects such as history, sociology, or psychology. Finally, theorists take a step back from a particular work of art or literature in an attempt to get a broader view. In looking at the entire social and historical context, they ask such questions as: How has photography affected portrait painting? What is the role of the devil in the American novel?

Research in the Humanities

The humanist deals in significance, insight, imagination, and the meaning of human experience. What does it mean, then, to research in the humanities? Interpreting and critiquing art and literature is one type of research conducted by humanists. Interpreters and theorists in the humanities attempt to "talk sense" about a work of art or literature to make the audience see what the artist or author meant and to link the work with other, larger human events and experiences. A second kind of humanistic research involves reconstructing humanity's past, reconstructing both the ideas (philosophical research) and the events that have occurred over time (historical research). All three types of humanistic research (literary and art criticism, philosophical research, and historical research) contribute to our understanding of the meaning of human experience.

Literary and Art Criticism

Critical researchers necessarily use their own interpretations of a work of art or literature in critiquing it. But those subjective interpretations are based on experience and reflective thought, and they are expressed in well-chosen language. Criticism in the humanities is not just a string of personal opinions. The critical researcher builds a solid argument to substantiate his or her interpretation or theory. Such an argument is based on research involving a close reading of the text itself (in literary criticism) or a close analysis of the work of art (in art criticism). The argument also takes into account social and historical factors that bear on the interpretation of the literary text or work of art. It incorporates research involving other related texts or works of art by the same author or artist or secondary criticism influencing the critic's own argument. A piece of good interpretive criticism is both insightful and true to life. A piece of good literary or art criticism is complete and comprehensive; it offers the audience a sound theory that fits with the experience of audience members and that ties together related threads in their understanding. A critical researcher investigates the complex context from which a work of art or literature has come to provide an understanding of how it fits into the larger realm of human experience. In this way, the critical researcher is much like a historical or social science researcher.

One example of a critical researcher who combined techniques of criticism with historical scholarship is John Livingston Lowes, who began with the question of what sources influenced the poetry of Samuel Coleridge, a nineteenth-century English poet and critic.[11] In an attempt to elucidate Coleridge's poetry, Lowes traced the sources the poet used in writing such poems as "The Rime of the Ancient Mariner" and "Kubla Khan." Richard Altick calls Lowes's book "the greatest true-detective story ever written."[12] Lowes began his research with Coleridge's *Gutch Memorandum Book,* a notebook containing the suggestions for reading that Coleridge had jotted down as he looked for ideas to translate into poetry. Next, Lowes looked at the records from the Bristol Library that showed the books Coleridge had borrowed. Following these and many other leads, Lowes was able to virtually reconstruct how certain of Coleridge's greatest poems took shape in the author's mind and took form on the written page.

Philosophical Research

The philosophical researcher investigates the truths and principles of being, knowledge, and human conduct. Alfred North Whitehead, in his book *Process and Reality,* describes the process of research in speculative philosophy:

> The true method of discovery is like the flight of an aeroplane. It starts from the ground of particular observation; it makes a flight into the thin air of imaginative generalization; and it again lands for renewed observation rendered acute by rational interpretation.[13]

Here Whitehead is describing the general process of inquiry that we have been discussing. As he says, the success of any imaginative speculation is the verification of it through extended application. He sees the work of philosophical research as an attempt to frame a coherent, logical system of the general ideas of humanity. In Whitehead's work, he presents a scheme that can be used to interpret or frame the "cosmology." He shows how his philosophical scheme can be used for "the interpretation of the ideas and problems which form the complex texture of civilized thought."[14] Thus, the philosophical laws are verified in their application to actual philosophical problems encountered in human experience.

Historical Research

Historical researchers proceed in much the same fashion as philosophy researchers, except that historical researchers investigate events as well as ideas. They research the events that have occurred in a person's life or at a particular time. Then they weave those events and ideas into a narrative that recounts and interprets the past. As in all the humanities, historians attempt to understand and interpret life itself. Historians also use the data gathered by social scientists—the surveys and statistical counts conducted by sociologists, economists, or political scientists. However, historians often present their understanding of the past in a story form intended to give the reader a picture of the past events, describing and recreating what those events were like for the participants. In this way the study of history bridges the gap between the social sciences and the humanities such as literature and the arts.

The research process used by historians is much like that of the theorists. The historian investigates the facts and data available about an individual or a period of time. Through those facts, carefully verified for their accuracy, the historian recreates the past to capture the truths that reside there. The historian is not reluctant to make individual judgments about the meaning and importance of past events. As in all humanities, the historian verifies those judgments by gauging their ring of truth, their resemblance to what is known intuitively about life, and their explanatory power.

One example of a historical researcher at work is Frank Maloy Anderson.[15] Anderson was confronted with the problem of who wrote the important "Diary of a Public Man," a document of questioned authorship that first appeared in 1879 in the *North American Review*. Many historical, little-known facts about Abraham Lincoln were revealed in the diary. Anderson spent nearly thirty-five years trying to identify the document's author, using every historical clue he could find. He searched congressional records, hotel registries, business documents, and newspaper subscriptions. From this extensive search, he posited two hypotheses: (1) the diary was a fiction or (2) it was a combination of fiction and truth. Anderson decided on the second hypothesis, because he could find nothing that was provably false in the document. He arrived at a probable author in Sam Ward but could never prove this beyond all doubt. Nevertheless, Anderson's historical case is a good one, based as it is on intuitive speculation combined with factual evidence.

Acceptable Evidence in the Humanities

In the humanities, there is no absolute proof that leads unerringly to a particular interpretation or theory. Rather, the humanist will make a claim and argue for that claim. What is demanded in the humanities is not proof but sensitivity and perceptiveness. The way of knowing required in the humanities can be cultivated by hard work and study.

The evidence that is acceptable in literary and art criticism or interpretation comes from the interpreter's sensibility, from the work of art or literature itself, and from the context. Some interpretations and theories may seem more insightful than others. They cast the work into a new light or integrate it into a wholeness we had not originally perceived. The claim or hypothesis made by a theorist is accepted as valid if it fits the work and helps the audience understand it. Critical and theoretical research can expand our consciousness, deepening and broadening our sensitivity to experiences. We could say, as did William

James, that the performance of a piece of violin music is "the scraping of the hair of a horse over the intestines of a cat."[16] Although the description is true enough, as Meiland points out, it is not all there is to violin music; in fact, the remark leaves out just about everything that is really important in the performance of a violin piece. A valid interpretation illuminates a work in a way that makes it more meaningful to us.

The evidence that is acceptable in historical and philosophical research is that which is based either on verifiable facts or adequate interpretations that fit known human experience. As Barzun and Graff put it, "The researcher who does historian's work can at least preserve his sense of truth by concentrating on the tangle of his own stubborn facts."[17] But in addition to those facts, the historian is also "aware of his duty to make individual judgments" regarding the meaning or significance of those facts.[18] As Whitehead states, the application of his philosophical scheme to life "at once gives meaning to the verbal phrases of the scheme by their use in the discussion, and shows the power of the scheme to put the various elements of our experience into the consistent relation to each other."[19] In both cases, these humanistic researchers insist on the role of the researcher's insight and imagination in elucidating experience and in describing and predicting what human beings are and how they think and act. Acceptable evidence in all the humanities is evidence that supports those imaginative and insightful descriptions and interpretations.

✦ QUESTIONS FOR DISCUSSION

1. What is the general goal of inquiry in the humanities?
2. How are written texts used in the humanities? Why are they important?
3. What three kinds of research are common in the humanities? How are they alike or different?
4. What constitutes acceptable evidence in the humanities?

✦ EXERCISES

1. Obtain a copy of an undergraduate catalog. In the catalog, find references to the academic disciplines and notice how they are classified. Are there differences in the categories you find in the catalog and those outlined in this chapter? In a paragraph, describe the major divisions of disciplines in the catalog.
2. In an undergraduate catalog, look up a discipline you are considering as a major, for example, prelaw, history, or mathemat-

ics. In addition to courses in that discipline, what other courses are required (for example, foreign languages, liberal arts, laboratory sciences)? In a paragraph, describe those "core" requirements and speculate on why they are included as a part of an undergraduate education.

3. In your classes in high school or prior to the courses you are currently taking in college, you have probably studied sciences, social sciences, and humanities. Describe in a short essay how classes in these three areas were similar or different.

4. Obtain a copy of a textbook from a course in the sciences, the social sciences, or the humanities. Read the preface and glance through the table of contents. Does the author mention research? Is there a chapter or section discussing research? Why or why not? What can you infer about the discipline's approach to research from the textbook? Does it seem to differ from the approach discussed in this text? If so, in what ways? In a paragraph or two, discuss your speculations about the assumptions made about research in the textbook you are examining.

5. For each problematical situation below, propose a solution and suggest in a short report how you would go about verifying that solution:

   A. For your dorm or for a church or other group to which you belong, you are in charge of collecting the money for a favorite charity or project. You must organize the collection drive.

   B. As president of your student association, you are in charge of getting your fellow students to voluntarily comply with the no-smoking rule in the college cafeteria. Or, as the president of the union local at your place of employment, you are in charge of getting the union rank and file to voluntarily comply with a new safety regulation. Or, as the president of the PTA at your child's school, you are in charge of getting parent volunteers to help with a new school program.

   C. A newspaper has assigned you to write an article on pollution and the environment. The editor wants you to report how students on your campus or co-workers at your place of employment really feel about pollution and other environmental issues.

6. Interview a friend whose major is different from yours. What kinds of research are required of your friend in his or her courses? Write your interview notes into a short report.

NOTES

1. Adaptation of excerpt from "The Four Stages of Inquiry," in Richard E. Young, Alton L. Becker, and Kenneth L. Pike, *Rhetoric: Discovery and Change* (New York: Harcourt Brace Jovanovich, Inc., 1970). Reprinted by permission of the publisher. This four-step problem-solving process (preparation, incubation, illumination, verification) was first outlined by Wallas in 1926 (*The Art of Thought*, New York: Harcourt, Brace).

2. Charles Nicolle, "The Mechanism and Transmission of Typhus," in Rene Taton, *Reason and Chance in Scientific Discovery* (New York: Philosophical Library, 1957), pp. 76–78. Reprinted by permission of Philosophical Library, Inc.

3. Taton, p. 85.

4. Taton, p. 88.

5. Stanley Milgram, *Obedience to Authority: An Experimental View* (New York: Harper & Row, 1974).

6. Milgram, p. 6.

7. Sigmund Freud, *Civilization and Its Discontents*, edited and translated by James Strachey (New York: W. W. Norton, 1961).

8. Freud, p. 62.

9. Jacques Barzun and Henry F. Graff, *The Modern Researcher*, rev. ed. (New York: Harcourt Brace and World, 1970), p. 245.

10. Jack Meiland, *College Thinking: How to Get the Best out of College* (New York: Mentor, 1981), p. 174.

11. John Livingston Lowes, *The Road to Xanadu: A Study in the Ways of the Imagination* (1927; reprint ed., London: Pan Books, 1978).

12. Richard Altick, *The Art of Literary Research* (New York: W. W. Norton, 1963), p. 100.

13. Alfred North Whitehead, *Process and Reality* (New York: Free Press, 1929), p. 5.

14. Whitehead, p. xi.

15. Frank Maloy Anderson, *The Mystery of "A Public Man": A Historical Detective Story* (Minneapolis: University of Minnesota Press, 1948).

16. As found in Meiland, p. 186.

17. Barzun and Graff, p. 250.

18. Barzun and Graff, p. 251.

19. Whitehead, p. xi.

2

♦ ♦ ♦

Library Resources

INTRODUCTION

Students' experience researching in libraries varies from expert to novice. Your own experience will fall somewhere along that continuum. But even if you have used libraries before, there is always more to learn. College libraries are typically large, complex entities that often seem to have a life of their own. They are constantly changing as new information and methods to access information are incorporated by librarians.

Your library contains many important general research tools with which you need to become familiar to conduct any research project. Also in your library are specific resources that are important for research in particular disciplines. This chapter covers information on general library resources; for specific library resources used in the sciences and technology, social sciences, humanities, and business, turn to the disciplinary chapters in Part Two. You may find that some of this chapter is review, but you will certainly also encounter sources of which you were not previously aware.

LIBRARIES AND GENERAL LIBRARY RESOURCES

The Library Reference Area

Most library research begins in the library reference area. Reference librarians are excellent resources when you need help finding information in the library. However, you need to know enough about libraries to ask the librarian to help you, just as you need to know enough about your car to suggest to a mechanic where to begin when your car needs repair. It is not productive to walk up to a mechanic and simply ask for help. You need to explain the specifics of your particular problem and describe the make, model, age, and condition of your car. Similarly, you need to tell a librarian what kind of project you are working on, what information you need, and in what form that information is likely to be stored. So that you can ask the right questions, you must first take the time to learn your way around the library. Working your way through this chapter is a good place to begin.

Librarians use terminology that you should become familiar with. Particular terms are defined throughout this chapter. We will start by looking at some major library sources and what distinguishes them.

In the heading of this section of the chapter you saw the word *reference*. As you might suspect, a reference is something that *refers* to something else. In your library there is an area designated as the reference area and a person called the reference librarian. The reference area may be a separate room or simply a section of the library. In the reference area you will find books containing brief factual answers to such questions as, What is the meaning of a particular word? What is the population density of a particular state? What is the birthplace of a certain famous person? Also in the reference area are books that refer you to other sources. These library tools—bibliographies and indexes—will help you find particular articles written about particular subjects. The reference area of the library is usually the place to begin any research project. Reference sources include the following general types of works:

Abstracts: Short summaries of larger works; may be included in an index

Almanacs: Compendia of useful and interesting facts on specific subjects

Atlases: Bound volumes of maps, charts, or tables illustrating a specific subject

Bibliographies: Lists of books or articles about particular related subjects

Biographies: Works that provide information on the life and writings of famous people, living and dead

Dictionaries: Works that provide information about words, such as meaning, spelling, usage, pronunciation

Encyclopedias: Works that provide concise overviews of topics, including people, places, ideas, subject areas

Handbooks: Books of instruction, guidance, or information of a general nature

Indexes: Books or parts of books that point to where information can be found, such as in journals, magazines, newspapers, or books

Reviews: Works that analyze and comment on other works, such as films, novels, plays, or even research

Serials: Periodicals (magazines) that are published at specific intervals and professional (scholarly) journals that contain articles and research reports in a specific field

General Reference Works

In most research projects, you need to discover general information relevant to your research. The most commonly used general reference works are dictionaries, encyclopedias, and biographies. Depending on your project, you may also need to consult atlases, almanacs, and handbooks.

Dictionaries

Dictionaries provide information about words: definitions, pronunciations, usage, origin, and changes of meaning. It is essential that you have a good desk dictionary to consult for all your writing. Some good ones include:

> *Random House Dictionary of the English Language,* 2nd ed. New York: Random House, 1987.
> *American Heritage Dictionary of the English Language,* 3rd ed. Boston: Houghton Mifflin, 1992.
> *Webster's Ninth New Collegiate Dictionary,* 9th ed. Springfield, Mass.: Merriam, 1989.

More comprehensive dictionaries are found in the reference area of your library. These include:

> *Oxford English Dictionary (OED),* 2nd ed. 20 vols. London: Oxford University Press, 1989, with supplements. The OED traces the chronological history of words and describes and illustrates with examples the changes in the meaning of words through the years.
> *Webster's Third New International Dictionary Unabridged: The Great Library of the English Language.* Springfield, Mass.: Merriam, 1986. This unabridged (complete) dictionary gives definitions of spoken as well as standard written English. It is a complete source of words in the English language.

Encyclopedias

Encyclopedias provide concise information on people, places, subjects, events, and ideas. Encyclopedias are particularly useful for general background information on a specific subject or person. Look in the encyclopedia's index for references to related subtopics and articles within the encyclopedia. Both general and specialized encyclopedias exist. The specialized encyclopedias, for example, the *Encyclopedia of American History*, cover information in particular disciplines or fields. These encyclopedias often contain bibliographies that can lead you to other sources in your research. (For specialized encyclopedias, see "Discipline-Specific Resources," in each chapter of Part Two.) Some general encyclopedias include the following:

> *Encyclopaedia Britannica.* Chicago: Encyclopaedia Britannica, 1992.
> *Encyclopedia Americana.* Rev. ed. New York: Grolier, 1993.
> *Academic American Encyclopedia.* Rev. ed. Danbury, Conn.: Grolier, 1993.

Biographies

Biographies provide information on the lives and work of famous people. As with encyclopedias, there are both general and specialized biographies. (Specialized biographies are covered in "Discipline-Specific Resources," in each chapter of Part Two.) General biographies include the following:

> *Biography and Genealogy Master Index.* Detroit: Gale, 1985, with updates. Combines into one listing access to biographical sketches found in biographical dictionaries, subject encyclopedias, volumes of literary criticism, and other indexes. Covers both current and retrospective biographies, mostly of notable Americans from all fields.
> *Current Biography.* New York: Wilson, 1940 to present. Covers important living people from all fields, including popular figures. Published monthly with bound annual cumulation (yearbook).
> *Dictionary of American Biography.* 17 vols. plus supplements. New York: Scribners', 1943 to present. Covers famous Americans who are no longer living. Includes biographies of noteworthy figures from America's colonization on.
> *The McGraw-Hill Encyclopedia of World Biography.* New York: McGraw-Hill, 1975. Covers famous men and women both living and dead. A good place to find biographies of people not traditionally covered in other works, for example, women and minority groups.

Who's Who. New York: St. Martin's, 1948 to present. Covers living people who are prominent in their fields. Primarily a source of information on famous British citizens. *Who Was Who* contains the biographies of those no longer living but previously selected for *Who's Who.*

Who's Who in America. Chicago: Marquis, 1899 to present. Covers living Americans who are noted for exceptional contributions to their fields. *Who Was Who* in America provides biographies of those no longer living but previously selected for *Who's Who in America.*

Bibliographies

Bibliographies are lists of books or articles about particular subjects. Some bibliographies are found at the end of articles or books; others are entire books in themselves. General bibliographies include the following:

Bibliographic Index. New York: Wilson, 1938 to present. Lists bibliographies found in other sources, including bibliographies in books, journals, and single volumes.

Guide to Reference Books, 10th ed. E. P. Sheehy. Chicago: American Library Association, 1986. Lists and describes reference works that can provide access to other works.

A World Bibliography of Bibliographies, 4th ed. 5 vols. T. Besterman. Totowa, N.J.: Rowman, 1963. Lists available bibliographies.

A World Bibliography of Bibliographies, 1964–1974. 2 vols. Compiled by A. F. Toomay. Totowa, N.J.: Rowman, 1977. Updates Besterman's bibliography for the subsequent ten-year period.

Reviews

Reviews are brief critical discussions of important works in a particular field. The following are some indexes that provide access to these reviews:

Book Review Digest. 1905 to present. (Annual). New York: Wilson. Provides excerpts of and citations to reviews of current books in English. Books on science for the general reader are included, but textbooks and technical books are not. The *BRD* is searchable by author, title, and subject.

Book Review Index. 1965 to present. (Annual). Detroit: Gale. Provides access to reviews of books and periodicals. *BRI* is a comprehensive listing of reviews that appear in more than

460 publications, representing a wide range of popular, academic, and professional interests. *BRI* is searchable by author and title only.

Combined Retrospective Index to Book Reviews in Scholarly Journals, 1886–1974. 15 vols. Compiled by E. Farber. Woodbridge, Conn.: Research Publications. Fills in the gap before comprehensive book review indexes were widely published. Searchable by author and title.

Current Book Review Citations. Annuals, 1976–1982. New York: Wilson. Author/title index to book reviews in 1,000 periodicals written during the dates listed above.

Index to Book Reviews in the Humanities. 1978 to present. Annual. Williamston, Mich.: Thomson. Provides access to book reviews in humanities periodicals; indexed by author only.

Index to Scientific Reviews. Semiannual. Philadelphia, PA.: Institute for Scientific Information. Comprehensive listing of scientific reviews covering the spectrum of over 100 subject disciplines in the sciences, medicine, and technology; indexes over 3,000 principal science journals and review publications by subject and author. An extremely useful index for those in science and technical fields because it is a quick way to find and read reviews of research.

Technical Book Review Index. New York: Wilson. Provides access to reviews in science and technology periodicals by author's name and also quotes from those reviews.

Abstracts

Abstracts are similar to indexes in that they provide access to sources by subject and often by author. They provide additional information through a brief summary (abstract) of each source cited. Abstracts are often compiled in two volumes, one for the abstract (with summaries) and one for the subject index. You look first in the subject index, which provides you with an abstract number. Then, using that abstract number, you can look up the abstract itself in the abstract volume (Fig. 2-1).

Abstracts reflect a specific area or field of interest. For example, *Sociological Abstracts* indexes journals in the field of sociology. Several abstracts are listed in the sections called "Discipline-Specific Resources," found in each chapter of Part Two.

One abstract of a general nature is *DAI: Dissertation Abstracts International.* Published in Ann Arbor, Michigan, by University Microfilms International, *DAI* provides a monthly compilation of abstracts of dissertations submitted to University Microfilms for publication. Abstracts are published in two sections: A = Humanities and Social Sciences, B = Science and Engineering. Complete copies of texts may be purchased in microfilm or photocopy from University Microfilms. The *DAI* is searchable by author, subject, and key word title.

The example of a subject listing in Figure 2-1 is from *Sociological Abstracts*, which indexes journals in the field of sociology.

Note the abstract number. You use it to locate the abstract (or brief summary) in the abstract volume (Fig. 2-2).

Locating Books and Resources: Computer Cataloging Systems

In an age of exploding information, many libraries have determined that their mission is no longer to attempt to physically house all of the information sources of potential use to their patrons. Rather than simply being book repositories, today's libraries provide "access" to information, often through computers. If they do not have a particular

Cultural Identity
    academic performance, minorities, contemporary industrial urban societies;
        9405254
    African Americans, contemporary cultural politics; 9405131
    Australian intellectual/cultural identity; 2-book review essay; 9404980
    black history education, cultural empowerment functions; classroom observations;
        Maryland suburb; 9405167
    cultural distinctiveness, Caribbean countries; 9405098
    cultural identity development, deaf people; scale data; 9405063
    cultural identity-liberation interdependence, Latin American philosophy; 9405255
    cultural identity; Latin America; 9405239
    cyberpunk, bodily devaluation, cultural identity implications; 9405827
    ethnic group dispersion/ethnocultural orientations, Leningrad, USSR,
        1970s–1980s; questionnaire data; Armenians/Estonians/Tatars; 9405152
    ethnicity-crime relationship, methodological problems; 9406479
    freedom/rationality/justice definitions, monoculture's worldwide domination,
        global discourse; 9405252
    gay clone lifestyle, political/economic construction, profit logic, 1971–1982;
        9406209
    gender relations-nationalism relationship, citizenship/culture/origin issues;
        9406751
    homosexuality, social construction, gay culture development barriers, Nicaragua,
        1980s; 9406195
    intercultural communication/assistance; 9405516
    Irish language, historical/sociolinguistic aspects; book review essay; 9405803
    Jewish identity/generation/space concepts, dispora meanings, Western discourse,
        Pauline sources; 9405105
    Latvian cultural/sociopolitical history, 17th–19th centuries; 9405816

FIGURE 2-1   Sociological Abstracts

9405131

Gray, Herman (Dept Sociology U California, Santa Cruz 95064), **African-American Political Desire and the Seductions of Contemporary Cultural Politics,** *Cultural Studies,* 1993, 7, 3, Oct, 364–373.

¶ Remarks on contemporary cultural politics as it pertains to African Americans, with consideration also given to the discourse & debates surrounding essentialism, postmodernism, & multiple subject positions. The localities & relationships of critical black intellectual engagements with postmodernism & essentialism are specified, & a case is made for intensifying the application of postmodern insights to the material conditions & social locations of people's lives. Comments on rap music as black self-representation are offered, & it is argued that essentialist discourses, expressed in totalizing forms of nationalism, have intervened in those public arenas, especially popular culture, where blacks do not enjoy the material privilege or the social space to construct themselves differently. 27 References. W. Howard (Copyright 1994, Sociological Abstracts, Inc., all rights reserved.)

FIGURE 2-2   Sociological Abstracts

item in their collection, for example, they may be able to tell you quickly, by a computer search, which nearby library does have a copy. Most libraries today have converted their card catalogs into computerized catalog access systems to provide their patrons with the most up-to-date information in the most timely fashion. (If your library still uses a card catalog, see The Card Catalog section in this chapter for information.)

Online Computer Catalogs

One of the most visible computer tools in libraries today is the online catalog. Such a system, which supplements or replaces the traditional card catalog, is designed to provide library materials service, such as circulation, cataloging, and location of materials within the library collection. Most online catalogs are searchable by author, title, and subject (as are card catalogs), but many are also searchable by keyword or by combinations of subjects or keywords.

You should become familiar with your library's online catalog as soon as possible. (Note: Some online catalogs cover only the most recent additions to the library's collection, in which case older books still may be found by looking in the card catalog.) Check with your librarian to find out exactly what materials (e.g., books, magazines, journals, government documents) are cataloged in your library's online catalog.

How to Search the Online Catalog

When you log-on to your library's online catalog, you will typically see a menu of choices listing the various databases available for searching. For example, the library at my university includes the following databases in its online catalog, all searchable from the same computer. To enter any one of these databases, you make the appropriate selection from the main menu.

> *General Book Collection* (OPAC, Online Public Access Catalog) lists the books, government documents, and audiovisual materials in the library.
> *General Periodicals Index* (WRGA, Wilson Readers' Guide to Periodical Literature) lists articles from popular magazines and journals and corresponds to the *Readers' Guide to Periodical Literature* from 1985 to the present.

To search for articles written in particular disciplines, our library also provides several specialized databases in the online catalog:

> *Wilson Guide to Business Periodicals, Education Index, and the Social Sciences Index* (WSOC) indexes journal articles in business, education, and social sciences.
> *Wilson Guide to Art Index and Humanities Index* (WHUM) indexes journal articles in humanities and arts.
> *Wilson Guide to Applied Science and Technology Index, Biological and Agricultural Sciences Index, and General Sciences Index* (WSCI) indexes journal articles in sciences, agriculture, and technology.
> *Current Contents Articles and Journals* (CART and CJOU) indexes the table of contents for recent journal issues in several fields of the sciences and social sciences (Fig. 2-3).

You will need to know enough about how information in your library is organized to be able to select the appropriate databases from the computer menu. Many libraries offer instruction in the use of their online catalog. If yours does not, plan to spend the time you need to become a confident user of your library's computer system. Take advantage of online help menus provided by the computer, and be sure to ask a librarian for help when stumped. Librarians are trained to be "user friendly."

Internet

Many libraries provide access to information in other libraries through Internet services via computer. The Internet is a computer "network of networks" from campuses as well as regional, national, and even international sources that are joined into a single network. It is like a worldwide network of information highways with all the freeways and byways connected. Internet in our library offers an opportu-

```
                    WELCOME
            UTAH STATE UNIVERSITY
               MERRILL LIBRARY

To select a database, type appropriate four letter
code, i.e. OPAC and press ENTER. To return to this
menu screen, type START.

                 MERLIN
OPAC             USU LIBRARY COLLECTION
                 JOURNAL/PERIODICAL INDEXES
*WRGA            POPULAR MAGAZINE INDEX
*WHUM            HUMANITIES & ART INDEXES
*WSCI            AGRICULTURE/BIOLOGY & SCIENCE
                 TECHNOLOGY
*WSOC            BUSINESS/EDUCATION & SOCIAL SCIENCES
                 CURRENT CONTENTS
*CART            CURRENT CONTENTS ARTICLES
*CJOU            CURRENT CONTENTS JOURNALS
             * Databases that require Sign-On.
--------------------Page 1 of 1------------------
HELP  Select a database label from above
NEWs (Library System News)


Database Selection:
Alt-Z FOR HELP3 VT100   3 FDX 3 19200 N81 3 LOG
CLOSED 3 PRINT OFF 3 OFF-LINE
```

FIGURE 2-3   Main Menu

nity to explore other Utah library catalogs, for example, or to find information through many different lists or "gophers" that store information. Students can use Internet to find information on sample job interview questions offered in a gopher by USU's career services. Or, you can locate the most recent White House press release on the budget. The best way to learn about Internet is to practice using it yourself.

Subject Headings

When using online catalogs, it is important to become familiar with the *Library of Congress Subject Headings* (*LCSH*), a listing of subject areas using specific terminology. To search the database by subject, you must provide the computer with exact subject headings, those officially used by the Library of Congress as listed in the *LCSH*. However, sometimes it is difficult to predict which terms will be used. The *LCSH* is your key or guide to the subjects recognized by the online catalog: it lists the subject headings that are assigned to books and materials in the library's collection. As there is often more than one way to describe a topic, the *LCSH* gives the exact format (wording and punctuation) for subject headings as they will appear in the database.

The *LCSH* is a large, three-volume work, usually kept near the computer terminals or somewhere in the reference area of your library. Look in the *LCSH* for as many variations on a subject as you can think of, starting with the most specific expression of your subject. For example, if your subject is the influence of classical Greece on ancient civilizations, you might begin first with "Civilization, Classical" since this is the heading listed in boldface type in the *LCSH*. The heading is followed by a scope note, describing those works listed under this particular heading. Note also the way the *LCSH* leads you to both broader (BT) and narrower (NT) subject headings, as well as telling you which ones are *not* subject headings (USE and UF "Used For") (Fig. 2-4).

The subject headings assigned to a particular book are listed by the computer as part of the entry for that book, known as the "tracings" because it traces, or keeps track of, the various subjects under which a work is cataloged. Multiple headings are assigned to a book to provide alternative access points by subject. You can often discover new terms to examine for information on a topic by checking the subject tracings in addition to using the *LCSH*.

On the other hand, if you have the wrong heading or the wrong terminology for your subject, the computer may not recognize your request and you may not discover anything in your online subject search. For example, if you are interested in classical Greek civilization, and you type into the computer "classical civilization," you might get the response that there are no holdings in your library on that subject. When checking the *LCSH*, you discover that the appropriate subject heading is "Civilization, Classical." (The heading "Classical civilization" is accompanied by the notation "UF" which means "Used For." This notation tells you that "Civilization, Classical" is *used for* "Classical civilization" in the catalog.) To get the computer to respond appropriately, you need to use the correct terminology, in this case, "Civilization, Classical."

Before beginning to search the online catalog, first check the *LCSH* to become familiar with all the possible subject terms related to your topic. Keep a comprehensive list of all the subject headings that you are using in your search of the library's holdings. These subject headings

Civilization, Classical

Here are entered works on both ancient Greek and Roman civilization. Works on the combined civilizations of Greece and Rome following the conquest of Greece in 146 B.C. are entered under Civilization, Greco-Roman. Works on the spread of Greek civilization and influence throughout the ancient world following the conquests of Alexander the Great are entered under Hellenism.

UF   Classical civilization
BT   Civilization, Ancient
RT   Classicism
NT   Aggada—Classical influences
      Art, Italian—Classical influences
      Art, Renaissance—Classical influences
      Arts, Modern—Classical influences
      Balkan Peninsula—Civilization—
         Classical influences
      Byzantine Empire—Civilization—
         Classical influences
      Catalonia (Spain)—Civilization—
         Classical influences
      Central Europe—Civilization—
         Classical influences
      Civilization, Greco-Roman
      Civilization, Western—Classical
         influences
      English literature—Classical
         influences
      Europe—Civilization—Classical
         influences
      Greece—Civilization—To 146 B.C.
      Greece—Civilization—Classical
         influences
      Greece—Intellectual life—Classical
         influences
      Mexico—Civilization—Classical
         influences
      Opera—Classical influences
      Public architecture—Classical
         influences
      Rome—Civilization
      Serbia—Civilization—Classical
         influences
      United States—Civilization—Classical
         influences
Civilization, Comparative
  USE Comparative civilization

FIGURE 2-4   The LCSH

will be useful to you not only for the library's book collection, but also when you begin searching for articles in magazines and journals.

Title and Author Searches   The computer can search quickly through its database when you provide it with a correct title or an author's name (T = Title; A = Author). If there is more than one work by an author, the computer lists them all, and then allows you to select the one you are looking for. You may need to request an expanded screen (or "long view") with more details about the specific work you have selected. The computer should also let you know whether or not the book has been checked out of the library and provide you with a call number to help you locate the book. In some libraries, it is possible to place a "hold" on a work through the computer, with a provision that you will be notified as soon as the book is back in circulation (Fig. 2-5).

Subject Searches   To search by subject, once again be certain to use the exact *LCSH* subject heading as found in the *LCSH* volumes. Tell the computer that you intend to search by subject by entering the appropriate command along with the exact subject heading (in our library, for example, you type "S = Subject"). The computer then tells you how many items in its database are cataloged under that subject heading (called the number of "hits") and provides you with a list of titles (Fig. 2-6).

If the computer tells you that there are several hundred books with your subject heading, you may need to narrow your subject search. The *LCSH* will provide you with narrower terms (labeled "NT"). Or you can narrow your search by combining key words (see Keyword Searching section in this chapter). On the other hand, if the computer tells you there are only one or two titles with your subject heading, you may need to broaden your subject search. Again, the *LCSH* will suggest related terms (labeled "RT") or broader terms ("BT") that you can try as well.

Call Number Searching.   This is an excellent way to locate materials similar to works for which you currently have a call number. By typing in the exact call number of a known work, you can ask the computer to list all of the call numbers that come before and after that work in the computer's memory. This means that it is possible to read titles on the computer screen by call number, just as you would browse a shelf in the library and retrieve other books found on surrounding shelves.

Keyword Searching.   Keyword searching allows for searching under the most important term or terms for your research project that

```
Search Request: T=HARD TIMES            USU CATALOG
      Record 1 of 10 Entries Found        Brief View

Author:     Terkel, Louis

Title: Hard times; an oral history of the great depression

Published: New York, Pantheon Books <1970>
--------------------------------------------------------------
LOCATION:          CALL NUMBER:   STATUS:
MERRILL LIBRARY    309.173 T272   Not checked out
STACKS



--------------------Page 1 of 1----------------------
STArt over         LONg view       <F6>  NEXt record
HELp               INDex
OTHer options
```

```
Search Request: T=HARD TIMES            USU CATALOG
BOOK - Record 1 of 10 Entries Found     LONG VIEW
--------------------------------------------------------------
Author: Terkel, Louis.

Title: Hard times; an oral history of the great depression

Published: New York, Pantheon Books <1970>
Description: xiii, 462 p. 25 cm.

Subjects: United States--Economic conditions--1918-1945
          United States--Social conditions--1933-1945
--------------------------------------------------------------
LOCATION:          CALL NUMBER:   STATUS:
MERRILL LIBRARY    309.173 T272   Not checked out
STACKS



--------------------Page 1 of 1----------------------
STArt over         BRIef view      <F6>  NEXt record
HELp               INdex
OTHer options

NEXT COMMAND:
Alt-Z FOR HELP3 VT100   3 FDX 3 19200 N81 3 LOG CLOSED 3
PRINT OFF 3 OFF-LINE
```

FIGURE 2-5 Online Title Search

```
Search Request:   S=ACUPUNCTURE                 USU CATALOG
BOOK - Results:   8 Entries Found               Subject Index
- - - - - - - - - - - - - - - - - - - - - - - - - - - - - - - - - - - - - -
    ACUPUNCTURE
1   CAUSES OF ACUPUNCTURE <1988>
2   CHINESE ACUPUNCTURE STANDARD PRACTICES LOCAT <1973>
3   CLINICAL ACUPUNCTURE A PRACTICAL JAPANESE AP <1988>
4   INTRODUCTION TO ACUPUNCTURE A PRACTICAL GUID <1987>
5   ZANG FU THE ORGAN SYSTEMS OF TRADITIONAL CHI <1985>

    ACUPUNCTURE- -PHYSIOLOGICAL ASPECTS- -CONGRESSES
6   SCIENTIFIC BASES OF ACUPUNCTURE <1989>
    ACUPUNCTURE ANESTHESIA
7   ACUPUNCTURE ANESTHESIA IN THE PEOPLES REPUBL <1976>
    ACUPUNCTURE ANESTHESIA- -CHINA
8   ACUPUNCTURE ANESTHESIA IN THE PEOPLES REPUBL <1976>

- - - - - - - - - - - - - - - - - - - - - - - - - - - - - - - - - - - - - -
STArt over         Type number to display record
HELp
OTHer options
NEXT COMMAND:
```

```
Search Request: S=ACUPUNCTURE                   USU CATALOG
BOOK - RECORD 1 of 8 Entries Found              Long View
- - - - - - - - - - - - - - - - - - - - - - - - - - - - - - - - - - - - - -
Author:            Stux, Gabriel.

Title:             Basics of acupuncture

Published:         Berlin ; New York : Springer-Verlag, c1988.
Description:       xi, 272 p. : ill. ; 19 cm.

Subjects:          Acupuncture.

Other authors:     Pomeranz, Bruce, 1937-

Notes:             Includes index.
                   Bibliography: p. 253-257.

- - - - - - - - - - - - - - -  + Page 1 of 2  - - - - - - - - - - - - - - -
STArt over         BRIef view      <F8>  FORward page
HELp               INDex           <F6>  NEXt record
OTHer options

NEXT COMMAND:
Alt-Z FOR HELP3 VT100    3 FDX 3 19200 N81 3 LOG CLOSED 3
PRINT OFF 3 OFF-LINE
```

FIGURE 2-6 Online Subject Search

continued

Figure 2-6 continued

```
Search Request: S=ACUPUNCTURE                        USU CATALOG
BOOK - Record 1 of 8 Entries Found                   Long View
-------------------------------------------------------------------
Author:             Stux, Gabriel.

Title:              Basics of acupuncture
Published:          Berlin ; New York : Springer-Verlag, c1988.
Description:        xi, 272 p. : ill. ; 19 cm.

Subjects:           Acupuncture.

Other authors:      Pomeranz, Bruce, 1937-

Notes:              Includes index.
                    Bibliography: p. 253-257.

-----------------    + Page 1 of 2   ------------------------
STArt over          BRIef view       <F8> FORward page
HELp                INDex            <F6> NEXt record
OTHer options

NEXT COMMAND:
Alt-Z FOR HELP3 VT100    3 FDX 3 19200 N81 3 LOG CLOSED 3
PRINT OFF 3 OFF-LINE

Search Request: S=ACUPUNCTURE                        USU CATALOG
BOOK - Record 1 of 8 Entries Found                   Long View
-------------------------------------------------------------------
Title:              Basics of acupuncture

-------------------------------------------------------------------
LOCATION:           CALL NUMBER:     STATUS:
SciTech LIBRARY     RM184.S79 1988   Not checked out
STACKS-4TH FLOOR

-----------------    + Page 2 of 2   ------------------------
STArt over          BRIef view       <F7>  BACk page
HELp                INDex            <F6> NEXt record
OTHer options

NEXT COMMAND:
Alt-Z FOR HELP3 VT100    3 FDX 3 19200 N81 3 LOG CLOSED 3
PRINT OFF 3 OFF-LINE
```

you have identified. The computer locates items in its database that use a particular keyword anywhere in a work's record. However, if the record doesn't happen to include that particular keyword or term, the computer typically will not be able to supply the synonym. Therefore, you still need to try as many keywords and subject headings as you can think of in a database search. For example, if you are searching the subject UFOs, you might use "UFO" as a keyword. But you might also want to try other keywords, such as "flying saucers" or "paranormal events."

Advanced Keyword Searching.   Using keywords, it is possible to perform combined searches of two or more terms. Combining keywords helps to limit an otherwise broad topic. For example, if you were interested in teenage pregnancy but only for the state of California, you could combine the terms "teenage pregnancy" and "California" to narrow your search, thus searching the collection only for those sources that include both keywords. This kind of focused searching offers distinct advantages over using a card catalog. If your library offers instruction in advanced database searching, you would be wise to take the opportunity to learn the "tricks of the trade" (Fig. 2-7).

Recording Bibliographic Information

Once you have a listing of books from the online catalog, you need to note each book's specific call number so that you can locate it in your library's collection. It may be possible for you to send a print command from your online catalog to request a printout of your search

```
Search Request: K=ACUPUNCTURE + CHINESE     USU CATALOG
BOOK  -  Record 1 of 1 Entry Found             Long View

Author:          Chuang, Yu-Min.

Title:           Chinese acupuncture : standard practices,
                 locations, illustrations / by Yu-min Chuang
                 (Yu-ming Chong).

Published:       Hanover, N. H. : Oriental Society, 1973.
Description:     98 p. : ill. ; 22 cm.

Subjects:        Acupuncture.

Notes:           English and Chinese.
------------------------------------------------------------
LOCATION:          CALL NUMBER:       STATUS:
SciTech LIBRARY    RM184 .C58x        Not checked out
STACKS-4TH FLOOR
------------------ Page 1 of 1  --------------------------
STArt over         BRIef view
HELp
OTHer options

NEXT COMMAND:
Alt-Z FOR HELP3 VT100    3 FDX 3 19200 N81 3 LOG CLOSED 3
PRINT OFF 3 OFF-LINE
```

FIGURE 2-7   Online Keyword Search

results. If not, you will need to be certain you write down the titles, along with their complete bibliographic information, on your working bibliography in your research notebook. Complete bibliographic information includes:

> Author(s) full name, including initials
> Title of the book, including subtitles and editions
> Place (city and state) where the book was published
> Name of the book's publisher
> Date of publication

Microforms

A few libraries organize their holdings on microforms rather than computer databases or catalog cards. Microforms are either microfilm or microfiche; both make use of methods to condense information in a very compact form. Machines called microform readers are necessary to read either form. Information stored on microform is similar to that found on traditional cards. If your library uses this system, check with the reference librarian for instructions about using the microform readers.

Locating Articles in Serials: Popular Periodicals

Periodicals are popular magazines and newspapers printed at regular intervals, such as daily, weekly, monthly, or quarterly. It is possible to search for magazines and journals through both online computer searching and print indexes. The reference section of your library contains several indexes to articles found in periodicals. Two important indexes of general-interest periodicals are:

> *Magazine Index.* Los Altos, CA.: Information Access, 1978 to present.
> *Readers' Guide to Periodical Literature.* New York: Wilson, 1901 to present.

Both sources index articles in popular magazines. The *Readers' Guide* is available in chronologically bound volumes; each contains an alphabetical listing of articles from a particular year. (The current issues are paperbound.) The *Magazine Index* is available on microform and online computer systems. This index is extremely useful for very current topics, because it indexes about twice as many articles as the *Readers' Guide.* In both sources, entries are arranged both by subject and author. These indexes may also be available in your library in a computer database.

Newspapers

Your library probably stores back issues of newspapers on microform. To gain access to articles in the *New York Times*, use the *New York Times Index*, which lists all major articles from the *Times* from 1913 to the present. The *Newspaper Index* lists articles from the *Chicago Tribune, Los Angeles Times, New Orleans Times-Picayune,* and *Washington Post.* Both indexes are arranged by subject. For business news, use the *Wall Street Journal Index.* Newspaper indexes may be available in your library in both print and database forms.

Finding Periodicals

Indexes such as the *Magazine Index* or the *Readers' Guide* may lead you to titles of articles related to your particular research topic. However, it is important to note that these indexes catalog general interest periodicals that may not be appropriate for some academic research projects. To find discipline-specific journals, you must use discipline-specific indexes (see the section in this chapter on Locating Articles in Serials: Professional Journals).

When researching your topic, write down or print out the *complete* citation of any relevant article. The citation includes:

the author (if given)
the title of the article
the name of the magazine
the volume number
the issue number
the date published
the inclusive pages of the article

For example, suppose you were researching artificial hearts. You might turn up the listing from the *Readers' Guide* shown in Fig. 2-8: You would write down in your research notebook the complete citations of any articles that look as though they might be related to your topic. For example:

Shiley saga leads to improved communication D. Farley. il FDA Consumer v28 p12–17 Ja/F '94

The title of the magazine may be abbreviated in the index. To find the full name of the magazine, look in "Abbreviations of Periodicals Indexed," usually found at the front of each volume of the index. You can also ask the online computer to provide you with the "long view," which includes the complete information on an article (Fig. 2-9).

HEART
Abnormalities
Mutant gene causes heart malformations [study by Donna Rounds] K. Fackelmann. *Science News* v145 p79 Ja 29 '94
Diseases
Nutritional aspects
See also
Cholesterol
Clean living [D. Ornish's program] N. Rotenier. il por *Forbes* v153 p173 Ap 25 '94
Fast—and lose [alleged harmfulness of high fat diet] J. Le Fanu. *National Review* v46 Pleasure p3-6 Ap 18 '94
Feet-first prevention [role of exercise in lowering triglycerides; research by Peter H. Jones] il *Prevention (Emmaus, Pa.)* v46 p9-10 Ja '94
Prevention
Headed for a heart attack? [quiz] il *American Health* v13 p32-3 Ja/F '94
Tummy chum [use of aspirin transdermal patch to prevent heart disease] il *Prevention (Emmaus, Pa.)* v45 p28 D '93
Psychological aspects
"I've been blessed with 16 more years of a good life." [J. Morrison] H. Dreher. il por *Good Housekeeping* v217 p74+ N '93
'Open heart' without surgery [D. Ornish's program focusing upon stress management and social interaction] il *Prevention (Emmaus, Pa.)* v46 p56-62+ F '94
Taking depression to heart [research by Nancy Frasure-Smith] N. Wartik. il *American Health* v13 p30 Ja/F '94
Therapy
Clean living [D. Ornish's program] N. Rotenier. il por *Forbes* v153 p173 Ap 25 '94
Too little, too late? [underutilization of thrombolytic agents; study by Vernon Anderson] J. Rennie. il *Scientific American* v270 p21-2+ F '94
Surgery
See also
Cardiac catheterization
Coronary bypass
Transmyocardial revascularization
HEART, ARTIFICIAL
Defects
Shiley saga leads to improved communication [monitoring safety of artificial heart valves] D. Farley. il *FDA Consumer* v28 p12-17 Ja/F '94
HEART ATTACKS *See* Heart—Diseases
HEART BEAT
See also
Pacemaker, Artificial (Heart)

FIGURE 2-8 Reader's Guide

Your library has a particular system for listing magazine and newspaper holdings. This serials listing may appear in the online catalog, in a separate catalog, in the main card catalog, on computer printouts, or on microform. Consult your librarian to determine which system your library uses. The serials listing tells you to which periodicals your library subscribes, where they are located in the library, the inclusive dates of the issues your library has, and whether the issues are in bound or unbound volumes or on microform.

Once you have obtained the call number of the magazine containing your article from the serials listing, you will be able to find the magazine itself, whether it is in a bound volume, in the current-periodicals section of the library, or on microform. Once you have the article in hand, be sure to copy down the complete publication information, which is often only abbreviated in the index (see p. 42). Writing everything down at this point will prevent your having to return to the library later for information you neglected to note originally.

```
Search Request:K=FAMILY AND COUNSELING  BUSINESS/EDUCATION & SOC
WILSON Record -- 2 of 18 Entries Found                   Long View
------------------------------------------------------------------
AUTHOR:       Aronen, Eeva.

TITLE:        The effect of family counselling on the mental
              health on 10-11-year-old  children in low- and
              high risk families: a longitudinal approach.

SOURCE:       The Journal of Child Psychology and Psychiatry
              and Allied Disciplines 34:155-65 Feb  '93

SPECIAL FEATURES:
              bibl.

SUBJECT DESCRIPTORS:
              School children--Mental health.
              Mental illness--Prevention.
              Family counseling.
---------------------------- Page 1 of 1  --------------------
STArt over          HOLdings            <F6> NEXt record
HELp                BRIef view          <F5> PREvious record
OTHer options       INDex
Held by library--type HOL for holdings information.
NEXT COMMAND:
Alt-Z FOR HELP3 VT100   3 FDX 3 19200 N81 3 LOG CLOSED 3 PRINT
OFF 3 OFF-LINE
```

FIGURE 2-9 Long View Journal Article

Evaluating Periodicals

If you find the title of a magazine but are unsure of its nature or scope, a useful evaluative tool is *Katz's Magazines for Libraries*, 5th ed. (New York: Bowker, 1986). This work describes and explains magazines. Katz's guide can give you some insight into the magazine's purpose, reputation, and scope.

Locating Articles in Serials: Professional Journals

When you are researching a technical subject, you want to refer to articles written on the subject by professionals in the field. Professional journal articles, sometimes called serials because they are printed in series, are indexed in much the same way as the general periodicals previously discussed. However, numerous specialized indexes and databases exist for professional articles, and each index or database covers a particular discipline or subject area. ("Discipline-Specific Resources," in Part Two, lists discipline-appropriate indexes for sciences and technology, social sciences, humanities, and business.)

Once you have located an appropriate index, begin looking up your topic in the most recent volume first. If you were researching the topic "drug abuse," Figure 2-10 provides an example of what you might find in the *Social Sciences Index.*

For articles that sound promising for your research, copy down the complete citation (see page 45). To find the full version of abbreviated journal names, turn to "Abbreviations of Periodicals Indexed," usually at the front of the index volume. For example, you would find that *Congr Q Wkly Rep* is the abbreviation for *Congressional Quarterly Weekly Reports.* Then locate the particular journal by using your library's listing of serial holdings, just as you did for magazines and newspapers. Professional journals are stored in bound or unbound volumes (the latter for very recent editions) or on microform. The citation you have obtained from the index is your key to finding a particular article. Thus, it is crucial that you copy down the citation information accurately and completely.

Many of the indexes to scholarly journals follow the format of the *Social Sciences Index* (see Fig. 2-10). However, there are sometimes variations in the index formats. Take the time to get acquainted with the arrangement of each index by reading the explanation in the index's preface. If you are still confused about how an index is organized, ask your reference librarian for help. As mentioned before, many indexes are now contained on databases so that they may be searched with computers. Check with your librarian to discover which indexes in your library may be searched on computer.

Dual career couples *See* Dual career families
Dual career families
>   *See also*
>   Commuter marriage
>   Work and family

Division of household labor and child care in dual-earner
    African-American families with infants. Z. Hossain
    and J. L. Roopnarine. bibl *Sex Roles* v29 p571-83 N '93
The division of household labor and wives' happiness:
    ideology, employment, and perceptions of support.
    D. L. Piña and V. L. Bengtson. bibl *J Marriage
    Fam Rev* v55 p901-12 N '93
The dual-career commuter family: a lifestyle on the
    move. E. A. Anderson and J. W. Spruill. bibl *Marriage
    Fam Rev* v19 no1-2 p131-47 '93
Dual-earner couples in Singapore: an examination of
    work and nonwork sources of their experienced burnout.
    S. Aryee. bibl *Hum Relat* v46 p1441-68 D '93
Female employment and first union dissolution in Puerto
    Rico. K. P. Carver and J. D. Teachman. bibl *J Marriage
    Fam* v55 p686-98 Ag '93
Dual career marriage *See* Dual career families

FIGURE 2-10   Social Sciences Index

Locating Government Documents

The U.S. government is one of the largest publishers of information and is a rich source of materials in almost every field, from aeronautics to zoology. Government documents are sometimes listed in a separate database or catalog from the main online or card catalog. Check with your reference librarian to discern how your library catalogs its documents.

The *Monthly Catalog of United States Government Publications* is the comprehensive bibliography that lists all publications received by the Government Printing Office for printing and distribution. The *Monthly Catalog*, established in 1895, is the best overall guide to finding government sources. At the back of each monthly register are indexes that provide access to the documents by authors, subjects, and series/report numbers. The monthly indexes are cumulated (that is, brought together into one volume) both semiannually and annually for ease of access.

Other ways to find government documents include the following indexes:

> *Index to U.S. Government Periodicals*
> *Public Affairs Information Services (PAIS)*
> *Resources in Education (RIE)*

U.S. Government Reports, Announcements and Index
(*NTIS*—National Technical Information Service)

The *Index to U.S. Government Periodicals* provides access by author and subject to 180 government periodicals. The *PAIS* lists by subject current books, pamphlets, periodical articles, and government publications in the field of economics and public affairs. *RIE* lists government-sponsored reports related to the field of education. The *U.S. Government Reports, Announcements and Index (NTIS)* lists government-sponsored research in the technical sciences by subject fields: aeronautics; agriculture; astronomy and astrophysics; atmospheric sciences; behavioral and social sciences; biological and medical sciences; chemistry; earth science and oceanography; electronic and electrical engineering; energy conversion; materials; mathematical sciences; mechanical, industrial, civil, and marine engineering; methods and equipment; military science; navigation, communications, detection; nuclear science and technology; physics; and propulsion and fuels.

Other Technologies

Online Database Services

To supplement the searches you have been able to conduct in your own library, online database searches may be conducted for you by trained search librarians who have access through a telecommunication link to a central databasing service such as DIALOG. When you want to conduct such a search, make an appointment with a librarian to discuss your search needs, possible databases, and likely subject headings. The librarian then conducts the search and provides you with a printout of sources or abstracts. The cost of the search is typically passed on to you, so you should discuss any search with a trained librarian first to decide whether it is feasible and economical.

CD-ROM Searching

Many libraries are now providing patrons with the opportunity to search databases themselves, using microcomputers connected to compact disk units (CD-ROMs). With compact disk technology, large databases can be made accessible and easy to use. For example, the education index ERIC (Education Research Information Clearinghouse) is now available in this format, as is the business index ABI-INFORM. Check your library reference area to see whether such tools are available to you. These databases are subject specific, so you need to find out just which journals or subjects they index. But they often can provide a quick alternative to searching the print indexes on your subject. Another bonus of using CD-ROMs is that the information found in your search can usually be sent to a printer or downloaded onto your own computer disk.

As with any computerized search, it is important to know your subject headings and terminology. Many of the computer databases use their own "controlled vocabulary," which may vary slightly from the subject headings listed in the *LCSH*. Check with your librarian to discern whether there is a "thesaurus" or listing of subject headings for the particular database you are using. ERIC on-disk, for example, uses the "ERIC Descriptors" as its method of cataloging by subject.

The section titled Discipline-Specific Resources in each chapter of Part Two indicates which indexes may be available to you through computerized database searching (Figure 2-11).

Accessing Information from Other Libraries

If, in your search, you discover that some item you need is not located in your library, it is still possible to find the item in another library. An online computer database called the OCLC (Online Computer Library Center) provides thousands of libraries with connections to each other's catalogs. By searching the OCLC database (by author or title), you can quickly ascertain if a nearby library contains the needed item; then you may request it through interlibrary loan or secure it yourself.

The Card Catalog

Your library may use cards to record some or all of the library's holdings; these cards are found in the card catalog. (Note: Library catalogs differ from institution to institution. A few libraries still use card catalogs, but most now use computer access systems or microforms, as previously discussed.) In a card catalog, each card lists a single work, and each work is represented by three cards: one for the author, one for the title, and one for the subject. Your library's card catalog may be divided into author/title cards and subject cards, and these may be filed together in one file or separately.

Each work has a unique number, the *call number*, in the upper left-hand corner of the catalog card. A book's call number is its address to help you locate it in the library. The two major systems of cataloging in the United States are the Dewey decimal system and the Library of Congress system. Both systems use call numbers to provide you access to the particular item. The accompanying examples shown in Figures 2-12 through 2-14 use the Library of Congress system. (If they used the Dewey decimal system, the call numbers would be somewhat differ-

Database— DIALOG File 1: ERIC - 66-84/Sep

service
date

EJ299865   HE518071
Many Colleges Limit Students' Use of Central Computers for
Writing.
Turner, Judith Axler
CAUSE/EFFECT, v7 n3 p6-7 May 1984
Available from: UMI
Language: English
Document Type: POSITION PAPER (120); PROJECT DESCRIPTION (141)
Allocating limited resources to an unlimited demand is an
issue faced by data processing management in higher education.
Use of the central computer for word processing is creating a
demand at many institutions that is stretching and exceeding the
available computing resources. (Author/MLW)
Descriptors: *College Students; *Computers; Data Processing;
Higher Education; *Time Management; Use Studies; *Word Process-
ing; *Writing (Composition)
Identifiers: *Computer Centers; Yale University CT

Education —— *Title*
Journal
(EI) iden- EJ298427   IR512505
tification A Dyslexic Can Compose on a Computer.————————— *Author*
number Arms, Valarie M.
Educational Technology, v24 n1 p39-41 Jan 1984 —*Journal*
Available from: UMI   *publication*
Language: English   *data*
Document Type: PROJECT DESCRIPTION (141)
Journal Announcement: CIJAUG84
Abstract ⌐Describes the strategies used by a technical writing teacher
         │who encouraged a dyslexic university engineering student to use
         │a microcomputer as an aid in composition writing, and discusses
         │how a word processing program was used to make the writing
         └process easier and increase the student's self-confidence. (MBR)
Subject ⌐Descriptors: College Students; Computer Assisted Instruction;
headings│*Dyslexia; Higher Education; Learning Disabilities; Learning Mo-
         │tivation; *Microcomputers; *Teaching Methods; *Word Processing;
         └*Writing (Composition)

EJ298270   FL515801
Computer-Assisted Text-Analysis for ESL Students.
Reid, Joy; And Others
CALICO Journal, v1 n3 p40-42 Dec 1983
Language: English
Document Type: PROJECT DESCRIPTION (141); POSITION PAPER (120)
Journal Announcement: CIJAUG84
Reports an investigation into possibilities of using word
processors and text analysis software with English as second
language (ESL) students to determine (1) if foreign students can
learn to use computer equipment, (2) if students feel time in-
vested is worthwhile, and (3) if ESL students' problems with

writing American academic prose can be remedied by this type of
assistance. (SL)
Descriptors: Comparative Analysis; *Computer Assisted In-
struction; *English (Second Language); Grammar; Modern Language
Curriculum; Second Language Learning; *Student Participation;
Vocabulary Development; *Word Processing; *Writing Skills

EJ298267   FL515798
Computer-Assisted Language Learning at the University of
Dundee.
Lewis, Derek R.
CALICO Journal, v1 n3 p10-12 Dec 1983
Language: English
Document Type: NON-CLASSROOM MATERIAL (055); POSITION PAPER
(120)
Journal Announcement: CIJAUG84
Presents an overview of activities in field of computer-as-
sisted language learning at the University of Dundee (Scotland).
These include: (1) use and testing of a self-instructional
teacher's package; (2) development of the computer-controlled
tape recorder; (3) cloze-type gapping exercises; and (4) pro-
jects aimed at the word processing translation skills of under-
graduates. (SL)
Descriptors: *Cloze Procedure; *Computer Assisted Instruction;
Foreign Countries; *Language Tests; Modern Language Curriculum;
*Second Language Instruction; *Student Participation; Transla-
tion; Undergraduate Students; *Word Processing; Writing Skills
Identifiers: Dundee University (Scotland)

EJ297923   CS729605
Pitfalls in Electronic Writing Land.
Oliver, Lawrence J., Jr.
English Education, v16 n2 p94-100 May 1984
Available from: UMI
Language: English
Document Type: POSITION PAPER (120)
Journal Announcement: CIJAUG84
Discusses the drawbacks of computer assisted instruction in
the composition classroom. (FL)
Descriptors: *Computer Assisted Instruction; *Computers; Ele-
mentary Secondary Education; Higher Education; *Problems;
*Teacher Role; *Word Processing; *Writing Instruction

EJ297016   IR512399
"Writing to Read"--Challenging an Age-Old Tradition.
Electronic Education, v3 n5 p21-22 Feb 1984
Language: English
Document Type: PROJECT DESCRIPTION (141)
Journal Announcement: CIJJUL84
Describes Dr. John Henry Martin's theory of how children can
learn to write phonetically before learning to read and how this
theory developed into a computer-based teaching system
(cont. next page)

FIGURE 2-11 Online Database

```
      ── Call number                          Author's name
    PR                                          /
    461      Buckley, Jerome Hamilton.'              Work's title
    B75      The Victorian temper : a study in literary culture
    1981     / by Jerome Hamilton Buckley.-- 1st pbk. ed.── Edition
  Imprint────Cambridge [Cambridgeshire] : Cambridge University
  (place of  Press, 1981, c1951.              Special features
  publication,   x, 282 p. ; 22 cm.           /
  publisher, date / Includes bibliographical references and index.
  of publication) /
                                                       Tracings
                                                      /
    Number of/  1. English literature--19th century--History and
   pages, size criticism. I. Title
   of book
    TxLT        bo                           ILUUnt    81-6142
```

FIGURE 2-12   Author Card

ent.) On author cards the author's name is at the top, on title cards the title is at the top, and on subject cards the subject heading is at the top.

✦ EXERCISES

1. In the reference section of the library, find a major biographical work. To become familiar with major biographical sources, look

```
            Title──·The Victorian temper
    PR
    461      Buckley, Jerome Hamilton.    ─Complete title
    B75       The Victorian temper : a study in literary culture
    1981      / by Jerome Hamilton Buckley.-- 1st pbk. ed.--
              Cambridge [Cambridgeshire] : Cambridge University
              Press, 1981, c1951.
                 x, 282 p. ; 22 cm.
                 Includes bibliographical references and index.


                 1. English literature--19th century--History and
              criticism. I. Title

    TxLT        bo                           ILUUnt    81-6142
```

FIGURE 2-13   Title Card

```
         ⎯ Call number                          Author's name
   PR                                          ╱
   461      Buckley, Jerome Hamilton. ╱              ╱ Work's title
   B75        The Victorian temper : a study in literary culture
   1981       / by Jerome Hamilton Buckley.-- 1st pbk. ed. ⟵ Edition
   Imprint ⎯⎯⎯ Cambridge [Cambridgeshire] : Cambridge University
   (place of    Press, 1981, c1951.            ╱ Special features
   publication,   x, 282 p. ; 22 cm.         ╱
   publisher, date / Includes bibliographical references and index.
   of publication) ╱
                                                   ╱ Tracings
                                                 ╱
      Number of ╱ 1. English literature--19th century--History and
      pages, size criticism. I. Title
      of book
      TxLT     bo                            ILUUnt    81-6142
```

FIGURE 2-14   Subject Card

up information on a famous person who is or was important in
your major field or in your specific research project. (Be sure to
look in an appropriate biography in accordance with whether
the person is living or dead, American or British, and so on.)
Take notes on that person's life and work. Write a one-page report on some aspect of the person that seems interesting to you.
You may wish to consult more than one biography and compare
the entries.

2. In your library's online or card catalog, look up a subject area
   that interests you as a possible research topic. (For ideas, browse
   through the *Library of Congress Subject Headings* list.) Write down
   the author, title, and call number of any book that seems interesting. Using the call number, find the book in the library stacks.
   Write a complete citation for the book, including the author's
   full name, the title and edition of the book, and the publication
   data. Then write a one-paragraph annotation describing the
   book. (An annotation is a short critical or explanatory note.)

3. Using one of the indexes to periodicals (either online or in
   print), look up the subject you looked up in question 2. Again,
   note one article listed in the index that sounds interesting. Find
   the article itself in the library by using your library's serials listing of magazine holdings and their locations. Make a photocopy
   of the article. On your copy, underline key ideas in the article.
   Turn in your underlined copy.

4. Look up the magazine you used in question 3 in *Katz's Magazines for Libraries*. Write down the information you find about the magazine. (Note: If your library does not have Katz's work, find out if it carries a similar work, such as *Farber's Classified List of Periodicals for the College Library*.)

5. Using the *Social Sciences Index*, or another index appropriate for your field, look up a current issue, for example, a social problem (alcoholism, child abuse, or prison reform). Find the title of one current article in a scholarly journal. Write down or print out the citation from the index, find the complete journal name in the front of the index, and using that information find the journal article in your library. (Remember, you will need to look up the journal name in the serials listing just as you did for a popular magazine.) Make a photocopy of the article. On your copy, underline key ideas. Then construct an outline of the article. Turn in the photocopy with your outline.

6. Find any information your library has about online computer searches and discuss computer searching in your particular field with the librarian responsible for computer searches.

7. Find out whether your library has any databases on videodisk or CD-ROM that you can search using a microcomputer. Try out any such tools, using appropriate subject headings and key words for your topic, and turn in the printout generated from your search.

8. Interview one of your professors about library research in his or her field. How does that professor gather information needed for his or her work? How has the research process changed over the years? How much does the professor rely on computer searching? Write a short paragraph summarizing the interview.

9. Interview a reference librarian at your campus library. How has information access changed? How many new information sources have come to campus in the past year or so? What does the librarian foresee in the libraries of the future? Write a short paragraph summarizing the interview.

3

✦ ✦ ✦

Library Research
Methods

INTRODUCTION

Successful research depends on knowing what library resources are available, but it also depends on knowing how to find and use those resources. Developing a search strategy will help you to find materials on your research topic and to use library resources efficiently. First, you need to use library tools to locate source materials; then you must evaluate those sources and interpret them so that they will be useful to your particular research project.

PREPARATION AND INCUBATION

As a college student, you are uniquely prepared to conduct a research project. Your experiences and prior schooling have given you a wealth of information to draw from. A research project may begin in one of the following ways: you may have been assigned to do a research paper in a particular college class or you may have discovered an interesting question or problem on your own that you decided to investigate. Although the former impetus, a course assignment, might seem artificial or contrived at first, in reality it may give you the opportunity to investigate something that has always intrigued you.

Finding a Topic

A good place to begin looking for a research topic is in the textbooks you are currently using for the courses you are taking. Scan the table of contents with an eye toward a topic that you'd enjoy investigating. Or if you have no idea at all, begin by browsing through a specialized encyclopedia, such as the *Encyclopedia of Psychology* or the *Encyclopedia of Education*. (Other specialized encyclopedias are listed by discipline in the chapters of Part Two.) A third resource for finding topics is Editorial Research Reports (ERR). If your library subscribes to ERR, it receives a weekly description of a wide variety of contemporary events, problems, and issues, such as acid rain, homelessness, or women in business. A bibliography listing several recent articles, books, and reports on each topic covered by ERR is also included. Skimming these reports may spark an interest in a particular topic, as well as get you started on finding relevant materials and information.

Once you have an idea for a topic, you might discuss your idea with a reference librarian, with your teacher, and with other students in your class. They may have ideas or suggestions related to your topic or may be able to direct you to aspects of the topic you may not have considered. Your goal is to focus your topic by asking pertinent starting questions that your research will attempt to answer. So, if your general topic is "acid rain," your specific starting question might be "What have the effects of acid rain been on the forests of New York?" Or, "What is the EPA currently doing to control pollutants that cause acid rain?" Such questions, which should be neither too trivial nor too broad, will help you to sort through information in search of an answer and may prevent you from aimlessly reading on a topic area that is too general.

Gathering Research Materials

The Research Notebook

To keep track of all your research, you need to obtain a notebook to serve as your "research notebook." In the notebook, you record your specific topic area and the starting questions you wish to answer, outline your plans for searching the library (called a library search strategy), and begin a list of sources (called a working bibliography). Your research notebook is also the place where you can begin to articulate for yourself your own understanding of the answer to your starting question as it evolves through your research. It is crucial that, as you investigate your topic, you record in the research notebook not only what others have said on the subject, but also your own impressions and comments.

Your research notebook, then, will be the place for tracing your entire research process: the starting questions, the search strategy, the sources used in your search, your notes, reactions to and comments on the sources, the tentative answers you propose to your starting question, a thesis statement articulating the main points to be covered by your paper, an informal outline or an organizational plan for your paper, and all preliminary drafts of your paper. Many students like to take notes from sources in their research notebooks instead of on note-cards, in order to keep all their research information in a single conve-nient place. If you decide on this approach, be sure to record your notes and evaluative comments in separate parts of the notebook. I suggest to my students that they leave a blank page for comments in their note-books adjacent to each page of notes. Also, remember to reserve a place in your notebook for recording any primary research data (such as in-terview, survey, or questionnaire data) that you collect in connection with your research project.

A Computer Research Notebook

If you are using a word processor, you can take advantage of the storage capabilities of your computer to develop a computer research notebook. Create a file or directory on your computer and label it your research notebook file. All of the items previously listed for a research notebook can be gathered together in this one file or directory on your computer. For example, you could include your topic and starting questions, search strategy, working bibliography, notes and evaluative comments on sources, and so on. In this way, your research project can proceed systematically as you gather information and build your own expertise on your topic through your evolving computer file. Using word processing, then, you can revise your notebook file, organize your information, and even write your paper based on the stored in-formation on disk.

For example, a student who had to write a research report for a computer science class decided to write about computer crime. In thinking about the subject, he determined that first he needed to cate-gorize the types of computer crimes so that he could arrange the infor-mation in his research notebook in an organized way. As he read books and articles on the subject, he began to sort materials into the following subheadings: computer as object or target of crime, computer as subject or site of crime, computer as instrument used to create crime, and com-puter as symbol for criminal deception or intimidation. After entering these subheadings onto his computer file, he gradually built up the re-port; as he encountered information for the various sections of his re-port, he added it under the appropriate subheading in his file. You could use a similar method for your own research notebook.

The Working Bibliography

A bibliography, as you learned in Chapter 2, is a list of books and articles on a particular subject. Your working bibliography, your preliminary list of sources, grows as your research progresses, as one source leads you to another. It is called a "working" bibliography—as opposed to the finished bibliography—because it may contain some sources that you ultimately will not use in your paper.

A working bibliography need not be in final bibliographic form, but it is important to record accurately all the information eventually needed to compose your final bibliography to keep from having to backtrack and find a book or article again. Oftentimes, a student finds a book, reads a relevant section and takes notes, but neglects to write down all of the bibliographic information, that is, the author(s), complete title, publisher, date and place of publication, and so on (see pp. 43–45). Then, when compiling the final bibliography in which are listed all of the sources referred to in the paper, the student discovers that he or she has not written down the date of publication, for instance, or the author's first name. This means another trip to the library to find the book or journal, which may or may not still be on the shelf!

The working bibliography should be comprehensive, the place where you note down all sources that you run across—in bibliographies or databases, for example, whether your library has them and whether they turn out to be relevant to your topic. So, the working bibliography is a complete record of every possible path you encountered in your search, whether or not you ultimately followed that path. In contrast, the final bibliography lists only those sources that you actually read and used as references for your own paper.

The example below of a working bibliography comes from a student's research project on the body's immune system. The student used the CBE citation style commonly used in sciences and technology.

                    Working Bibliography

        Golub, E. S. 1987. Immunology: A synthesis.

            Boston: Sinauer Associates.

        Bellanti, J. A. 1978. Immunology II.

            Philadelphia: W. B. Saunders.

        Bass, A. 1985. Unlocking the secrets of immunity.

            Technology Review 88: 62.

        Getzoff, E. 1987. Mechanisms of antibody binding

            to a protein. Science 235: 1191.

        Herscowitz, H. 1985. Cell-mediated immune

            reactions. Philadelphia: W. B. Saunders.

Silberner, J. 1986. Second T-cell receptor found.

Science News, 180: 50.

Wise, H. 1987. Man bites man. Hippocrite 100: 93.

Quinn, L. Y. 1968. Immunological concepts. Ames,

IA: Iowa State University Press.

Reissig, J. L. 1977. Microbial interactions. New

York: Chapman and Hall Press.

Notecards and Bibliography Cards

Many students and teachers like to record information from library sources on index cards. If you choose this method, you will develop two sets of cards: bibliography cards and notecards. The bibliography cards are used to record bibliographical information from the source (author, title, and publication data). The notecards are used to record actual notes (either paraphrased or directly quoted) from the source. See the examples of a bibliography card and a notecard that a student used in his research on computer crime (Figs. 3-1 and 3-2).

Each notecard contains a descriptive title and the notes themselves. Take notes on only one side of each card to allow for easy sorting and scanning of information later on. As you paraphrase material from your source, you must be careful to transcribe the meaning without using the author's wording. When you quote directly, be sure to mark words or phrases from the original with quotation marks. Provide a page reference for all notes, both quotations and paraphrases.

A number appears in the upper right-hand corner of the notecard. This is the control number that allows you to match the notes with the source. On the notecard in Figure 3-1, the number 3 tells you that this note was found in the third source, *Encyclopedia of Computer Science and Engineering*. The number 1 in 3.1 indicates that this note was the first one taken from source 3. Notes are numbered consecutively for each source. It is important that you number every notecard in this way, since you will be relying on this system later in documenting the source of your information.

The Bibliography Card for a Book or Journal

On the bibliography card for a book, write down the library call number of the book (in case you need to look up the book again) and its complete citation: the author(s) of the book (if known), the complete

---

3.1

Crime and Computer Security
Origin

When computers began to be used for classified
government documents, the need for security was
recognized (p. 426).

FIGURE 3-1   Notecard

---

title and edition number of the book, and the publication data (place of publication, publishing company, and date). The bibliography card for a journal is similar to that for a book, except the details of the citation vary somewhat. For journals, write down the author's (or authors') complete name(s); the complete title of the article; the complete name of the journal; the volume, issue number, and date of publication; and the inclusive page numbers of the article you are citing.

Developing a Search Strategy

Once you have decided on some starting questions and have gathered the necessary research materials, you are ready to outline a preliminary search strategy. Many library research projects begin in the reference area of the library, since the library tools that refer you to other sources are kept there. Often you will begin with reference works (dictionaries, encyclopedias, and biographies), in which can be found background and contextualizing information on your topic. Then, you may proceed to more specific reference works (abstracts, indexes, and databases). To make your library search an orderly and thorough process, you should design a search strategy, beginning with general sources and working to more specific sources. In most fields, a search strategy includes the following major components:

1. Background sources—dictionaries and encyclopedias (including discipline-specific sources)

QA   3
76.15
E 48

The Encyclopedia of Computer Science and
Engineering, 2nd ed. *Anthony Ralston, ed. N.Y.: Van*
Nostrand Reinhold, 1983.

FIGURE 3-2   Bibliography Card

2. Biographies (on people relevant to your topic)
3. Reviews of literature and research reports (to discover how others outline or overview the subject)
4. Print indexes and bibliographies (for listings of source materials
   by subject) (Remember to use the LCSH for subject headings)
5. Library online catalog and other databases (including CD-ROMs)
   for subject and keyword searching of books and journal articles
   on your topic (Use your library's serials listing to locate sources
   available in your library)
6. Primary research (for firsthand information such as interviews or
   surveys)

One student designed the following search strategy to help him
begin his research on computer crime:

1. Look up "computer crime" in dictionaries and encyclopedias, including *Chambers' Dictionary of Science and Technology* and *The Encyclopedia of Computer Science and Engineering* for definitions.
2. Look up any reviews already done on computer crime, using the
   Index to Scientific Reviews and *Current Contents* for background
   overviews on the subject.
3. Use the *Applied Science and Technology Index* to look up current
   works on computer crime. Check headings to be sure that the keyword is "computer crime." (Note: This student discovered that
   this particular index listed articles on computer crime under the

heading "Electronic Data Processing—Security Measures.") Use the *Science Citation Index* for a forward search on key sources.
4. Look up "computer crime" in the *Library of Congress Subject Headings* (LCSH) list to determine whether it is the subject heading used in the online catalog. Then, using the online catalog, search for sources on "computer crime" and other related headings by subject and keywords to find books and articles on computer crime.

Notice that this student's search began in the reference area and ended with use of the online catalog. Many students make the mistake of using the catalog before they really know enough about their topics to make it useful. You would be wise to order your search strategy to begin in the reference area as well.

You may need to change or modify your search strategy as you go along; do not feel that the strategy must be rigid or inflexible. However, using a search strategy enables you to proceed in an orderly, systematic fashion with your research. On your working bibliography, write down the complete citation for each source you encounter in your search. As you read in the general and specialized encyclopedias, for example, you may find related references listed at the end of articles. Write down in your working bibliography complete citations for any references that look promising so that you can look them up later. Similarly, as you look through the reviews, the indexes, and the card catalog, write down the citations to any promising sources. In this way, you will build your working bibliography during your library search.

✦ EXERCISES

To begin preparation for your own research project, follow these steps:

1. Select and narrow a research topic, that is, limit the topic in scope so that it is of a manageable size. Talk your topic over with others, including your classmates, your teacher, and your librarians.
2. Articulate several starting questions that you would seek to answer during your research.
3. Gather your research materials—notebook and notecards. Or create a computer file or directory for a computerized notebook.
4. Reserve space in your research notebook or computer file for both notes from sources and the evaluative comments that you will write down as you are reading.

5. Reserve space in your research notebook or computer file for your working bibliography in which you will list all of the sources you encounter during your search.
6. Outline your search strategy (refer to Chapter 2 for specific library tools to use in your search and to Chapters 6, 7, 8, or 9 for a sample search in your chosen discipline).

Outlining a Time Frame

After writing down your search strategy, you will have at least some idea of how long your research is likely to take. Now is the time to sit down with a calendar and create a time frame for your entire research project. Your teacher may have given you some deadlines, and if so, they will help you decide on a time frame. If not, you will have to set your own dates for accomplishing specific tasks so that you can proceed in an orderly fashion toward the completion of the project. If you have never done a research project before, you might be overwhelmed at the thought of such a large task. However, if you break the job down into smaller parts, it will seem more manageable.

Allow yourself three to four weeks for locating, reading, and evaluating sources. As you begin to work in the library, you will see that a library search is a very time-consuming process. Just locating sources in a large library takes time; perhaps one book you need will be shelved in the third sub-basement and another on the fourth floor! Sometimes a book you want will have been checked out; in such a case you will have to submit a "recall notice" to the librarian asking that the book be returned and reserved for you. You may also find that you need to obtain materials from another library through an interlibrary loan, another time-consuming process. Plan to spend two to three hours in the library each day for the first month of your research project. After that, you may find you can spend less time in the library.

If your research project involves primary research (see Chapter 4), begin to plan for that research while you are writing your search strategy. Allow one to two weeks for conducting your primary research, depending on its nature and scope.

Schedule one to two weeks for preliminary writing. To make sense of your subject and answer your starting question, you need to spend time and effort in studying and evaluating your sources, in brainstorming and writing discovery drafts. Eventually, you ought to be able to express your understanding of the subject in a thesis statement, which helps control the shape and direction of the research paper and provides your readers with a handle on your paper's main idea or argument.

Finally, give yourself enough time to plan, organize, and write the complete draft of your research paper. You need time to plan or outline your paper and to construct your argument, using your source information to reinforce or substantiate your findings in a clearly documented way. Allow yourself one to two weeks for organizing and writing rough drafts of your paper and an additional week for revising, polishing, and editing your final draft. If you intend to hire a typist or if you need to type your paper in what may turn out to be a busy computer lab, allow an extra week for the typing of the paper.

As you can see from this overview, most research projects take an entire college term to complete. Recall from Chapter 1 the stages in the research process: preparation, incubation, illumination, and verification. You need to consider all four stages as you plan your research project. Allow time for your library search, time for ideas to incubate in your subconscious, time for arriving at an understanding of your topic, and time to verify that understanding in writing.

What follows is a sample time frame to give you some idea of how you might budget your own time:

<u>Week 1</u>:   Select preliminary research topic; articulate starting questions; gather and organize research notebook; draw up tentative search strategy; plan research time frame; read general background sources; begin to focus topic.

<u>Week 2</u>:   Build working bibliography by using indexes, online catalogs, and databases; begin to locate sources in library.

<u>Week 3</u>:   Read and evaluate sources; take notes on relevant sources; in research notebook, comment on sources, that is, their importance to topic and their relationship to other sources.

<u>Week 4</u>:   Arrange and conduct any primary research; complete reading and evaluating of sources; identify gaps in research and find more sources if necessary.

<u>Week 5</u>:   Begin preliminary writing in research notebook—summary, synthesis, critique activities; initiate brainstorming and discovery drafting; begin to define an answer to the starting question.

<u>Week 6</u>:   Write a tentative thesis statement; sketch a tentative plan or outline of the research paper.

<u>Week 7</u>:   Write a rough draft of the research paper; keep careful track of sources through accurate citation (distinguish quotes from paraphrases).

<u>Week 8</u>:   Revise and edit the rough draft; spellcheck; check correct usage and documentation of sources.

<u>Week 9</u>:   Print and proofread final copy carefully; have a friend or classmate proof as well.

✦ EXERCISES

1. Outline the time frame of your research project; refer to a current academic calendar from your school and to any deadlines provided by your teacher.

2. Plan any primary research you intend to conduct for your project. For example, if you need to contact someone for an interview, do so well ahead of time.

Locating Sources

After defining your search strategy and outlining a time frame for your project, you can begin the actual research process in the library. Refer to the relevant section of Chapter 2, "Library Resources," and to the model searches in Part Two to begin listing possible sources for your own topic.

✦ EXERCISE

Begin your library search, writing down source citations in your working bibliography. Refer to the relevant section of Chapter 2 and to the model search outlined in Chapters 6, 7, 8, or 9 for explicit direction in the process of research for your chosen discipline.

Working with Sources

One of the most crucial aspects of the research process is the development of the skills needed to pull the appropriate information from the source materials you have gathered.

Reading for Meaning

The sources you locate in your library search are the raw material for your research paper. You might supplement these sources with primary data, but generally your research paper will be based on information from written secondary sources. Your job is to read carefully and actively. Reading is not a passive process by which the words float into your mind and become registered in your memory. If you read passively, you will not comprehend the author's message. You have probably had the experience of rereading a passage several times and still not understanding a word of it. In such cases, you were not reading actively. In active reading, the reader is engaged in a dialogue with the author.

To be fair in your interpretation of what you are reading, you must first be receptive to what the author is saying; approach anything you read with an open mind. Before actually beginning to read, look at any nontextual materials that accompany the source, including information about the author, the publisher, the origin of the work, the title, and the organizational plan or format of the work.

The Author.   Questions to consider about the author include the following: Who is the author? Is the author living or dead? What other works did the author write? What are the author's qualifications and biases on this particular topic? Is the author affiliated with any organizations that might espouse a particular point of view (e.g., the National Rifle Association or the National Organization for Women)? Is the author a faculty member at a reputable college or university? Does the author work for a government agency, a political group, or an industry?

The Publication.   You should look at the publication information for the source. What was the date of publication? Would the particular context help you understand the work? It is also important to evaluate the medium in which the work appears. Was this an article published in a popular magazine, such as *Ladies' Home Journal,* or was it a paper in a scholarly journal, such as *College and Research Libraries*? The title of the work itself may reveal some important information. Does the title seem significant? Does it indicate the probable conclusions or main points of the article or book? Does it provide a clue to some controversy? Authors provide titles as indicators of what the work will contain, so we should be sensitive to the title of any work we read.

The Organization.   Finally, before you read the work, look at the author's organizational plan. For a book, look at the table of contents, the introduction or preface, the chapter headings, and the major subdivisions. Judging from these clues, ask yourself what the author's main points are likely to be. What does the author seem to consider important about the subject? For articles, read the abstract (if provided) and look at any subdivisions or headings. These will help you to understand the overall structure of the article.

Active Reading and Notetaking

Once you have completed your preliminary overview of the work, you are ready to begin the actual reading process. Plan to read a work that you need to understand thoroughly at least twice. During the first reading, go through the work at a relatively quick pace, either a section or a chapter at a time. If an article is relatively short, you can read it through entirely at one sitting. As you go along, pay attention to key words or phrases and try to get a general idea of the author's main points. This reading will be more than a skimming of the work; you should be able to generally understand what you have read on this first time through.

Then read the work again, carefully and slowly. Use a highlighter or a pencil to underline key ideas and to write in the margins of your own books or photocopied articles, called annotating the article. Of course, if you are borrowing a book from the library, you will not be able to underline on the book itself. In that case, record key ideas, using your own words, on your notecards or in your research notebook, along with the author's name and the page number on which the material was found.

The second time you read, stop frequently to absorb the information and interpret it in your own mind. For each paragraph or section of the article or chapter, jot down on the page itself or on notecards a summary sentence or two that captures the main idea. Be sure that these marginal notes are in your own words. It is crucial that you paraphrase the author's ideas and that you note down the page number on which you found the information.

Paraphrasing Appropriately and Avoiding Plagiarism

Paraphrasing.   Paraphrasing may be defined as restating or rewording a passage from a text, giving the same meaning in another form. The objective of paraphrasing, then, is to present an author's ideas in your own words. When paraphrasing fails, it may be because the reader misunderstood the passage, the reader insisted on reading his or her own ideas into the passage, or the reader partially understood but chose to guess at the meaning rather than fully understanding it. To paraphrase accurately, you must first read closely and understand completely what you are reading. Here are five suggestions that will help you as you paraphrase:

1. Place the information found in the source in a new order.
2. Break the complex ideas into smaller units of meaning.
3. Use concrete, direct vocabulary in place of technical jargon found in the original source.
4. Vary the sentence patterns.
5. Use synonyms for the words in the source.

Plagiarism.   Plagiarism is defined as the unauthorized use of the language and thoughts of an author and the representation of them as one's own. Oftentimes students taking notes from a source will inadvertently commit plagiarism by careless copying of words and phrases from the author that end up in the student's paper and appear as if written by the student himself or herself. If you set the original piece aside while you are taking notes, you are less likely to copy the author's wording. Then go back and double check your notes against the original.

Sometimes plagiarism is not inadvertent at all, but rather overt theft of one author's work by another, as the accompanying article by Gregg Easterbrook attests. However, whether the plagiarist is a Stanford author or a newspaper reporter, it is always unethical to present someone's words or ideas as if they were your own. Nor is providing a footnote alone always sufficient. Any of the author's words or phrases should be enclosed in quotation marks to signal to the reader that exact wording and phrasing as written by the original author is being used; in addition, a footnote or parenthetical citation to the source should be provided.

The Sincerest Flattery

Thanks, but I'd rather you not plagiarize my work

Gregg Easterbrook

It was the best of times, and pretty much the worst of times. I felt borne back ceaselessly to the past. Maybe that's because days on the calendar creep along in a petty pace, and all our yesterdays but light fools the road to dusty death.

OK, the above words are not really mine. But hey, I changed them slightly. I thought nobody would notice.

Some kind of harmonic convergence of plagiarism seems to be in process. A Boston University dean, H. Joachim Maitre, was caught swiping much of a commencement address from an essay by the film critic Michael Medved. Fox Butterfield of The New York Times then cribbed from a Boston Globe story about the swipe. The Globe, in turn, admitted that one of its reporters was disciplined for stealing words from the Georgia politician Julian Bond. Laura Parker of The Washington Post (which owns NEWSWEEK) was found poaching from The Miami Herald's John Donnelly. And the president of Japan's largest news service, Shinji Sakai, announced his resignation, taking public responsibility for 51 plagiarized articles that were discovered last May.

I personally entered the arena last week when the Post reported that a Stanford University business-school lecturer plagiarized me in a recent book,

"Managing on the Edge." Chapters about the Ford Motor Co. contain approximately three pages nearly identical in wording to an article on Ford that I wrote five years ago for The Washington Monthly magazine.

What's it like to discover someone has stolen your words? My initial reaction was to feel strangely flattered that another author had liked my writing well enough to pass it off as his own.

OK, I plagiarized that last sentence. It comes from the writer James Fallows, who last week in a National Public Radio commentary described the two times he has been plagiarized. In one case a San Jose State professor published a textbook in which an entire chapter was nearly identical to an article Fallows had written. For good measure, another chapter was nearly identical to an article by the economic analyst Robert Reich. The professor claims this happened because of computer error. The publisher sent Fallows a letter saying that, since we disseminated your copyrighted work without permission, could we have permission now?

Plagiarism is the world's dumbest crime. If you are caught there is absolutely nothing you can say in your own defense. (Computer error?) And it's easy to commit the underlying sin—presenting as your own someone else's work—without running the risk of sanction, merely by making the effort to reword.

Yet figures as distinguished as Alex Haley, John Hersey, Martin Luther King Jr., and D. M. Thomas have been charged with borrowing excessively from the work of others. One factor is sloth. Another is ego: there are writers who cannot bear even tacit admission that someone else has said something better than they could. The line between being influenced by what others have written, and cribbing from it outright, is one nearly every writer walks up to at some point.

About that last sentence. The Post quoted me as saying that: does that mean I just plagiarized myself? It can happen. Conor Cruise O'Brien was accused of self-plagiarizing when he sold, to The Atlantic, an article hauntingly similar to one previously run under his byline in Harper's.

Perhaps word rustlers tell themselves they will never be caught, and indeed, unlikely combinations of events may be necessary for a theft to be exposed. Some no doubt further tell themselves that if they are caught no one will sue. Most writers don't make serious money and so are uninviting targets for litigation.

I might never have learned about "Managing on the Edge" if an alert reader named Robert Levering had not been researching Ford Motor Co. Shortly after reading my article, he saw a "Managing" excerpt from the Stanford business-school magazine. He not only realized he was reading the same words, but more important, remembered where he encountered them first. Levering wrote to Stanford. I heard about his letter, got a copy of the book, and my jaw dropped. Particularly galling, on the book's facing page, was the phrase

"Copyright 1990 by Richard Tanner Pascale." The author was asserting ownerships of words I composed.

Elegantly crafted: Unlike the Boston University incident, where the dean stole words for an unpaid speech, in this case there was money involved. "Managing" is a commercial book published by Simon & Schuster, a reasonable seller with 35,000 copies in print and another run pending. It's been well received by critics: mainly, I suspect, because of three particularly elegantly crafted pages. Another person was not only presenting my words as his own, but doing so for gain.

The author of "Managing" apologized for what happened but contended it was not plagiarism, because my name is in the book's footnotes. Footnotes my foot. Footnotes mean the place a fact can be found; they do not confer the right to present someone else's words as your own work. Any Stanford undergraduate who attempted that defense would not get far.

My case dragged on inconclusively for a while. But the moment a reporter for The Washington Post called Simon & Schuster, the pace of cooperation accelerated dramatically. Simon & Schuster is now preparing corrections for future editions of "Managing." Stanford has an academic committee investigating its end of the incident.

The wave of plagiarism disclosures poses an obvious question: are dozens of authors now quaking in their shoes, worried about whether some alert reader will stumble across the resemblance between those pages in their book and, say, that article in some obscure little journal no one ever reads?

Frankly, Scarlet, I don't give a damn. ✦

Easterbrook, G. (1991, July 29). The sincerest flattery: Thanks, but I'd rather you not plagiarize my work. *Newsweek*, pp. 45-46.

How to Paraphrase Appropriately

The examples below show acceptable and unacceptable paraphrasing:

ORIGINAL PASSAGE

During the last two years of my medical course and the period which I spent in the hospitals as house physician, I found time, by means of serious encroachment on my night's rest, to bring to completion a work on the history of scientific research into the thought world of St. Paul, to revise and enlarge the *Question of the Historical Jesus* for the second edition, and together with Widor to prepare an edition of Bach's preludes and fugues for the organ, giving with each piece directions for its rendering. (Albert Schweitzer, *Out of My Life and Thought*. New York: Mentor, 1963, p. 94.)

Embarrassing Echoes

In both journalism and academia, plagiarism is close to mortal sin. Sometimes writers are tempted to stray, giving themselves credit for the work of another. A side-by-side comparison can be withering.

Gregg Easterbrook, Oct. 1986:
"On a very dark day in 1980, Donald Peterson, newly chosen president of Ford Motors, visited the company design studios. Ford was in the process of losing $2.2 billion, the largest single-year corporate loss in U.S. history."

Richard Pascale, March, 1990
"On a dark day in 1980, Donald Peterson, the newly chosen President of Ford Motor Company, visited the company's Detroit design studio. That year, Ford would lose $2.2 billion, the largest loss in a single year in U.S. corporate history."

Sources: The Washington Monthly: "Managing on the Edge"

Michael Medved, Feb. 2, 1991:
"Apparently, some stern decree has gone out from the upper reaches of the Hollywood establishment that love between married people must never be portrayed on the screen."

H. Joachim Maitre, May 12, 1991:
"Apparently, some stern advice has come from the upper reaches of the Hollywood establishment that love between married people must never be portrayed on the screen."

Source: The Boston Globe

A POOR PARAPHRASE

Schweitzer said that during the last two years of his medical course and the period he spent in the hospitals as house physician he found time, by encroaching on his night's rest, to bring to completion several works.

[Note: This paraphrase uses too many words and phrases directly from the original without putting them in quotation marks and thus is considered plagiarism. Furthermore, many of the ideas of the author have been left out, making the paraphrase incomplete.

Finally, the student has neglected to acknowledge the source through a parenthetical citation.]

A GOOD PARAPHRASE

Albert Schweitzer observed that by staying up late at night, first as a medical student and then as a "house physician," he was able to finish several major works, including a historical book on the intellectual world of St. Paul, a revised and expanded second edition of *Question of the Historical Jesus,* and a new edition of Bach's organ preludes and fugues complete with interpretive notes, written collaboratively with Widor (Schweitzer 94).

[Note: This paraphrase is very complete and appropriate; it does not use the author's own words, except in one instance, which is acknowledged by quotation marks. The student has included a parenthetical citation that indicates to the reader the paraphrase was taken from page 94 of the work by Schweitzer. The reader can find complete information on the work by turning to the bibliography at the end of the student's paper.]

Making Section-by-Section Summaries

As an alternative to close paraphrasing, you may wish to write brief summaries (three or four sentences) on your notecards or in your notebook. Again, use your own words when writing these summaries. If the material is particularly difficult, you may need to stop and summarize more frequently than after each section or chapter. If it is relatively simple to understand or not particularly pertinent to your topic, take fewer notes and write shorter summaries. At any rate, be certain that you are internalizing what you read—the best gauge of your understanding of the material is your ability to put it into your own words in the form of paraphrases or short section-by-section summaries. Again, as with paraphrases or quotes, note down the page numbers on which the material was found.

Reviewing

After completing your marginal notes, paraphrases, or summaries, go back and review the entire piece, taking time to think about what you read. Evaluate the significance of what you learned by relating the work to your own project and starting questions. Your research notebook is the place to record the observations and insights gained in your reading. How does the work fit in with other works you read on the same topic? What ideas seem particularly relevant to your own research? Does the work help to answer your starting question? Answering such questions in your research notebook will help you to put each work you read into the context of your own research.

Perceiving the Author's Organizational Plan

In writing, you should attempt to make your organizational plan clear to your potential readers. Similarly, while reading, you should attempt to discern the organizational plan of the author. One of the best ways to understand the author's plan is to try to reconstruct it through outlining. For an article or book that seems especially important to your research project, you may want to understand the material in a more complete and orderly way than that gained through paraphrasing or summarizing. You can accomplish this goal by constructing an outline of what you have read.

In a well-written piece, the writer will have given you clues to important or key information. Your summaries should have identified main ideas that are most likely to be the main points of the outline. However, you may still need to go back to the work to identify the author's secondary, supporting points, including examples, illustrations, and supporting arguments used to make each individual argument clearer or more persuasive. In outlining a key source, you can come to understand it more fully. Again, be sure that all the points in your outline have been stated in your own words rather than the words of the author.

✦ EXERCISE

The following article has been included to illustrate how to go about underlining, annotating, summarizing, and outlining a key source. Read the article carefully, noticing which ideas have been underlined and which annotated. Do you agree with my identification of key ideas? Why or why not? Is there a right or wrong identification of key ideas? The final third of the article has not been underlined, summarized, or included on the outline that follows. Try out these four techniques (underlining, annotating, summarizing, outlining) by finishing the interpretation of the article, beginning immediately after the quotation from Paul Dirac:

1. Underline key ideas.
2. Annotate the article by putting notes in the margins that paraphrase the author's words.
3. Summarize in your own words the main ideas of the last section of the article, as you would on a notecard or in your research notebook (three to four sentences).
4. Complete the outline following the article, using your own marginal notes and annotations on the article.

The Scientific Aesthetic

K. C. Cole

Opening quote from physics textbook.

"Poets say science takes away from the beauty of the stars—mere globs of gas atoms. Nothing is 'mere.' I too can see the stars on a desert night, and feel them. But do I see less or more? The vastness of the heavens stretches my imagination—stuck on this carrousel, my little eye can catch one-million-year-old light . . . For far more marvelous is the truth than any artists of the past imagined! Why do the poets of the present not speak of it? What men are poets who can speak of Jupiter if he were like a man, but if he is an immense spinning sphere of methane and ammonia must be silent?"

Feynman rejects idea that science makes nature ugly.

This poetic paragraph appears as a footnote in, of all places, a physics textbook: *The Feynman Lectures on Physics* by Nobel laureate Richard Feynman. Like so many others of his kind, <u>Feynman scorns the suggestion that science strips nature of her beauty,</u> leaving only a naked set of equations. Knowledge of nature, he thinks, deepens the awe, enhances the appreciation. But Feynman has also been known to remark that the only quality art and theoretical physics have in common is the <u>joyful anticipation that artists and physicists alike feel when they contemplate a blank piece of paper.</u>

There is both beauty and creativity in science and art, says Feynman.

What is the relationship between science and art? There must be a link, as so many scientists are also artists.

What is the kinship between these seemingly dissimilar species, science and art? Obviously there is some—if only because so often the same people are attracted to both. The image of Einstein playing his violin is only too familiar, or Leonardo with his inventions. It is a standing joke in some circles that all it takes to make a string quartet is four mathematicians sitting in the same room. Even Feynman plays the bongo drums. (He finds it curious that while he is almost always identified as the physicist who plays the bongo drums, the few times that he has been asked to play the drums, "the introducer never seems to find it necessary to mention that I also do theoretical physics.")

One commonality is that art and science often cover the same territory. A tree is fertile ground for both the poet and the botanist. The relationship between mother and child, the symmetry of snowflakes, the effects of light and color, and the structure of the human form are studied equally by painters and psychologists, sculptors and physicians. The origins of the universe, the nature of life, and the meaning of death are the subjects of physicists, philosophers, and composers.

Art and science cover same ground— examples.

Yet when it comes to approach, the affinity breaks down completely. Artists approach nature with feeling; scientists rely on logic. Art elicits emotion; science makes sense. Artists are supposed to care; scientists are supposed to think.

Differing approaches: art = emotion, science = logic; but many scientists disagree, arguing that emotion in science is integral to the process.

At least one physicist I know rejects this distinction out of hand: "What a strange misconception has been taught to people," he says. "They have been taught that one cannot be disciplined enough to discover the truth unless one is indifferent to it. Actually, there is no point in looking for the truth unless what it is makes a difference."

The history of science bears him out. Darwin, while sorting out the clues he had gathered in the Galapagos Islands that eventually led to his theory of evolution, was hardly detached. "I am like a gambler and love a wild experiment," he wrote. "I am horribly afraid." "I trust to a sort of instinct and God knows can seldom give any reason for my remarks." "All nature is perverse and will not do as I wish it. I wish I had my old barnacles to work at, and nothing new."

The scientists who took various sides in the early days of the quantum debate were scarcely less passionate. Einstein said that if classical notions of cause and effect had to be renounced, he would rather be a cobbler or even work in a gambling casino than be a physicist. Niels Bohr called Einstein's attitude appalling, and accused him of high treason. Another major physicist, Erwin Schrodinger, said, "If one has to stick to this damned quantum jumping, then I regret having ever been involved in this thing." On a more positive note, Einstein spoke about the universe as a "great, eternal riddle" that "beckoned like a liberation." As the late Harvard professor George Sarton wrote in the preface to his *History of Science*, "There are blood and tears in geometry as well as in art."

Examples of scientific passion— Einstein.

Instinctively, however, most people do not like the idea that scientists can be passionate about their work, any more than they like the idea that poets can be calculating. But it

Artists and scientists are both passionate and in control of their work.

Creativity needed in science; control needed in art.

Scientists often proceed based on their own "vision of beauty."

Illustrations from science: aesthetics serve as "delicate sieve" for science.

would be a sloppy artist indeed who worked without tight creative control, and no scientist ever got very far by sticking exclusively to the scientific method. Deduction only takes you to the next step in a straight line of thought, which in science is often a dead end. "Each time we get into this log jam," says Feynman, "it is because the methods we are using are just like the ones we have used before . . . A new idea is extremely difficult to think of. It takes fantastic imagination." The direction of the next great leap is as often as not guided by the scientist's vision of beauty. Einstein's highest praise for a theory was not that it was good but that it was beautiful. His strongest criticism was "Oh, how ugly!" He often spoke about the aesthetic appeal of ideas. "Pure logic could never lead us to anything but tautologies," wrote the French physicist Jules Henri Poincaré. "It could create nothing new; not from it alone can any science issue."

Poincaré also described the role that aesthetics plays in science as "a delicate sieve," an arbiter between the telling and the misleading, the signals and the distractions. Science is not a book of lists. The facts need to be woven into theories like tapestries out of so many tenuous threads. Who knows when (and how) the right connections have been made? Sometimes, the most useful standard is aesthetic: Erwin Schrodinger refrained from publishing the first version of his now famous wave equations because they did not fit the then-known facts. "I think there is a moral to this story," Paul Dirac commented later. "Namely, that it is more important to have beauty in one's equations than to have them fit experiment . . . It seems that if one is working from the point of view of getting beauty in one's equations, and if one has really a sound insight, one is on a sure line of progress."

Sometimes the connection between art and science can be even more direct. Danish physicist Niels Bohr was known for his fascination with cubism—especially "that an object could be several things, could change, could be seen as a face, a limb, and a fruit bowl." He went on to develop his philosophy of complementarity, which showed how an electron could change, could be seen either as a particle or a wave. Like cubism, complementarity allowed contradictory views to coexist in the same natural frame.

Some people wonder how art and science ever got so far separated in the first place. The definitions of both disciplines have narrowed considerably since the days when science was natural philosophy, and art included the work of artisans of the kind who build today's fantastic particle accelerators. "Science acquired its present limited meaning barely before the nineteenth century," writes Sir Geoffrey Vickers in Judith Wechsler's collection of essays *On Aesthetics in Science.* "It came to apply to a method of testing hypotheses about the natural world by observations or experiments. . . ." Surely, this has little to do with art. But Vickers suspects the difference is deeper. People want to believe that science is a rational process, that it is describable. Intuition is not describable, and should therefore be relegated to a place outside the realm of science. "Because our culture has somehow generated the unsupported and improbable belief that everything real must be fully describable, it is unwilling to acknowledge the existence of intuition."

There are, of course, substantial differences between art and science. Science is written in the universal language of mathematics; it is, far more than art, a shared perception of the world. Scientific insights can be tested by the good old scientific method. And scientists have to try to be dispassionate about the conduct of their work—at least enough so that their passions do not disrupt the outcome of experiments. Of course, sometimes they do: "Great thinkers are never passive before the facts," says Stephen Jay Gould. "They have hopes and hunches, and they try hard to construct the world in their light. Hence, great thinkers also make great errors."

But in the end, the connections between art and science may be closer than we think, and they may be rooted most of all in a person's motivations to do art, or science, in the first place. MIT metallurgist Cyril Stanley Smith became interested in the history of his field and was surprised to find that the earliest knowledge about metals and their properties was provided by objects in art museums. "Slowly, I came to see that this was not a coincidence but a consequence of the very nature of discovery, for discovery derives from aesthetically motivated curiosity and is rarely a result of practical purposefulness." ✦

Cole, K. C. (1983). *The Scientific Aesthetic.* New York: Discover Publications, Inc. Reprinted by permission.

OUTLINE BASED ON MARGINAL NOTES

I. Opening quote from physics text to introduce the topic (Feynman)
  A. Feynman rejects the idea that science makes nature ugly
  B. There is both beauty and creativity in science and art, says Feynman
II. What is the relationship between science and art?
  A. There must be a link because so many scientists are also artists
  B. Art and science cover the same ground (examples to illustrate)
  C. Differing approaches: art is emotional, science is logical
  D. But many scientists disagree; they argue that emotion, caring in science is integral to the process.
  E. Examples of scientific passion, including Einstein
III. The importance of control and creativity in both science and art
  A. Scientists often proceed based on their own "vision of beauty"
  B. Illustrations from science
  C. Aesthetics serves as "a delicate sieve" for science
IV. Links between art and science can be quite straightforward

[Continue outline]

Illumination and Verification

An essential part of your research is the evolution of your understanding of the subject. As you read and evaluate your sources, you will be seeking a solution to your starting question. Several preliminary writing tasks can help you evaluate your sources and understand your topic better.

Evaluation

In your working bibliography, you record the information needed to find a source in the library. Once you have located a source, you need to evaluate it for its usefulness to your particular research project and to your starting question. Every library search will entail the systematic interaction of examination, evaluation, and possibly elimination of material. It is not unusual for an article with a promising title to turn out to be totally irrelevant. Do not be discouraged by dead ends of this sort—they are an accepted and expected part of the library search. You must not hesitate to eliminate irrelevant or unimportant information. As you read each source, consider the following criteria (see also the section on Active Reading).

Evaluative Criteria

1. The relevance of the work to your topic and starting question
2. The timeliness or recency of the work (particularly important in scientific research projects)
3. The author of the work (based on all available information)
4. The prestige or nature of the journal (scholarly or popular press)
5. The controversial nature of the source (whether it agrees with or contradicts other sources)

As you encounter new sources, you will be the best judge of whether or not a particular source contains useful information for your research project. Record your evaluative comments in your research notebook.

✦ EXERCISE

1. Write an evaluation of one book or article you have located in your library search (or an article assigned by your teacher). Use the above criteria for evaluating the source.

2. Read the article on pp. 87–93. First consider what information you know about the author, the publication, and the organization of the piece. Do these give you any insight into the possible coverage/approach/biases of the article?

Writing from Sources

Reading actively and taking accurate and careful notes in the form of paraphrases and summaries are the first important techniques for working with sources. Your reading notes will form the basis for all your subsequent writing about that particular source. In this section, we will discuss three important approaches to source books and articles that result in three different kinds of writing. These are (1) summarizing the main points of the source book or article in condensed form, (2) synthesizing the information found in two or more related sources, and (3) critiquing the information found in one or more sources.[1] These three kinds of writing differ from each other in the approach the writer takes to the source in each instance. Your purpose for writing summaries will be different from your purpose for writing syntheses or critiques. Although the source or subject may remain the same, your approach to that source or subject can change, depending on your purpose. Using different approaches to the same sources will help you to understand those sources better.

Summarizing

When summarizing, the writer takes an entirely objective approach to the subject and the source. The writer of summaries is obliged to accurately record the author's meaning. To do this, of course, the summarizer must first understand the source and identify its key ideas during active reading. Since, in general, a summary is about one third as long as the source itself, this means that two thirds of the information in the original is left out of the summary. So, what do you as summarizer eliminate? Typically, it is the extended examples, illustrations, and explanations of the original that are left out of a summary. The summarizer attempts to abstract only the gist of the piece, its key ideas and its line of argument. If a reader desires more information than that provided in a summary, he or she may look up the original.

To write a summary, first transcribe your short marginal reading notes onto a separate sheet of paper (see the outline on p. 80). Read these notes and decide what you think the author's overall point was. Write the main point in the form of a thesis statement that encapsulates the central idea of the whole article.

> *Thesis:* Cole thinks that there are close
> connections between science and art that stem
> from the creative spirit of humanity.

Be sure not to use the author's words; rather, paraphrase the author's central idea in your own words. Then, by combining the thesis sentence with the marginal notes, you will have constructed the first outline of your summary. Revise the outline for coherence and logical progression of thought.

Next, write the first draft of your summary, following your outline rather than the source. Use your own words, not the words of the author, paraphrasing and condensing his or her ideas. If you want to use the author's own words for a particular passage, use quotation marks to indicate the author's exact words and insert a page reference in parentheses:

> Cole observes that "a tree is fertile ground
> for both the poet and the botanist" (54).

In the first few sentences of your summary, introduce the source book or article and its author:

```
In the article "The Scientific Aesthetic"

(Discover, Dec. 1983, pp. 16-17), the author,

K. C. Cole, discusses the relationship of

aesthetics and science.
```

Follow this context information with the thesis statement, which reflects the author's position, and then with the summary itself. Do not insert your own ideas or opinions into the summary. Your summary should reflect the content of the original as accurately and objectively as possible.

When you have completed the first draft of your summary, review the source to be certain that your draft reflects its content completely and accurately. Then reread your draft to determine whether it is clear, coherent, and concise. Next, revise the summary for style and usage, making your sentences flow smoothly and correcting your grammar and punctuation. Finally, write and proofread the final draft. Remember, your summary will recount objectively and in your own words what someone else wrote, so you should refer often to the author by name.

Synthesizing

When synthesizing, you will approach your material with an eye to finding the relationships among sources. Your purpose will be to discern those relationships and present them coherently and persuasively to your potential readers. Again, the process begins with the active reading of the sources. As you read, highlight and summarize key ideas from your sources in the margins. But instead of simply summarizing the information in one source, look for relationships between ideas in one source and those in another. The sources may be related in one or more of the following ways:

- They may provide examples of a general topic, or one source may serve to exemplify another.
- They may describe or define the topic you are researching.
- They may present information or ideas that can be compared or contrasted.

You must decide in what way or ways your sources are related. When you have decided on the relationships among the sources, write a thesis sentence that embodies that relationship. This thesis sentence should indicate the central idea of your synthesis.

Write an outline of your synthesis paper based on the organizational plan suggested by the thesis statement. This outline should articulate the relationship you have discerned among the sources. For example, if the passages you read all served to describe the same topic (perhaps life in colonial New England), the structure might look like this:

1. Opening paragraph with contextualizing information about the sources and the particular situation, life in colonial New England.
2. Thesis statement describing the relationship to be discussed: Life in colonial New England is described by historians and participants as rigid in its social structure.
3. Description 1 (based on source 1: a historical work about the New England colonies).
4. Description 2 (based on source 2: a diary or journal written by an early colonist).
5. Description 3 (based on source 3: a sermon written by a colonial preacher).
6. Conclusion: All the sources combined contribute to a description of the rigid social structure in colonial New England.

After outlining your synthesis, write the first draft of your paper. In the introductory section of your synthesis, just as in the summary, introduce the sources and their authors. Follow the introduction of sources with your thesis expressing the relationship among the sources. As you write your first draft, keep your thesis in mind, selecting from your sources only the information that develops and supports that thesis. You may want to discuss each source separately, as in the example above, or you may prefer to organize your paper to present major supporting points in the most logical sequence, using information from the sources to develop or support those points. Be sure that you acknowledge all ideas and information from your sources each time you use them in your synthesis.

Upon completion of your first draft, review the sources to be sure you have represented the authors' views fairly and cited source ideas and information properly. Reread your first draft to make sure it is organized logically and that it supports your thesis effectively. Be certain that you have included sufficient transitions between the various sections of your synthesis. Revise your synthesis for style and correctness. Finally, write and proofread the final draft of your synthesis. In general, a synthesis should give the reader a persuasive interpretation of the relationship you have discerned among your sources.

Critiquing

In the third kind of writing from sources, critiquing, the writer takes a critical or evaluative approach to a particular source. When writing critiques, you argue a point that seems important to you based on your own evaluation of the issues and ideas you have encountered in your sources. Critiques are necessarily more difficult to write than summaries or syntheses, because they require that you think critically and come to an independent judgment about a topic. However, critiques are also the most important kind of writing from sources to master, because in many research situations you are asked to formulate your own opinion and critical judgment (as opposed to simply reporting or presenting the information written by others).

As in the other forms of writing from sources, critiquing begins with active reading and careful notetaking from a source. You must first identify the author's main ideas and points before you can evaluate and critique them. Once you understand the source and the issues it addresses, you are in a position to appraise it critically. Analyze the source in one or more of the following ways:

> What is said, by whom, and to whom?
>
> How significant are the author's main points and how well are the points made?
>
> What assumptions does the author make that underlie his or her arguments?
>
> What issues has the author overlooked or what evidence has he or she failed to consider?
>
> Are the author's conclusions valid?
>
> How well is the source written (regarding clarity, organization, language)?
>
> What stylistic or rhetorical features affect the source's content?

Other questions may occur to you as you critique the source, but these will serve to get you started in your critical appraisal. To think critically about a source, look behind the arguments themselves to the basis for those arguments. What reasons does the author give for holding a certain belief? In addition, try to discern what assumptions the author is making about the subject. Do you share those assumptions? Are they valid? It is your job to evaluate fairly but with discerning judgment, since this evaluation will be the core of your critique. Formulate a thesis that states your evaluation. Do not feel that your evaluation must necessarily be negative; it is possible to make a positive critique, a negative critique, or a critique that cites both kinds of qualities.

Write an outline of your critique, including the following:

1. An introduction of the subject you wish to address and the source article you wish to critique. Be sure to include a complete citation for the source.
2. A statement of your judgment about the issue in the form of a thesis. In that thesis statement, give your own opinion, which will be supported in the critique itself.
3. The body of the critique. First, briefly summarize the source itself. Then review the issues at hand and explain the background facts and assumptions your readers must understand to share your judgment. Use the bulk of your critique (about two thirds) to review the author's position in light of your judgment and evaluation.
4. Your conclusion, which reminds the reader of your main points and the reasons you made them.

After completing your outline, write the first draft of your critique, using your outline as a guide. Make certain that all your points are well supported with specific references to the source. Also, make certain that your main points are related to each other and to the thesis statement.

Review the source to be sure you have represented the author's ideas accurately and fairly. Reread your first draft to determine whether your thesis is clearly stated, your paper logically organized, and your thesis adequately and correctly supported. Revise your critique for content, style, and correctness. Finally, write and proofread the final draft of your critique.

Unfortunately, because critiques are subjective, it is not possible to be any more explicit in guiding your writing of them. The substance of the critique will depend entirely on the judgment you make about the source. Remember, though, that a critique needs to be well supported and your opinion well justified by evidence drawn from the source itself. In the exercises that follow, you will have the opportunity to practice writing summaries, syntheses, and critiques. It will also be valuable to write summaries, syntheses, and critiques of sources you are using in your research project as a way to better understand that topic. Do all such preliminary writing in your research notebook.

◆ EXERCISES

1. *Summary*
   Carefully read, underline, and annotate the brief article that follows or another article you have encountered in your own re-

search. Using the procedure described above, write a summary of the article. Be certain to turn in to your teacher both your summary and a photocopy of the article you are summarizing.

2. *Synthesis*

   A. Use two or more articles you have encountered in your research as the basis for an extended definition of an important concept. For example, perhaps you are researching the Senate hearings held prior to Clarence Thomas's confirmation for the U.S. Supreme Court. Because of the testimony of Anita Hill, an important by-product of those hearings was a heightened awareness of sexual harassment in the workplace. You could write an extended definition of sexual harassment based on the explanations you find in articles on the hearings.

   B. Use two or more articles to compare and contrast an idea presented by different authors. Again, using the sexual harassment example, perhaps two or more articles seem to disagree about whether or not a particular action was harassment. You could write a paper that contrasted their views.

   C. Use the illustrations and examples from two or more articles to describe something. For example you could write a paper that described sexual harassment in the workplace. For such a paper, you would cite specific cases or examples of sexual harassment as reported by the authors but divide your examples into categories or types of harassment behaviors.

3. *Critique*

   Write an evaluative critique of the following article or of an article you have encountered in your own research. Remember, in a critique it is appropriate to include your opinions and experiences as well as your reactions to the article itself. Some issues you might want to focus on are (1) the fairness of the definition of sexual harassment to men in the office, (2) the fairness of making women provide proof of harassment, (3) the relationship of harassment to office politics in general, and (4) the assumption that sexual harassment happens only to women.

Innovative Steps to Take in Sexual Harassment Prevention

Rebecca A. Thacker

For organizations concerned with preventing sexual harassment in the workplace, the time to investigate prevention policies is now. Passage of the

1991 Civil Rights Act allows for punitive damages to be paid to victims of sexual harassment, an option that was not previously available. Recent information from the Equal Employment Opportunity Commission should prove alarming for organizations hoping to minimize their liability for sexual harassment claims. The EEOC reports a 50 percent increase in the number of sexual harassment complaints filed in the first three quarters of 1992. Apparently, complainants are asking the courts to judge whether they have been wronged by sexual harassment in the workplace.

The courtroom need not be the place to make such a determination. Top management of any company can set up internal prevention policies that, if implemented effectively, can provide the necessary outlet for someone who is the target of sexual harassment. Standard prevention policies, however, are not adequate for creating an environment in which targets can feel comfortable complaining about unwelcome social-sexual behavior in the workplace. This article provides guidance for top management in revising sexual harassment prevention policies and designing programs to educate and train employees.

The Problem with Most Sexual Harassment Prevention Policies

Most sexual harassment prevention policies provide for informal and formal complaint procedures. The informal route allows the harassed individual to complain to a member of management or a person designated to receive such complaints. The formal route provides for a formal, written complaint, usually accompanied by a documented investigation.

What is the problem with these policies? The problem is that individuals who are targets of the harassment are required to file a complaint. However, almost half of them do not feel comfortable complaining, either formally or informally, about the unwelcome sexual harassment. For these people, the response is likely to be passive, acquiescent, perhaps even compliant. A policy that requires passive targets to complain is similar to having no prevention policy at all.

Conversely, for those who do feel comfortable filing a complaint, the written policy is probably sufficient. For more than half the targets of sexual harassment, complaining is a natural response, along with telling the harasser to stop, or saying forcefully, "No!"

Ultimately, however, passive, acquiescent targets are harmed by a policy that requires complainant behavior. For these individuals, there is fear of retaliation, or fear that a harassing supervisor may use coercion to make the target comply ("Go out with me or lose your job"). To understand how to design prevention policies that ease the way for passive targets to complain, management must understand what is motivating them to respond in such a manner.

Targets who display passive, acquiescent responses are exhibiting learned helplessness behavior. Learned helplessness is a cognitive state in which individuals perceive that, in spite of their efforts, unpleasant outcomes cannot be averted. For targets of sexual harassment, feelings of learned helplessness may result from an organizational culture that condones sexually harassing behaviors in the workplace, particularly from supervisors and managers. In addition, learned helplessness can come from perceptions that the organization condones sexual discrimination in other forms, such as differential promotion and pay rates for males and females. Regardless of the accuracy of these perceptions, the overall effect is one that prompts targets to believe that they lack the capability of controlling their work environment and terminating unwelcome harassment.

Some passive, acquiescent targets eventually file suit, usually when a negative workplace outcome (a demotion, poor performance appraisal, or even termination) occurs. These people have already experienced retaliation and suffered the consequences of sexual harassment; as a result, they have nothing to lose by filing a suit. Management has the ability and the responsibility to prevent such devastating and costly events by providing internal mechanisms to assist passive, acquiescent targets in feeling comfortable with complaint behaviors. Not only will the organization benefit in terms of reduced litigation costs, but the target will not have to suffer emotional and physical distress as a result of the harassment.

Emphasize Commitment to Eliminating Sexual Harassment from the Workplace

All organizations should have a written sexual harassment prevention policy that includes the following:

• Confidentiality of complaint. The target should be assured that the complaint will be kept in confidence. This is a critical step in raising the comfort level of otherwise passive targets.

• Prompt, tactful investigation. This is extremely critical to providing an incentive for passive targets to file a complaint. Tactful investigation should involve speaking only to the parties involved— the target and the accused harasser. If satisfactory settlement of the complaint occurs at this step, no one else need know that the complaint was filed.

• A written guarantee that there will be no retaliation against targets for filing a complaint. Management must provide this guarantee by investigating claims of retaliation, and when necessary, disciplining supervisors and managers who retaliate against those filing sexual harassment complaints.

• Discipline proven harassers. This can follow the firm's standard disciplinary procedure. If management perceives that the problem is wide-spread, immediate disciplinary action, such as suspension, may be necessary. Again, for passive targets to be comfortable in filing a complaint, management must send a strong signal that sexual harassment will not be tolerated. Disciplining proven harassers can send such a signal.

• Provide visible top management support. Top management must signal that sexual harassment prevention is of top priority in the workplace. One way to accomplish this is to have a member of top management come to every training session to articulate the company's commitment to eliminating sexual harassment from the workplace.

• Carefully choose the person who will handle complaints. He or she should be tactful, kind, warm, and capable of conducting an objective investigation. If the person who might naturally receive complaints, such as the human resources manager, does not possess these characteristics, then top management should designate someone else who does. Top management should also be careful not to place into this position a person who has a hidden personal agenda (such as an individual who has previously filed a sexual harassment complaint or been the target of a complaint).

• Introduce the person who is responsible for receiving sexual harassment complaints. This should be done during each training session to help enforce top management's commitment to sexual harassment prevention. It should also increase the comfort level of passive targets, giving them an opportunity to meet and talk to the person who will receive and investigate their complaints.

Modify Your Sexual Harassment Prevention Training Programs

Because management often fails to understand the complexity of sexual harassment as a workplace phenomenon, prevention training programs are inadequate. The following are important criteria to take into account when designing these programs:

• Discuss openly both types of target response. Explain that passive, acquiescent responses are not abnormal, and that people who feel inclined to respond in this way should not feel guilty or embarrassed. A frank discussion of both types of response will make those who are passive targets feel as if they are not alone, which can remove some of the reluctance to come forward and complain.

• Discuss positive and negative aspects of both types of target response. The positive aspect of strong, forceful, complaint response is that the target gives the message that harassment is unwelcome. The potential for retaliation is also present when the target resists strongly; however, as mentioned before, the prevention policy should include a statement that retaliation for complaint behavior will not be tolerated.

There are no readily visible positive aspects to passive, acquiescent target response, but there are many negative aspects. The passive target sends a signal that the harassment is welcome, which encourages the harasser to continue. Moreover, the passive target often suffers emotional and psychological distress. Productivity may decrease and absenteeism may increase as he or she finds it increasingly difficult to deal with the harassment.

• Allow employees to role-play both the harasser and the target, and to respond both passively and forcefully in the case of the latter. Observers and participants can then discuss both types of response. Harassers can discuss the kinds of signals sent by targets displaying both types of response.

• Do not rely on sexual harassment prevention training films to do your training for you. Films are appropriate for explaining the different types of sexual harassment, providing visual examples, stimulating discussion, and illustrating target response. However, they should only be used to supplement the rest of the training.

Understand the Role of the Supervisor

Supervisors should provide the first line of defense for organizations attempting to handle sexual harassment complaints internally. However, supervisors often fail to understand their responsibilities in sexual harassment prevention as well as the concept itself. In particular, supervisors often fail to understand that hostile environment harassment (one of the two types of sexual harassment, the other being *quid pro quo* harassment, in which the harasser demands sexual favors in return for benefits of some kind) can involve almost any form of social-sexual behavior—sexual jokes, sexual comments, touching, or leering. Training programs must emphasize the definitional components of sexual harassment for supervisors.

However, in defining harassment, supervisors often fail to understand that *their* definition is not important: it is the *target's* definition that determines whether the unwelcome behavior is sexual harassment. Therefore, when supervisors observe social-sexual behavior in the workplace, the appropriate question is whether the target is bothered by it, not whether the supervisor perceives it as sexually harassing. For example, if supervisors believe that targets who passively accept the social-sexual behavior actually welcome it, they are not fulfilling their responsibility to remove sexual harassment from the workplace. Supervisors typically believe that the appropriate response to sexual harassment is to request an investigation, either internally or externally, or to file a grievance. Supervisory training must emphasize that failure to exhibit either of these responses does not mean that the target finds the social-sexual behavior to be welcome

Even more critical is the problem of supervisors not understanding their responsibility in preventing harassment on the job. As representatives of management, supervisors must aid in providing a workplace that is free from sexual harassment by assuming the following responsibilities:

• Understand the definitions of sexual harassment as described in the EEOC guidelines. Supervisory training and sexual harassment films can take care of this responsibility.

• Be observant. Supervisors must use their understanding of the definitions of sexual harassment to "police" their work area. If they see social-sexual behavior of any sort, they should take active steps. They might approach tactfully, without being obvious, to ask those exhibiting such behavior if they realized they are engaging in potential sexual harassment. In addition, supervisors might have to ask targets if they are offended by such behavior, for it is always possible that a target is passive and acquiescent.

• Demonstrate listening skills. Listen to employees who have problems in their work area. Passive targets may be willing to articulate a personality conflict or a level of discomfort caused by working around a certain person, but they may be reluctant to mention sexual harassment. By listening, the supervisor can sometimes uncover discomfort caused by sexual harassment. Additional training in listening and communication skill development may be necessary to achieve this step. Such training, which has benefits far beyond sexual harassment prevention, is worth the training dollars spent. Improving listening and communication skills can enhance the supervisor's ability to conduct performance appraisal and disciplinary sessions, as well as enhance the supervisor's ability to motivate problem-solving teams of subordinates.

• Enforce the company's sexual harassment prevention policy. As mentioned before, someone should be designated as the recipient of sexual harassment complaints. The supervisor, as a representative of the company, is obliged to investigate such behavior. If he or she is uncomfortable conducting an investigation, then the appropriate step is to notify the company's designated complaint recipient. Once sexual harassment is observed, the company has immediate liability and must take prompt action. The supervisor then has a responsibility to follow up to ensure that the complaint has been dealt with fairly, and that the target has suffered no retaliation for complaining.

• Appraise performance objectively. Use objective criteria as much as possible to avid a sexual harassment lawsuit. A target who is terminated, demoted, or given a poor performance appraisal may claim that the negative outcome occurred because the supervisor sexually harassed the target, who refused to go along with the harassment. An objective performance evaluation supports the company's position that the negative outcome resulted from poor performance, and is therefore job-related.

Organizations can do much to encourage targets of sexual harassment to file complaints internally. By understanding the nature of target response, management can design prevention policies that increase the likelihood that passive, acquiescent targets will use internal mechanisms to deal with unwelcome sexual harassment in the workplace. Given the incentive for courtroom litigation prompted by the monetary damages clause of the 1991 Civil Rights Act, management would do well to address these issues. Much can be done by supervisors in the workplace, whose role in sexual harassment prevention needs to be strengthened with training and education. Ultimately, organizations and employees will benefit. ✦

References

EEOC Guidelines on Sexual Harassment, *Federal Register,* 45 (1980), No. 72: 25025.
Meritor Savings Bank v. Vinson (106 S.Ct. 2399), 1986.
R. A. Thacker, "A Descriptive Study of Behavioral Responses of Sexual Harassment Targets: Implications for Control Theory," *Employee Responsibilities and Rights Journal,* 5 (1992), June: 155–171.

R. A. Thacker and G. R. Ferris, "Understanding Sexual Harassment in the Workplace: The Influence of Power and Politics Within the Dyadic Interaction of Harasser and Target," *Human Resource Management Review, 1* (1991): 23–37.

United States Merit Systems Protection Board, *Sexual Harassment in the Workplace: Is It a Problem?* (Washington, DC: Government Printing Office, 1981).

United States Merit Systems Protection Board, *Sexual Harassment in the Federal Government: An Update* (Washington, DC: Government Printing Office, 1988).

Rebecca A. Thacker is an assistant professor of management at the College of Business and Public Administration, University of Louisville, Kentucky.

Thacker, R. A. (1994, January–February). Innovative steps to take in sexual harassment prevention. *Business Horizons,* pp. 29–32.

4

♦ ♦ ♦

Primary Research
Methods

INTRODUCTION

In all disciplines, the primary research methods are the customary ways in which investigators gather information and search for solutions to problems they have posed. For example, when a chemist performs an experiment in the lab, that is primary research, and when an archaeologist goes on a dig, that is also primary research. When conducting primary research, researchers are gathering and analyzing data. Secondary research, in contrast to primary research, involves studying and analyzing the primary research of others as it has been reported in books and journals. So when the chemist reads the relevant journals in the field and the archaeologist reads topographical maps of the area to be studied, they are doing secondary research. Many research projects are based on a combination of primary and secondary research methods.

This chapter discusses primary research methods used by researchers in the sciences, social sciences, humanities, and business. We will begin with a discussion of primary research methods in the natural and physical sciences, since primary research in many fields is based on the scientific method.

PRIMARY RESEARCH IN THE SCIENCES

Lab Experiments and Reports

Central to an understanding of research in the sciences is an understanding of the scientific method. In the sciences, the method by which an experimenter solves a problem is as important as the result the experimenter achieves. Guided by the scientific method, researchers investigate the laws of the physical universe by asking and answering questions through empirical research. The scientific method begins with a scientist formulating a question and developing a hypothesis that may answer the question posed. On the basis of the hypothesis, the scientist predicts what should be observed under specified conditions and circumstances in the laboratory. Next, the scientist makes and records observations, generally using carefully designed, controlled experiments. Finally, the scientist either accepts or rejects the hypothesis, depending on whether or not the actual observations corresponded with the predicted observations. As you may have discerned from this description of the scientific method, writing plays a role at every step. A researcher must describe in great detail both the method used in the experiment and the results achieved. A report of the experimental findings is based on the laboratory notes taken during the experiment. All researchers must keep written records of their work. In the natural sciences, such records generally take the form of a laboratory notebook. The researcher uses the notebook to keep a complete, well-organized record of every experiment and each experimental variable (phenomena not constant in the experiment). The researcher must record information in a clear, easy-to-understand format so that he or she (and coworkers) will have easy access to it when it is time to draw conclusions from the experiment.

In your undergraduate science courses, you are expected to conduct scientific experiments and record your methods and results in a laboratory notebook. You may also be expected to report your experiments in a systematic way. A good lab report introduces the experiment, describes the materials and methods used in collecting the data, explains the results, and draws conclusions from those results.

Your scientific experiments in your coursework will typically be connected with a laboratory. For example, many courses in the physical sciences, such as chemistry or physics, are accompanied by laboratory sections for practical lab experimentation. However, laboratory courses still involve writing. It is important for you to realize that the scientific method employed by laboratory researchers necessitates the careful, organized, and complete presentation of methods and results through written reports.

✦ EXERCISE

To help you understand the scientific method, the following exercise takes you through the design and implementation of a simple experiment. Or, you may use an experiment of your own choosing, following the same method as scientists would use. You may wish to work collaboratively in groups of three to five to complete this exercise.

Television advertisers tout their particular brand of popcorn as the "biggest and fluffiest." Is there any basis in fact to their claims of superiority? Is Orville Redenbacher's gourmet popcorn REALLY better than other brands?

1. Write a hypothesis related to popcorn that you can test experimentally. For example, "Orville Redenbacher's gourmet popcorn leaves fewer unpopped kernels than the generic store brand."
2. Predict what you should observe under specified conditions and circumstances in your popcorn "laboratory." For the above hypothesis, you might specify that when comparable bags of microwavable popcorn are popped in the same microwave for the same amount of time, the number of unpopped Redenbacher's kernels will be fewer than the unpopped kernels of the competition. Be certain to control for all variables, such as the weights of the unpopped bags.
3. Conduct your experiment, taking careful laboratory notes based on your experimental design and your observations during your controlled experiment.
4. Compare how your actual observations correspond to your hypothesis: Were there fewer unpopped kernels of the Redenbacher popcorn? If so, your hypothesis is proven correct; if not, your hypothesis is disproved. Either way, you have learned something about truth in advertising (or at least about the scientific method).

Field Observations and Reports

In some scientific disciplines, empirical or experimental work is supplemented by field observations that occur outside the laboratory. For example, a biologist interested in moose behaviors might visit Yellowstone National Park and observe juvenile moose and their parents to determine whether maternal or paternal examples are imitated in feeding behaviors. In this section, we will discuss a field experiment and report assigned to students in a physical geography laboratory.[1] This field experiment illustrates one approach to problem solving that incorporates both scientific data and field observation.

The students in the physical geography lab at Texas Tech University study landforms. In their laboratory research assignment, students are asked to investigate the urban flood hazard in Lubbock, Texas, and to report their findings. The students work in groups of four or five to gather the necessary data. It is not unusual in the scientific community for researchers to work in teams, collaborating on both the actual research and the written report of the research. For this assignment, the teacher provides important background readings to help students identify the potential problem of urban flooding. Students must apply general knowledge obtained in the class discussions and course readings to the particular problem of urban flooding in the city where they are attending college.

In this assignment, students are using a common approach to problem solving. The instructor gives them a potential problem, and their first step is to identify and define that problem carefully. In the outline below, provided by the geography professor, notice the similarity to the inquiry steps discussed in Chapter 1 (preparation, incubation, illumination, verification) and to the scientific method (pp. 95–96).

Students must

1. Clearly identify and define the problem.
2. Define an objective or goal that might lead them to a solution to the problem.
3. Gather information from their own backgrounds and from books, printed matter, media, other people, observations, and laboratory experiments.
4. Define the constraints that might limit the solution; generate possible solutions (hypotheses).
5. Evaluate all the possible solutions to determine which is most likely to solve the problem, which satisfies the basic objective, and which is the most feasible, practical, economical, safe, legal, and so on.
6. Prepare a written report that describes the problem, the experimental and field-data-collection methods, and the proposed solution to the problem. In the report, the evidence gathered is used to support the proposed solution.

What follows is an excerpt from a collaborative student report on urban flooding written for an introductory geography course. To complete the assignment, students used primary research methods—observation, experimentation, and report. They also used secondary research methods, incorporating into their report the pertinent ideas they found in books and articles read for their course. As you read this report, notice how the students have followed the approach to problem solving outlined above. Also, notice how they have used the various sources as evidence to support their position.

Geography 113 Report: Group 5

Leslie Bayer

Kim Springer

Charlotte Wedding

Pat Cates

The main objective of this report is to present a flood hazard reduction plan for Maxey Park in Lubbock, Texas. Within this scope we plan to:

1. Determine the specific boundaries around the park that would be flooded with a heavy rain.

2. Conduct discussions with other individuals who can give in-depth information about Lubbock's existing flood-management program.

3. Establish satisfactory or possible solutions for the flooding around Maxey Park.

To begin, a description of the location and nature of the flood problem in Lubbock is in order. Lubbock is located on the Texas South Plains. This area is relatively flat with only minor changes in elevation, which decreases the ability of water to drain easily. Because of this, Lubbock's drainage system is designed around what are known as playa, or man-made lakes. These lakes receive run-off, which is channeled mainly by streets and other man-made drainage channels. Therefore, Lubbock's flooding is called inflooding, because the lakes within the city fill up and overflow the surrounding areas.

The specific area of consideration, Maxey Park, is located in the western central part of Lubbock. The park and the immediate surrounding residential and commercial areas lie in a slightly depressed area, which increases the likelihood of flooding around this particular park.

[Students included drainage-basin analysis data from laboratory experiments.]

Three other problems that increase flooding are that (1) Lubbock is a semiarid region, which somewhat reduces infiltration capacity; (2) Lubbock streets are squared off, increasing flood peaks because run-off has reduced time to occur; and (3) Lubbock's rainfall is short and intense, increasing the demand on the drainage system.

The present flood problems facing Lubbock are definitely more acute than those of the past. Such a situation is caused by increased urbanization as a result of years of growth. The only time in the past during which Lubbock has had a rainfall close to the 6.4-inch rainfall of October, 1983, was in 1967, when

5.7 inches fell. An interview with Emory Potts, a Lubbock City Engineer, suggests that the flood in October, 1983, was between a 50- and 100-year flood. Regarding the amount of rainfall (6.4 inches) during a 24-hour period, the flood was closer to a 50-year flood. However, the total accumulation over the 4-day period was 9 to 10 inches, which classifies the flood as a 100-year flood.

From the facts given, it is evident that Lubbock has a serious problem regarding flooding. The city has implemented several measures to curb flooding. Its primary action has been to pass a Lakes ordinance to protect residential and commercial areas. This ordinance is designed to decrease flooding of these areas by building parks around natural playa lakes so that no homes or buildings will be constructed within the immediate area.

The city's second measure has been the construction of a storm sewer system that empties into the Canyon Lakes. Unfortunately, this system is not very extensive.

[Students went on to describe the city's current storm-sewer and flood-prevention systems.]

One possible solution to alleviate flooding around Maxey Park is to dredge the accumulation of silt in Maxey Lake. This action would probably allow the lake to hold more water and possibly increase the natural percolation. Another solution is to build the

homes and buildings on a higher or elevated
foundation to help protect them from the water.
However, Mr. Potts (city engineer) also emphasized
that very little can be done to "counteract mother
nature."

Because of the potential flooding situation
around Maxey Park, with few possible solutions to the
problem, none of the members of our group would want
to purchase a house immediately adjacent to the area.
However, those who own homes in the area should
acquire adequate flood insurance. Owners should also
be prepared to sandbag the lawn, plan alternate
routes of travel, and have a plan for safe and quick
evacuation if it should become necessary.

[Students included charts and graphs illustrating the Maxey
Lake area and its flood problems.]

✦ QUESTIONS FOR DISCUSSION

1. What are the stated objectives of the report?
2. What is the nature of the flooding problem described by the report?
3. Where did the group get its information? What kinds of primary and secondary sources did the students use? Did they acknowledge those sources?
4. What possible solutions were posed for lessening the hazard? What measures should home owners take to reduce the flood problem?

✦ EXERCISE

To help you understand the process of observation and report, this exercise encourages you to think through a problem-solving task. You may use the same steps to problem solving outlined in the geography assignment just described as you explore possible solutions to a problem that you have identified in your community. The task that follows outlines problem solving for a traffic hazard. You may wish to find an equivalent project of your own design and follow similar steps to complete it. For this exercise, work in groups of four or five people; be sure that you divide the work evenly among the members of your group.

1. Identify a traffic hazard (or comparable problem) that you have observed in your community. Perhaps it is an intersection where accidents occur frequently or a school crossing zone that has no painted crosswalk. Describe the problem as carefully as you can, giving the location of the problem area (maps might be appropriate).

2. Define an objective or goal that might lead to the solution of the problem you have identified. For a traffic hazard, perhaps a stoplight, a painted crosswalk, or a crossing guard would eliminate the problem.

3. Gather information from your own observations and from books, printed matter, media, other people, and observations. You may want to attend a public meeting, perhaps of the local traffic commission, or you might wish to study the commission's long-range plans for the community. You may want to speak to the principal of an elementary school about a school crossing hazard.

4. While gathering data, generate possible solutions and define the constraints that might limit them. For a traffic hazard, perhaps the city budget precludes installing any more traffic lights. In such a case, you might look for alternative sources of funding that the city has not yet explored.

5. Evaluate the possible solutions you have posed in number 4, to determine which is most likely to solve the problem, which satisfies the objective, which is the most feasible, practical, economical, safe, legal, and so on.

Prepare a report three to five pages long that describes the problem, the data-collection method, and the proposed solutions. In the report, use the evidence gathered to support the proposed solution.

Make an oral presentation of your report to your class, talking from a one-page outline of your report (which you should prepare after the report is finished). Your group will need to meet to work out the details of the oral presentation, but all should participate.

PRIMARY RESEARCH IN THE
SOCIAL SCIENCES

The social sciences have incorporated many of the research techniques of the natural and physical sciences and have developed some research methods of their own as well. Remember, as we discussed in Chapter 1, the primary aim of the social sciences is to study human beings and their interaction with society and the environment. Social scientists seek to help us understand the events that happen around us and to communicate that understanding to others. Systematic inquiry is essential in the social sciences. Because researchers must communicate the social knowledge they acquire through their research, they need a clear written form for transmitting their insights. As in the natural and physical sciences, researchers in the social sciences employ a version of the scientific method. The following steps (discussed in detail in later paragraphs) are generally utilized in the researching of a social scientific question:

1. Choosing the research problem and stating the hypothesis
2. Formulating the research design and method of gathering data
3. Gathering the data
4. Analyzing the data
5. Interpreting the results of the data analysis in order to test the hypothesis

Step 1—Problem and Hypothesis

Obviously, the first step must be preceded by extensive study and preparation in the discipline under investigation. To choose a research problem that is significant, fresh, and researchable, the social scientist must have an intimate knowledge of the field of study. Often, researchers will choose a problem based on the prior research of other social scientists, or they will seek to test their hypotheses of reality against actual social reality. It is crucial for researchers to keep abreast of the current research in their fields by reading professional journals, attending national meetings of professional societies, and maintaining contacts with other researchers doing similar studies. Research problems are not formulated in a vacuum. The first two inquiry steps discussed in Chapter 1, preparation and incubation, precede the actual formulation of a hypothesis.

Once a significant research problem has been chosen, a working hypothesis can be formulated, that is, the researcher sets forth a proposition (hypothesis) that may explain the occurrence of the phenomenon observed. For example, an education researcher interested in the writing processes of children might hypothesize that the type of learning environment could influence the children's willingness to write.

Step 2—Research Design

The researcher must decide how to test the hypothesis posed in step 1. To do this, he or she needs to determine which concepts or events being studied are constant and which are variable. Variables are phenomena that change or differ. Temperature, for example, is a scientific variable that differs by degrees. Thus, the variable "temperature" contains the idea of more or less heat, and this variable influences the physical world. Similarly, the social variable "religion" may be expressed differently: Protestant, Catholic, Muslim, and so on. Just as temperature influences physical nature, a social variable such as religion influences human nature. Public opinion polls have discovered that Protestants and Catholics differ predictably in their preference for political parties. Thus, the variable "religion" influences social behavior. In the example given from education, the variable is "learning environment," which refers to the formal or informal structure of the classroom—whether open or highly rigid.

Once the variables have been identified, the researcher must decide how best to measure them. The methods used by social scientists include experiments, surveys and questionnaires, interviews and case studies, and observations. These methods are discussed in detail on pp. 107–112.

Step 3—Gathering the Data

The researcher gathers data (both quantitative and qualitative) based on the research design chosen as most appropriate for testing the hypothesis. Social science researchers pay close attention to matters of accurate sampling and the accurate recording of data. Table 4-1, taken from FBI Crime Reports, illustrates the kind of data often used by social scientists.

Step 4—Analyzing the Data

Researchers analyze their data quantitatively (using numbers) to discern its relationship to the hypothesis. Depending on the research method used, the researcher relies to a greater or lesser degree on statistical analyses of the data. Often, researchers code their data to make

TABLE 4-1 FBI Uniform Crime Reports

Area	Population	Crime Index Total	Modified Crime Index Total	Violent Crime	Property Crime	Murder and Non-Negligent Manslaughter	Forcible Rape	Robbery	Aggravated Assault	Burglary	Larceny-Theft	Motor Vehicle Theft
ALASKA												
Metropolitan Statistical Area	231,039											
Area actually reporting	100.0%	13,746		1,025	12,721	15	154	285	571	2,113	9,491	1,117
Other Cities	168,591											
Area actually reporting	87.4%	8,100		590	7,510	9	69	62	450	1,081	5,581	848
Estimated totals	100.0%	9,267		675	8,592	10	79	71	515	1,237	6,385	970
Rural	125,370											
Area actually reporting	100.0%	5,219		691	4,528	28	108	28	527	1,743	2,319	466
State Total	525,000	28,232		2,391	25,841	53	341	384	1,613	5,093	18,195	2,553
Rate per 100,000 inhabitants		5,377.5		455.4	4,922.1	10.1	65.0	73.1	307.2	970.1	3,465.7	486.3
ARIZONA												
Metropolitan Statistical Area	2,587,955											
Area actually reporting	100.0%	204,538		17,226	187,312	206	1,208	4,262	11,550	46,196	128,869	12,247
Other Cities	422,312											
Area actually reporting	98.3%	30,282		2,267	28,015	17	139	347	1,764	6,145	20,379	1,491
Estimated totals	100.0%	30,803		2,305	28,498	17	141	353	1,794	6,251	20,730	1,517
Rural	375,733											
Area actually reporting	91.0%	7,342		1,103	6,239	27	43	66	967	2,378	3,366	495
Estimated totals	100.0%	8,064		1,211	6,853	30	47	72	1,062	2,612	3,697	544
State Total	3,386,000	243,405		20,742	222,663	253	1,396	4,687	14,406	55,059	153,296	14,308
Rate per 100,000 inhabitants		7,188.6		612.6	6,576.0	7.5	41.2	138.4	425.5	1,626.1	4,527.3	422.6

it suitable for computer processing. Computers can quickly and accurately process data and correlate variables. As an example of data analysis, students in a political science class were asked to analyze the crime statistics data in the accompanying Table 4-1. First, the students were asked to compare the data for two states, in this case Alaska and Arizona, to see whether the differences were statistically significant. Then they were asked to explain or interpret their results.

Step 5—Interpreting the Results

The relationship among variables suggested by the hypothesis is tested at this stage in the research, often through statistical measures. In the social sciences, a hypothesis can never be proved or disproved "beyond the shadow of a doubt." However, researchers can statistically calculate the probability of error for the hypothesis and thus can strongly suggest the truth or validity of the hypothesis. In other words, a social scientist may be able to either reject or fail to reject a hypothesis based on a careful marshaling of the evidence. For example, in comparing the crime reports for Alaska and Arizona, the students noticed that the rates per 100,000 population differed in potentially interesting ways: Arizona exceeded Alaska in total property crimes (burglary, larceny-theft, motor vehicle theft) and in total violent crimes (murder, rape, robbery, assault). But for individual crimes, Alaska topped Arizona in murders, rapes, and vehicle thefts. The students needed first to find out whether these perceived differences were significant, using statistical tests. If so, they then could interpret their results by positing plausible explanations (hypotheses) to further explore and test. The students, for example, hypothesized that the high number of rapes in Alaska could be related to the scarcity of women. This hypothesis could be tested, perhaps by comparisons with other states with similar demographics.

Social Science Research Designs

The research designs used in social science research include the following:

1. Experiments
2. Surveys and questionnaires
3. Interviews and case studies
4. Observations

Outlined in the paragraphs that follow are the research designs most commonly used by social science researchers. Each has both advantages and disadvantages. Researchers must keep the relative merits in mind as they design a research project.[2]

Experiments

The social scientific experiment is a highly controlled method of determining a direct link between two variables—for example, between high temperature and riots. The researcher must have control over the research environment so that no external variables can affect the outcome. Unlike experimental methods in the sciences, in social scientific research it is often difficult to control the research environment totally. A researcher who is interested in the causes of riots should not attempt to create a riot in the laboratory for study. However, social science researchers can study laboratory animals and posit hypotheses about human behavior based on their experimental results. For example, to test the hypothesis that overcrowding can cause riots, some researchers studied populations of rats and varied the population density to test their hypothesis. They found that for the rat populations, overcrowding did indeed cause antisocial behavior. From this result, the researchers hypothesized that a similar phenomenon may exist for people—that is, overcrowded cities may contribute to antisocial behavior. Although experimental research is the best means of definitively establishing causal links (variable A causes variable B; overcrowded living conditions cause antisocial behavior), experiments may be limited in applicability. In the case of the above experiment, people may or may not behave as rats do.

Surveys and Questionnaires

Ideally, we would study an entire population to gain insights into its society; finding out how all Americans intend to vote in an upcoming election would accurately predict the outcome. However, polling an entire population is seldom feasible, so pollsters sample small segments of the entire population at random. The most frequently used sampling is random-digit-dialing over the telephone. Researchers have refined sampling techniques to the point that polls can be quite accurate. Thus, CBS news can announce the outcome of a presidential election hours before the returns are in for much of the country.

One particular kind of survey is the questionnaire, a form that asks for responses to a set of questions. Large numbers of people can be polled for their opinions by means of questionnaires over the telephone, through the mail, or in person. The advent of computers has radically changed the survey business: it is now possible to survey large populations, input and code their responses into a computer database, and obtain immediate analyses of the data.

The Hypothesis.   As with most other research in both the sciences and social sciences, the first, and perhaps most important, step in survey research is the articulation of a hypothesis. "Developing the hypothesis provides the key ingredient to structure all subsequent parts of the project: the questionnaire, the sample, the coding, the tabulation forms, and the final report itself."[3] A questionnaire is not given simply to gather random facts; rather, it is a problem-solving enterprise. The researcher poses a hypothesis in an attempt to shed light on a particular research problem. The questionnaire works to either support or counter the hypothesis. For example, in a study of the relationship between the elderly and the police, the researchers presumably would try to solve a problem, for example, that the elderly do not see the police in a positive light and therefore hesitate to call on them in an emergency situation. The researcher, then, might hypothesize that the real problem lies in the elderly population's erroneous perceptions of the police. A questionnaire could be designed to elicit their perceptions and to try to understand the origins of their distrust. In fact, when a study like this was conducted in a major metropolitan area, researchers discovered that an elderly person's distrust of the police was in direct proportion to the number of hours of TV viewed, in particular TV crime shows.

Question Design.   The survey researcher must design each question on the questionnaire carefully to ensure that it is clear, direct, and understandable to the target population. Questions should be pretested so that initial responses can be reviewed and the questions revised to eliminate any ambiguity prior to their use in the actual study. Researchers should also design questionnaires that are reliable (measure the same thing each time) and valid (measure what they claim to measure). In addition, the population sampled should represent the larger group being studied.

Two basic kinds of questions are used on questionnaires: open-ended questions and closed questions. The open-ended questions may require an interviewer, since research has shown that self-administered open answers tend to yield less usable data. Fowler says that "generally speaking, if one is going to have a self-administered questionnaire, one must reconcile oneself to closed questions, that is, questions that can be answered by simply checking a box or circling the proper response from a set provided by the researcher."[4] On the other hand, Labaw says that open questions have gotten a lot of undeserved bad press in the survey business in recent years. She says they "provide absolutely indispensable insight into how respondents interpret complex but apparently single-issue questions"[5] and, in general, recommends the strategic coupling of both closed and open-ended questions. She also states that "the most basic principle of question wording, and one very often ignored or simply unseen, is that only one concept or issue or meaning should be included in a question."[6]

The accompanying questionnaire was designed by a student to discover the attitude of foreign students toward Utah State University and the education they were receiving. He hypothesized, based on his own experiences as a foreign student, that their responses would be generally very favorable. The student researcher polled sixty foreign students, collected during several visits to the library, representing a variety of nationalities. He found that, in general, foreign students were satisfied with university administrative policies but less satisfied with interpersonal relationships between them and their teachers and classmates.

Questionnaire
1. What is your nationality?
2. How long have you been a student at USU?
3. What is your native language?
4. Do you feel classes at USU are designed with consideration of the needs of foreign students?   yes   no
5. Do you feel your instructors are unbiased toward you and your nationality during class?   yes   no
6. Do you feel you have received an undeserved grade from an instructor due to a bias against foreign students?   yes   no
7. Do you feel any language difficulties (limited vocabulary, accent, etc.) cause communication barriers between you and your instructors?   yes   no
8. Do you feel accepted as an equal by your American classmates?   yes   no
9. Do you feel USU's administrative policies regarding foreign students are fair and unbiased?   yes   no
10. Do you feel USU provides an equal opportunity for a sound education for its foreign students?   yes   no

✦ QUESTIONS FOR DISCUSSION

1. Based on the previous discussion of questionnaire design, how would you rate this student's questionnaire?

2. Do the questions asked match the hypothesis?

3. Are there any ambiguous words or phrases that could be misunderstood?

4. Do you see any way this questionnaire could be made better?

Interviews and Case Studies

Interview studies are one particular type of survey. Their advantages over the questionnaire include flexibility (the questioner can interact with the respondent), response rate (the questioner immediately knows the respondent's answer), and nonverbal behavior (the questioner can gather nonverbal clues as well as verbal). Interviews have other advantages as well, but the disadvantages are also great. Primarily, the time and expense of interviews makes them difficult to conduct. Consequently, fewer responses can be gathered. In addition, the interview is actually a complex interaction between individuals and thus can hinge on the characteristics of the individuals involved. If a respondent is put off by the interviewer, for example, his or her interview answers may be affected. Nevertheless, interviewing is an important research method in the social sciences that results in rich, high-quality data.

Some considerations when designing interviews follow:

1. Be certain that the questions are written down and asked exactly as worded.
2. Be certain that you probe any unclear or incomplete answer.
3. Be certain that inadequate or brief answers are not probed in a biasing (directive) way.

The accompanying interview was conducted by a student who was interested in the relationship between emotions and the onset of asthma attacks in asthmatic children. Prior to the interview, she obtained the subject's permission to tape-record for later data analysis.

Interview with Dr. John W. Carlisle, September 10, 1988
(Pediatrician with extensive experience treating asthmatic children)

1. *Do emotions cause asthma?* Dr. Carlisle feels that the misconception "emotions cause asthma" is easily explained by the fact that stressful emotional situations frequently trigger asthma attacks. People who may have already been prone to asthma may experience their first attack in an emotionally stressful situation. In actuality, asthma is a physical disease that can be irritated by emotional stress or trauma.

2. *What emotional or psychological effects on your asthmatic patients have you observed?* Dr. Carlisle targeted several detrimental effects of asthma on children's emotional and psychological well-being. Older children (8–12 years) feel "defective" in some way because they are suddenly different from their peers (they often have to take medicine or other precautions to prevent an attack). Older children may rebel against parents who expect

them to take on the extra responsibility for controlling their own disease. Younger children tend to regress, become very frightened, and cling to parents because they are not yet capable of understanding their disease.

3. *What suggestions do you have for treating the emotional aspects of asthma?* In Dr. Carlisle's opinion, the best emotional support parents can give childhood asthmatics is to make sure they understand the disease and what is happening to them. At the same time, try to reinforce the fact that there will always be someone there to help them if they need help. This can alleviate a great deal of the anxiety that can aggravate their condition.

Observations

The survey method is important for obtaining a person's opinion on a particular issue. The observation, on the other hand, is best suited to the collection of nonverbal data. In this method, the observer takes notes on people behaving in customary ways in a particular environment or setting. In this way, the researcher accumulates "field notes," which are used to analyze trends and discern customary behaviors. The disadvantages of observation include lack of control over the environment, lack of quantifiable data, and small sample size. Also, whenever an observer enters the environment to observe people, the participants' behavior may no longer be natural.

The goal of social research based on observation and description is a general one: to describe and perhaps evaluate a culture or subculture in as much detail as possible. An example of this type of observational research is sociologist Margaret Mead's book *Coming of Age in Samoa*. In this book, Mead describes the complex culture of the Samoan island, paying particular attention to customs surrounding the transition from adolescence to adulthood.

The following excerpt from a report written for a speech communications course illustrates an observation and description of a particular cultural setting—the country singles bar.[7] The researcher was observing particular nonverbal behaviors exhibited by the patrons of the bar. As you read the report, notice the descriptions and categorizations of the patrons in this subculture.

Red Raider Romances

by Lee Guyette

The following study was conducted at the Red Raider Club in Lubbock, Texas. The study is a brief survey of the nonverbal communication displayed in this particular club. The following observations were made by me not only in the recent few days, but also over a seven-month period in which I worked as a cocktail waitress there. I made my observations from the standpoint of a nonperson/waitress and from the person/female customer. The Red Raider Club is a Country and Western club that caters primarily to a crowd of people between the ages of 25 and 50. It is for the most part a blue-collar, lower-middle class crowd.

Body Types, Shapes, and Sizes

Attractiveness:

A majority of the people, both male and female, were only average in appearance. There were a few exceptionally attractive males and females, and they did seem to get preferential treatment; for example, the attractive men were turned down less when they asked a woman to dance, and the attractive women were asked to dance more frequently.

Body Image and Appearance:

Many of the individuals were slightly overweight. They did not seem to be very aware of or satisfied with their bodies. Their body concept seemed low. In the more attractive individuals, the reverse was true. The attractive individuals were more aware of their bodies; they noticed what they were doing with their bodies, and they smiled more and seemed in general more comfortable with themselves. I did notice that the less attractive people seemed to worry less about their unsightly bodies as they became intoxicated.

Body Messages:

Most of my subjects were definitely endomorphic, and they certainly seemed viscerotonic. Most of the men were slightly overweight. There were women as tall as six feet and men as short as five feet. Nearly all my subjects were white. Perhaps two percent were Hispanic and there were no blacks. Many of the men had beards and moustaches, perhaps to indicate masculinity. Most of the women wore their hair either long and curly or short and straight.

Clothing and Personal Artifacts

Function of Dress:

The main function of dress in this club was cultural display more than comfort or modesty. Nearly all of the subjects of both sexes wore jeans. The men wore Wranglers and most of the women wore designer jeans. Chic, Lee, Wrangler, Sergio, and Vanderbilt were the most commonly worn for the women. A few

women wore western dresses. I did not see any man not
wearing cowboy boots and most of the women also wore
cowboy boots. A few women wore high-heeled shoes. All
of the women wearing dresses wore heels. Most of the
people, both female and male, wearing jeans and boots
also had their names on the back of their belts. For
the men, it was their last names on the belt; for the
women, their first names.

Communication Components of Dress:

It is difficult to say whether or not these
people were intentionally or unintentionally
communicating messages through dress. They all seemed
to communicate their preference for western dress.
They did not wish to communicate, however, that they
were from a lower socioeconomic background by wearing
western dress. Although this conception has changed in
recent years, it still is thought that lower-middle-
class people wear western clothes.

Personality Correlates of Dress:

It is extremely difficult to assess personality
types of a large group just from their clothing
styles. However, I did notice that most of the women
in dresses were there with dates. I also noticed that
women wearing red western blouses danced more
frequently. For the most part, both men and women
dressed conservatively. The colors were usually solid

black, brown, and white for the men, and red, purple,
or blue for the women.

Perception of Dress:

    Most of the people were dressed in the
conventional stereotype of western dress. Indeed, it
was almost as if there were an unspoken dress code.
The young attractive girls, wearing red and purple
blouses with ruffles, tight jeans, boots, belts, and
wearing their hair long, seemed to be thought the
sexiest and most likeable. They were asked to dance
more frequently than any others. The young attractive
men with beards and moustaches wearing black or white
western cut shirts seemed to be the most popular with
the women. No one wore very much jewelry of any kind.
A few women had small earrings or hair barrettes.
Nearly everyone smoked cigarettes continuously. I saw
no pipes or cigars.

The Effects of Dress:

    The main effect I observed was that everyone
seemed able to identify with each other and feel a
sense of belonging to the group because of their
similar style of dress.

[Researcher goes on to describe behaviors observed according to the
following categories: body movements and gestures; facial
expressions and eye behavior; responses to environment; personal
space, territory, and crowding; touching behavior; voice
characteristics; taste and smell; culture and time.]

Discussion

I feel that the nonverbal communication that I
have described may be representative of lower-middle-
class America in Lubbock, Texas. The nonverbal
communication described in this report may illustrate
lower-middle-class values: the tendency to be slightly
overweight in both sexes; the conservative,
traditional, western-style dress; the traditional use
of male/female regulators and posture; the overcontrol
of masculine expressions of emotion and the lack of
control in feminine emotional expressions; the
environment, with its tacky chairs and dirty carpet;
the use of territory by the men; the fact that women
have no true territory, personal space, or value (the
women are treated as possessions and property and
they have only as much value as they are granted by
men); the way in which the men have absolute control
over when and how they will be touched, but the women
have very little to say about when or how the men
will touch them; the way the women plead with soft
cooing pitch at the end of their voice or remain
silent while the men speak loudly and uninterruptedly;
the use of substandard speech; the accepted deception
on the part of the males; the overwhelming smell of
tobacco and liquor and stale urine in the restrooms;
the taste of cheap wines, beer, and whisky; the time
being measured by the sets the band plays. All of
these things are often associated with lower-middle
classes. Women and men may be poorly educated and

thus rely on tradition and myth. I felt that the
nonverbal communication that I observed was
representative of this particular subculture.

✦ QUESTIONS FOR DISCUSSION

1. What is the relationship between the observer and those she is observing?

2. Observation research tends to both describe and classify behaviors of individuals in order to predict future behaviors within the setting. List the classifications used by this writer. Do they seem appropriate to the behaviors observed? Why or why not?

3. Does the writer overgeneralize from a small sample; that is, does she jump to conclusions based on insufficient data? Why or why not? Do her conclusions follow logically from her evidence? Why or why not?

4. Is it likely that the observer's presence changed the dynamics of the situation so that her subjects' behavior was no longer natural? Why or why not?

5. Do the writer's personal opinions and biases come through? Why or why not?

6. How much can an observer infer about the subjects' thoughts and emotions from observing their behaviors? For example, in the subsection "Communication Components of Dress," the author states that "they did not wish to communicate, however, that they were from a lower socioeconomic background. . . ." Is this a valid inference or a reflection of a personal bias? Justify your response.

✦ EXERCISES

The exercises below are provided to give you an opportunity to try out some of the primary research techniques frequently used by social scientists. Or, you may wish to adapt these methods to find information pertinent to your own research topic with an eye toward incorporating the primary research data you discover into your larger research paper.

1. To understand observing and reporting, begin by observing the behavior of a particular group or subculture and report on that observation. You may find that an observation report would be

a helpful component in a larger research paper project. As in the sample paper above on the country singles bar, first choose subjects in a "field" to observe. Some possibilities include customers at a fast-food restaurant, patrons at a theater, participants in a sport, spectators at a rock concert, students in a dorm, customers in a department store elevator, and so on.

Procedure:

A. Identify the field you have chosen to observe. Describe the setting, location, and the time you spent observing. Describe your research method. (Are you an observer or participant?)

B. Take field notes as you observe the behaviors of the individuals in your chosen group. Look for verbal and nonverbal behaviors.

C. Categorize your field notes into related behaviors and personality types.

D. Speculate on the meaning of the behaviors you observed. What did you learn about the people in your study and how they act? Give possible reasons for why they behaved as they did.

E. Write up your field observations in a report three to five pages long.

2. To understand the processes of interviewing and reporting, conduct an actual interview, working by yourself or with a classmate. You may find that an interview with an expert is a useful component of a larger research paper project.

Procedure:

A. Find someone in your intended major field. Write or phone the person to introduce yourself. Set up an interview with that person, explaining that you want to find out what a person in your chosen career actually does.

B. Prior to the interview, draw up a list of interview topics similar to the following:

- education and background
- job title and general description of the job
- description of the company or organization
- years at the job
- prior positions within the same company
- tasks performed in the job
- tools used in the job (for example, computers, books)

- career plans or aspirations
- job satisfaction
- advice for someone just beginning in the field

Use this topic list as a model only in developing your questions. The questions you ask will vary in accordance with your career choice. It is important to think through the questions you intend to ask your informant very carefully. If you want to tape the interview, be certain to ask for permission.

C. Once you have collected your data, analyze and categorize it into a report three to five pages long. Someone reading your report should be able to discern what the career is like for participants.

PRIMARY RESEARCH IN THE HUMANITIES

Just as in the sciences and social sciences, researchers in the humanities employ standard research methods. There are standard methods used in the production of fine arts (painting, sculpture, music, drama, and so on) just as there are standard methods in the humanities that interpret fine arts, literature, history, and experience. Since production of fine arts is beyond the scope of this book, we will focus here as in Chapter 1 on interpretation. The goal of the humanities is to explore and explain the human experience, so humanities researchers make extensive use of written records of experience. Such written records are called primary texts and can include literary texts (poems, stories, novels, plays), other kinds of texts (letters, diaries, journals), and historical records (court proceedings, government records). All these texts provide the raw data from which the researcher in the humanities works.

Using Primary Texts

Research in the humanities often begins with a primary text of particular interest to the researcher. The researcher must read the text very carefully as preparation, noting any significant events, themes, characters, and so on. After finishing the close reading, much as researchers in the social sciences do, the humanities researcher posits a hypothesis, that is, a plausible interpretation of the work and its significance. Then the researcher collects evidence from the text itself and from other, related sources: works written by the same author, sources used by the author, and historical works on events occurring during the period when the work was written. These related sources are used to help verify or refute the initial hypothesis. Ultimately, the humanities researcher seeks to explain and interpret a primary text in such a way that its richness of meaning is increased for its readers.

An example of an interpretation of a primary text is Eugene K. Garber's article, " 'My Kinsman, Major Molineux': Some Interpretive and Critical Probes."[8] One of the aspects of the work Garber investigates is Hawthorne's use of myth in the story. Garber points out that the story is "a very old archetypal story—the story of the young hero whose quest for personal, religious, or cultural identity necessarily leads him down into the underworld." In tracing this myth, Garber draws parallels between Hawthorne's hero, Robin, and the archetypal hero who encounters not only "the darkness in the world" but also "the darkness in his own psyche." To a casual reader of the story, this mythical pattern may not have been immediately apparent. By reading Garber's interpretation, the complexity of the story and its rich resonances are brought to our attention. Once we grasp the parallels between mythical heros and Robin's quest for manhood, we not only understand the story better we also understand ourselves better.

The student who wrote the excerpt below, in her paper titled "Jim as a Romantic," followed a similar kind of interpretive probe to that used by Garber. In this paper, Stephanie Owen uses the characteristic beliefs of the romantic age as an interpretive grid with which to better understand the underlying motivations of the character Jim in Joseph Conrad's *Lord Jim.*

Jim as a Romantic

by Stephanie J. Owen

English 201

The Romantic Age took place in Western Europe between the years of 1780 and 1850. It was an age that emphasized the importance of the individual. The use of the imagination and the emotions were considered necessary for the discovery of deep, hidden truths (Knoebel 260) in the Romantic quest for the

"ideal state of being" (Miller 383). These truths
were thought simple, based on the moral behavior of
man (Knoebel 260).

The completion of the Romantic Age in 1850 did
not end the characteristics, beliefs, and sensibili-
ties that accompanied the age, however. Fifty years
after the end of this period, Jim, the main character
of Joseph Conrad's book Lord Jim, was described
within the book as "excessively romantic" (Conrad
416). After listening to the story of his life,
Stein, another character in the book, claimed, "I
understand quite well. He is romantic" (212). In trying to explain how a romantic person viewed the world
and what he must do to live happily within the world,
Stein used a metaphor which I believe is fundamental
to understanding Jim's behavior, both his failures and
his successes, throughout the book. He stated, "A man
that is born falls into a dream like a man who falls
into the sea. If he tries to climb out into the
air . . ., he drowns. The way is to the destructive
element submit yourself, and with the exertions of
your hands and feet in the water make the deep, deep
sea keep you up" (Conrad 214). I believe that Jim's
romantic characteristics induced his failures when he
tried to escape from that which surrounded him and
his successes when he submitted himself to his dream,
to his ideal response to his environment.

The Romantics placed a strong emphasis on the
value of imagination (Knoebel 260). Jim, too, was

very imaginative. As Marlow, the main narrator of the book, stated, "He was a poor gifted devil with the faculty of a swift and forestalling vision" (Conrad 96). He often imagined himself in the positions of the heroes of books that he had read and believed that, when the necessity arose, he would be able to act in the manner that he imagined. He felt that his imagination had prepared him for any danger that might occur (6). This type of imagination ruled his life throughout the first half of the book; he lived more within his dream life than in reality. In the second part of the book, though, Jim began to realize his dreams. In Patusan, Jim acted heroically on several different occasions, often because his imagination helped him to discover the best method to approach a difficult matter. He lived very much as one of his fictional characters would live (Martin 205).

Another aspect of the Romantic Movement was the value it placed on individualism. Each person was considered to have importance, and variation was considered to be beneficial (Miller 383). Jim again proved to be romantic in the value that he placed on individuals. Throughout most of the book, however, the only individualism that he understood was his own, as Conrad expressed through the omnipotent narrator; "his thought was contemplating his own superiority" (23). In Patusan, however, Jim began to value the lives of others. He cared deeply for the lives and happiness

of the Patusans, and he involved himself in their
politics to help assure their freedom. Because he had
learned the value of individual expression, he may
have placed more value on Gentleman Brown's life than
he should have. He had learned, however, that one
individual should not necessarily judge another.

Jim also displayed a similarity with the
Romantics in his wide range of emotions. The
Romantics felt that emotions were important for true
understanding of self, and their works continually
expressed a high emotional content (Knoebel 260). Jim
may not have fully understood his emotional swings,
but Marlow certainly noticed them. He claimed, "Your
imaginative people swing further in any direction, as
if given a longer scope of cable in the uneasy
anchorage of life" (Conrad 224). Immediately after
having jumped off of the Patna, Jim's unhappiness and
guilt were strong enough to have nearly driven him to
suicide. However, another equally strong emotion, his
anger at the others in the boat, prevented him (118).
As Chester explained, "[He] takes it to heart" (165).
After the inquiry, his inability to forget his
extreme guilt caused Jim to continually run away from
any incident or situation that might heighten his
feelings of unhappiness. After finally having arrived
in Patusan, Jim began to succeed, and his happiness
and pride reached the same levels as his guilt and
discomfiture had previously.

The imagination, individualism, and emotionalism
already described were, for the Romantics, the basis

and means for the discovery of deep, hidden truths
(Knoebel 260). They thus rejected materialism (Miller
383) and the morals of their time period (Knoebel
260) in deference to humanitarianism and efforts to
reform the world. They sought after "ideal states of
being" (Miller 383). I believe that Jim's feelings of
superiority and his constant search after heroism were
a result of his own desire to idealize his own "state
of being." He did have the sense of moral obligation
and correctness that was characteristic of the
Romantics, but he occasionally failed in his actions.
According to Stein, the way to discover truth was to
"follow the dream" (Conrad 215), and several times
throughout the book, Jim did "follow the dream" to
which his imagination, his individualism, and his
emotions led him. In those times, he immersed himself
"in the destructive element" (214), and then he
succeeded. He failed only when he forgot to "follow
the dream."

Jim made three major mistakes throughout his
career as both a seaman and a leader of Patusan. In
my opinion, each of these failures was caused,
directly or indirectly, by some aspect of his
romanticism that emerged when he attempted to "climb
out" of the dream rather than submit himself to it.
Jim's jump from the Patna, his inability to hold a
job after the inquiry, and his misjudging of Brown
were all actions that resulted from his uncontrolled
romanticism.

[Student goes on to describe each of the three mistakes made by Jim]

A reader can hardly keep from admiring Jim's giving up his life to "follow the dream" at the end of the novel, but Conrad seems almost to condemn rather than support the action. This condemnation raises the question of whether or not Jim's romantic characteristics could be considered his tragic flaw. I personally prefer to view Jim's death as a success, as a final proof that he was capable of controlling his own destiny and a final atonement for all of his mistakes, but I do recognize that his romanticism, his submission "to the destructive element," actually did destroy him. This is the question with which Marlow struggled and with which each reader must also struggle when studying Conrad and Lord Jim.

Works Cited

Conrad, Joseph. Lord Jim. 1920. New York: Oxford UP, 1989.

Epstein, Harry S. "Lord Jim as a Tragic Action." Studies in the Novel: Northern Texas State 5 (1973): 229-247.

Knoebel, Edgar E., ed. "Romantic Poetry." Classics of Western Thought: The Modern World. New York: Harcourt, 1988.

Martin, Joseph. "Conrad and the Aesthetic Movement." Conradiana 17 (1985): 199-213.

Miller, James E., Jr., et al., eds. "The Romantic Age." England in Literature. Glenview, IL: Scott-Foresman, 1976.

Reichard, Hugo M. "The Patusan Crises: A Reevaluation

of Jim and Marlow." <u>English Studies</u> 49 (1968):

547-552.

Stevenson, Richard C. "Stein's Prescription for 'How

to End the Problem of Assessing Lord Jim's

Career.'" <u>Conradiana</u> 7 (1975): 233-243.

✦ QUESTIONS FOR DISCUSSION

1. What significant event, theme, or character did Stephanie identify in Conrad's work?
2. What hypothesis did Stephanie pose to help us interpret the work?
3. What parallels did Stephanie find between the main character, Jim, and the romantics?
4. By reading Stephanie's interpretation, what new insights were you able to gain about Conrad's work?

Life-History Interviewing

The methods of humanities research may at times approximate the methods in social science research even more closely than the above description suggests. Historical research, for example, may include surveys and interviews of participants in a significant historical event, and very often historical research relies on the statistics gathered by social scientists.

One example of a humanities researcher is Studs Terkel, author of the book *Hard Times: An Oral History of the Great Depression,* which chronicles life during the 1930s.[9] Terkel's primary sources for his work were people who had lived through the Depression. He interviewed people from various walks of life and parts of the country, inquiring into their own life histories. The interviews were taped and transcribed. From the transcripts, Terkel wrote his version of the life history of each individual, bringing his own interpretations and explanations to the interview data. Terkel presented these explanations to readers in story form; the pieces describe and recreate events in each informant's life and together give a composite picture of life during the Depression.

The following excerpts show how Terkel transformed the taped material from his interview with Emma Tiller into a "story." As you read these excerpts, notice the differences between the taped original and Terkel's narrative. What kinds of changes did he make? Why do you think he made the changes he did?

Emma Tiller (transcribed tape)

Studs Terkel

a white in the south is like they is i guess in most other places they will not give and help especially the ones who is turned out to be tramps and hoboes uh they come to their door for food they will drive them away white tramps they will drive them away but if a negro come they will feed him they always go and get something another and give him something to eat and they'll even give them a little do you smoke or do you you dip snuff or uh or any do you use anything like that yes ma'am yes ma'am well they would uh give him a quarter or uh fifty cents you know and give him a little sack of food and a bar of soap or something like that well uh but they own color they wouldn't do that for them then the negro woman would uh uh say you know well we've got some cold food in there we'll give you she said oh no i don't give them nothing he'll be back tomorrow you know so so they won't dispose it Terkel: Oh, you mean the Negro woman [who works] yes [for the white] yes [mistress] yes [the white- -] she would take food and put it in a bag and sometimes wrap it in newspaper and ah we would hurry out and sometimes we'd have to run down the alley because he'd be gone down the alley and holler at him hey mister and he would stop you know and say come here and he'd come back and said look you come back by after while and i'll put some food out there in a bag and i'll put it down side the can so that you don't see it if we could see soap we'd swipe a bar of soap and face rag or something or you know and stick it in there for them negroes always would feed these tramps even sometimes we would see them on the railroad track picking up stuff and we would tell them you know come to our house and give them the address and tell him to come back that we would give him a old shirt or a pair of pants or some old shoes and some food we always would give them food many times i have gone in in my house and taken my husband's old shoes and his coat and some of them he he needed them hisself but i didn't feel he needed them as bad as that man needed them because that man to me was in a worser shape than he was in regardless of whether it was negro or white i would give them to him.

Emma Tiller (pages 60–61)

When tramps and hoboes would come to their door for food, the southern white people would drive them away. But if a Negro come, they will feed him. They even give them money. They'll ask them: Do you smoke do you dip snuff Yes, ma'am, yes, ma'am. They was always nice in a nasty way to Negroes. But their own color, they wouldn't do that for 'em. They would hire Negroes for these type jobs where they wouldn't hire whites. They wouldn't hire a white woman to do housework, because they were afraid she'd take her husband.

When the Negro woman would say, 'Miz So-and-So, we got some cold food in the kitchen left from lunch. Why don't you give it to 'im?' she'll say, 'Oh, no, don't give 'im nothin'. He'll be back tomorrow with a gang of 'em. He ought to get a job and work.'

The Negro woman who worked for the white woman would take food and wrap it in newspapers. Sometimes we would hurry down the alley and holler at 'im: 'Hey, mister, come here!' And we'd say, 'Come back by after a while and I'll put some food in a bag, and I'll sit down aside the garbage can so they won't see it.' Then he'd get food, and we'd swipe a bar of soap and a face razor or somethin', stick it in there for 'im. Negroes would always feed these tramps.

Sometimes we would see them on the railroad tracks pickin' up stuff, and we would tell 'em: 'Come to our house.' They would come by and we would give 'em an old shirt or a pair of pants or some old shoes. We would always give 'em food.

Many times I have gone in my house and taken my husband's old shoes some of 'em he needed hisself, but that other man was in worser shape than he was. Regardless of whether it was Negro or white, we would give to 'em. ✦

From Terkel, Studs (1970). *Hard Times: An Oral History of the Great Depression.* New York: Pantheon Books. Copyright © 1970 by Studs Terkel. Reprinted by permission of Pantheon Books, a division of Random House, Inc.

✦ QUESTIONS FOR DISCUSSION

1. What do you think Emma Tiller's job was?
2. Compare Emma's description of the treatment of hoboes by whites with that by blacks.
3. What attitude toward poor people does Emma exemplify?
4. What role do you think compassion played during the Depression?
5. How does Terkel use language to illustrate Emma Tiller's character?
6. Choose one line from the original transcript and compare it to Terkel's rendition of the same line. What changes did Terkel make? Why do you think he made those changes?
7. Which version is easier to read? Why?
8. How does Emma Tiller's story help make life during the Depression vivid and real?
9. Relate Terkel's work *Hard Times* to what you have learned about humanities research. Does Terkel's approach satisfy the goals of humanities research?

✦ EXERCISE

In this exercise, you will use some of the tools and procedures of researchers in the humanities as you research and write an auto-biographical report. This assignment can also help you become familiar with locating and using primary sources in your library.

Procedure:

A. First, locate a primary text. In this case, locate a newspaper that was printed on the day you were born. Old newspapers are probably kept in your library on microfilm, so you will need to learn how to use the microfilm readers. If possible, choose a newspaper from a city near where you were born. For example, if you were born in the East, you could read the *New York Times* or the *Washington Post.*

B. Read the newspaper completely, looking for significant events, people, and ideas. Take notes about any important events, people, or ideas that you find in the newspaper.

C. Once you have finished reading and taking notes, formulate a hypothesis that tells something about the times in which you were born. For example, you might hypothesize that very little has changed in the kinds of news stories written then and now. Or you might find that prices are drastically different and spec-ulate about the reasons for the change. Or you might find a sig-nificant article (on a political event or a social issue, such as the first busing for desegregation in a major city and the consequent rioting) that would provide the basis of your paper. Whatever the idea or event you choose, the task is to determine its signifi-cance and interpret it for your readers.

D. Write a short autobiographical account illustrating the times in which you were born. Or, alternatively, find something striking about the newspaper records and develop your own hypothesis. If possible, include your own experiences as a point of depar-ture for your paper.

PRIMARY RESEARCH IN BUSINESS

Just as the social sciences have incorporated many of the research techniques of the sciences, so the field of business has adopted many of the research techniques and methods of the social sciences. The types of research questions commonly asked in business situations have im-mediate and practical consequences: Should Company A take on a new product? How can Company B improve its image? How well do customers understand the sales offer of Company C? Does bottle color affect customer perception of beer taste? Such questions arise out of particular business needs and concerns. But to answer these questions, familiar research techniques are practiced.

For example, if Company A wants to know whether it should take on a new product, it will need to conduct a consumer survey using questionnaires or interviews to ascertain the market potential. Company A might also wish to compare the market shares of competitors and perhaps fieldtest its product with samples to consumers, monitoring their reactions. Or if a company wishes to discover whether bottle color influences perception of taste in beers, an experimental design (using taste tests) might be in order. These research techniques should sound familiar, since they are those customarily employed in the social sciences: surveys, questionnaires, interviews, case studies, and experiments.

Researchers in business, just like their counterparts in the social sciences, are especially interested in statistical compilations of information to help with decision making. There are many government and corporate agencies that provide information to researchers in business. For example, Table 4-2, produced by the U.S. Department of Commerce, might be of interest to business people in the grocery business.

Presenting Business Information

Much of the research information in business is presented in the form of tables, graphs, flow charts, or diagrams for easy access. The accompanying flow chart (Fig. 1), for example, outlines the process by which a researcher in business would conduct a skills survey. The purpose of such a survey would be to determine the level of employees' skills, knowledge, and ability so that they can be utilized more fully to meet the employment objectives and the staffing needs of a particular organization. As you look over the accompanying flow chart, notice its similarity to the five research steps outlined previously for the social sciences: problem or hypothesis, research design, gathering data, analyzing results, interpreting results.

Conducting a Survey in Business

Mike Smith, a student in business administration, encountered a problem at his place of employment and decided to investigate the extent of the problem by conducting a survey. As a line supervisor at a computer manufacturing plant, Mike had become aware that the workers he supervised were under considerable occupational stress. He wondered just what the origins of that stress were and how the work-

TABLE 4-2 Weekly Food Cost for Families, by Type of Family: 1975 to 1988 (in dollars, as of December, except as indicated. Based on moderate-cost food plan; assumes all meals are eaten at home or taken from home)

Urban Family Type	1975	1980	1981	1982	1983	1984	1985	1986	1987	1988 Jan.	1988 May
Couple, 25–54 years old*	37.10	52.00	53.40	54.60	54.70	56.50	58.30	60.40	63.50	63.90	64.20
Couple, 55 years and over*	32.40	45.90	47.10	48.10	52.00	53.90	55.70	57.80	60.70	61.40	61.70
Couple with children:											
1 child, 1–5 years old	44.90	62.90	64.70	66.00	66.90	69.20	71.30	73.90	77.50	78.10	78.60
1 child, 15–19 years old	53.50	74.80	76.80	78.50	77.80	80.50	83.00	85.50	90.10	90.90	91.40
2 children, 1–5 years old	51.80	72.60	74.70	76.20	77.80	80.50	82.90	85.80	90.00	90.70	91.40
2 children, 6–11 years old	63.00	88.10	90.70	92.60	93.50	97.10	99.80	103.30	108.30	109.20	110.00
2 children, 12–19 years old	67.20	93.80	96.50	98.60	98.00	101.60	104.60	108.20	113.50	114.50	115.20

*Beginning 1983, costs based on revised food plans with age groups 25–50 years old and 51 years old and over.

Source: *Statistical Abstract of the United States*, 1989. U.S. Department of Commerce, Bureau of the Census. (Washington, D.C.: Government Printing Office, p. 100).

Reprinted from U.S. Dept. of Agriculture, Human Information Service, *News*, monthly.

Skills Survey Process Flow Chart

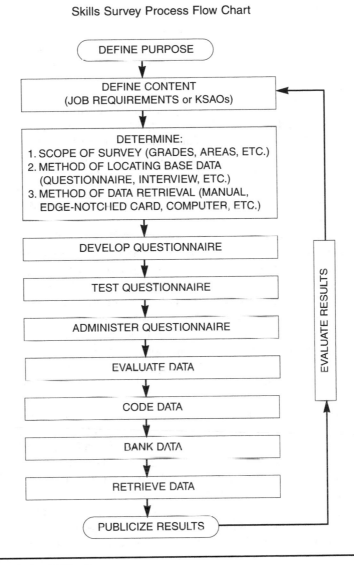

FIGURE 4–1   Skills Survey

Source: U.S. Civil Service Composition, *The Skills Survey: What It Is and How It Works* (Washington D.C.: U.S. Government Printing Office, October 1977), p. 24.

ers were coping with it. First, Mike defined for himself the problem: line workers at Bourn Enterprises seemed to be working under considerable occupational stress. Second, Mike designed a survey questionnaire and tested it on ten workers at Bourn in order to refine the questions and eliminate any ambiguities. Mike gathered his data by having sixty-nine of the line workers at Bourn write their answers to nine questions before their work shift began. Then, once his data was gathered, Mike began to analyze it by compiling the statistical results of each question (see below). Mike presented the information gathered in his survey to his business administration class in the form of an oral report.

In his data analysis, Mike pointed to the high percentage of his sample who felt stressed because of work: 82 percent. Responses to question 7 yielded some explanations of where that job stress originated. Respondents mentioned their job duties and tasks as the number one cause of their work stress. In a follow-up interview, Mike learned that many of the workers felt stressed by the repetitive nature of their work tasks and by the limited variety and lack of creativity in their jobs.

Respondents mentioned their supervisors as the second largest reason for stress on the job. Mike speculated that there is often a lack of communication between line workers and supervisors, causing a disparity between what the supervisor expects and what the worker is attempting to perform. Respondents listed equally stress from machines and stress from coworkers. When machines are broken or under repair, this becomes a frustrating stressor for production workers. Similarly, workers who have trouble getting along with others will find their job situation stressful. Again, Mike pointed to the need for supervisors to encourage communication between themselves and workers and among coworkers.

The respondents to Mike's survey also listed their three main ways of coping with stress in the workplace: relaxation, exercise, and talking to coworkers. Interestingly, the majority (70 percent) of the respondents all indicated that they thought a certain amount of stress was beneficial because it could motivate you to do better. Mike concluded from this survey that rather than eliminating stress altogether, the workplace goal probably should involve learning to lessen unproductive stress and providing an outlet for excessive stress through relaxation breaks, exercise programs, and effective communication.

Questionnaire Results
(69 people were surveyed)

1. Average years of service = 27 months
2. Average time assigned to present task = 47 weeks
3. Percentage of respondents who are main source of income = 44 percent
4. The three main reasons for working: a. Money b. Benefits c. Diversity of life (something to do)

5. Percentage of respondents who feel stress because of work = 82 percent
6. Percentage of respondents who feel stress at: a. Work—60 percent b. Home—34 percent c. Neither—6 percent
7. Three main stressors at work: a. Job duties (assigned tasks and responsibilities) b. Supervisors c. Machines and coworkers (equal number of responses)
8. Three ways to cope with stress: a. Relaxation b. Exercise c. Talking
9. Percentage of respondents who think stress is beneficial = 70 percent

✦ QUESTIONS FOR DISCUSSION

1. What was Mike's purpose for conducting the survey?
2. What is the nature of the workplace problem described by Mike?
3. Do you think the information Mike gathered is representative, complete, accurate, fair? Why or why not?
4. Do you agree with Mike's suggested solutions to the problem of workplace stress? Do you have other suggestions?
5. Have you experienced workplace stress yourself? Does your experience correspond with that described in Mike's report? How is it similar or different?

✦ EXERCISE

To help you practice some of the research techniques we have been discussing in this chapter so far, the following exercise suggests a written proposal to an employer or organization proposing a study of current procedures. The outcome of this assignment could be the proposal itself, or you could follow up the proposal by actually conducting the study described and reporting on its results.

1. Think of a problem or question that arose at a current or previous place of employment. Describe as clearly as you can the nature of the organization in which you were employed and the specifics of the problem or question. Perhaps your employer implemented a new procedure that caused workers to lose productivity (drive-in workers at a fast-food restaurant being required to wash their hands after each car served, for example); or perhaps your coworkers are taking long cof-

fee breaks in an effort to evade the work; or maybe the scissors at the fabric store in which you work are never kept sharp enough to cut the cloth cleanly, resulting in waste.

2. For the problem or question you identified, write a short proposal in the form of a memorandum to the logical recipient (supervisor, employer, business owner). In your memorandum, outline the problem and propose a study to determine the exact nature and extent of the problem in an effort to discover an acceptable solution. For the coffee break example, you might propose to your employer an anonymous observation by an unbiased observer of length of time for coffee breaks. Or in the example of dull scissors, you might propose an experiment comparing the fabric remnants from one employee using a recently sharpened pair of scissors and the fabric remnants of one whose scissors have not been sharpened.

3. (optional) Conduct the study proposed in 2 above. Write a short report in which you interpret the results of the study and draw conclusions from your data or make specific suggestions to the organization in question that will remedy the identified problem.

NOTES

1. I am indebted to Professor Judy Davidson of the Texas Tech University Geography Department for this assignment and student response.

2. Information for this section of the chapter is adapted and reprinted with the permission of The Free Press, a Division of Macmillan, Inc., from Kenneth D. Bailey, *Methods of Social Research,* 2nd ed. (New York: The Free Press, 1992).

3. Patricia Labaw, *Advanced Questionnaire Design.* (Cambridge, MA: ABT Books, 1981) pp. 35.

4. Floyd J. Fowler, Jr. *Survey Research Methods,* 2nd ed. (Newberry Park, CA: Sage Publications, 1993) p. 57.

5. Labaw, p. 134.

6. Labaw, p. 154.

7. I am indebted to Professor John Deethardt of the Texas Tech University Speech Communications Department for passing on to me this assignment and student response.

8. Eugene K. Garber, " 'My Kinsman, Major Molineux': Some Interpretive and Critical Probes," in Ben F. Nelms, ed., *Literature in the Classroom: Readers, Texts, and Contexts.* (Urbana, IL: National Council of Teachers of English, 1988) pp. 83–104.

9. Studs Terkel (1970). *Hard Times: An Oral History of the Great Depression* (New York: Pantheon Books).

5

♦ ♦ ♦

Planning and Writing Your Research Paper

INTRODUCTION

Through the process of planning and writing your research paper you will verify for yourself, and eventually for your readers, the answer to your starting question. You need to present that answer in the best possible fashion, using an appropriate research format and correct writing style. To handle in a reasonable way the large body of material you have accrued, it helps to approach the task systematically. To illustrate one student's writing process, throughout this chapter we will use a paper written for a sophomore-level research writing course by Kauleen Kershisnik.[1] Kauleen's research paper on acupuncture is appended at the end of this chapter.

PLANNING YOUR RESEARCH PAPER

After you have completed the primary research, library research, and preliminary writing on your topic, you are ready to begin planning the actual research paper. You should consider carefully the following two important components as you begin to plan: rhetorical situation and organization.

Rhetorical Situation

The context in which you are writing an assignment is called the rhetorical situation. The term rhetoric refers to written or spoken communication that seeks to inform someone of something or to convince someone of a particular opinion or point of view. For any writing assignment, you need to analyze the components of the rhetorical situation: (1) the writer's purpose, (2) the writer's persona, (3) the potential readers or audience, (4) the subject matter, and (5) the appropriate language or tone.

Purpose

When preparing to write, a writer must decide on the actual purpose of the piece. What is the goal that should be accomplished? Many times the goal or purpose is implicit in the writing task itself. For example, for a newspaper reporter, the goal is to present the facts in an objective manner, describing events for newspaper readers. For your research paper assignment, you need to determine your purpose or goal and define it carefully. The purpose does not have to be grandiose or profound—it may simply be to convince your readers that you have a fine grasp on the topic and are making some important points, or it may be to inform your readers of the current state of knowledge in a particular field. Kauleen's purpose statement read as follows: "My purpose in this paper is to tell readers who may know nothing about acupuncture in an informative manner how this ancient Chinese remedy is evolving into many modern day uses and cures."

Persona

You also need to decide just how to present yourself as a writer to those who will read your work. Do you want to sound objective and fair, heated and passionate, sincere and persuasive, or informative and rational? The term persona is used to describe the identity that the speaker or writer adopts. As you know, we all play many roles, depending on the situations in which we find ourselves: with our parents, we may be quiet and reserved; with our peers, outgoing and comical, and so on. Similarly, you can be flexible about how you portray yourself in your writing, changing your persona with your purpose and audience. First, establish your credibility by being careful and thorough in your research and by showing that you have done your homework and understand what you are writing about. Then, prepare your finished product with care and attention to detail. If you do not, your readers will assume that you are sloppy and careless and will largely discount anything you have to say. Many job applicants never even make it to the interview stage because their letters of application convey the subliminal message "here is a person who is careless and inconsiderate of others."

After discussions with her classmates and teacher, Kauleen decided that she wished to adopt a persona that reflected her balanced and fair appraisal of the medical treatment known as acupuncture. She felt that the public held many negative stereotypes and preconceptions about the use of acupuncture that she wanted to dispel by sounding logical and straightforward in her presentation of the facts.

Audience

Identifying those who may be reading your writing will help you to make decisions about what to include or not include in your research paper. Those who are the most likely to read your writing make up your audience. For example, a newspaper reporter assumes a general readership made up of members of the community. But the reporter must also assume that his or her readers were not present at the event being covered; thus, he or she must take care to reconstruct details for the readers.

In the case of a college research paper, the instructor of the course may suggest an appropriate audience or may in fact be the primary audience. You will wish to discuss the paper's potential audience with your teacher. If the instructor is the intended audience, you should assume that the instructor is knowledgeable about the subject, reasonably intelligent, and particularly interested in the accuracy of the research.

In Kauleen's research writing class, the teacher discussed questions of audience with the students who decided that their target readers would be each other, their peers, rather than their instructor. The class spent time in small groups discussing their papers with each other in order to obtain a better sense of their target audience's needs as readers. Kauleen discovered that the other students in her group had heard of acupuncture ("sticking needles in people") but knew very little of the details about its background or uses in medicine today. She determined that providing explicit and detailed information for these novice readers would be important.

Take time before writing to consider carefully who will read your research paper. Your readers make a difference to you, both in how you approach your topic (Are my readers novices or experts in the field?) and in the tone you adopt (Are my readers likely to agree with me or must I win them over to my point of view?). If your instructor has made no stipulations about the intended audience for your research paper, you should discuss the issue of audience with him or her. If your teacher is the target audience, it is especially important for you to know whether or not your teacher will be reading as a nonexpert (a novice in the field) or will assume the role of a knowledgeable expert. Your decisions about what to include in the paper and what level of tone and dic-tion to adopt will depend on whether you are writing for an expert or novice audience.

Subject Matter

The most important component of the rhetorical situation, however, is the subject matter. Although no piece of writing exists in isolation (hence the need for analyzing the purpose, persona, and audience), the content that you are presenting to your audience will be the core of any piece you are writing. You must decide from the mass of material you discover in your research what to include in your written presentation. These decisions are based on your starting question, your analysis and evaluation of your sources, and your thesis statement. Knowing what your ultimate goal is, how you wish to sound, and who your readers are will help you decide what source materials to use. Kauleen had run across several source citations when using the MedLine CD-ROM database. However, as she read the abstracts, the articles seemed far too technical for the general readers she had identified as her audience, and she decided to eliminate most of them from her search.

Appropriate Language or Tone

Knowing your purpose, persona, audience, and subject matter will lead you also into appropriate decisions about language and tone. If your purpose is to inform a general audience on a technical subject, you will need to take particular care with defining terms and using general words in place of technical jargon. You might also consider providing your readers with a glossary of terms to help them through technical information. Kauleen, for example, was careful in her paper to define the medical words she was using.

If you are addressing an audience of specialists, your rhetorical decisions about language and tone will be quite different. In this case you may wish to use technical vocabulary to identify yourself with the expert audience and to build your own credibility. You will need to take care not to bore an expert reader by providing too much background information, which such readers will not need.

Organization

Once you have gathered and evaluated source materials on your topic, completed your preliminary writing assignments, and analyzed the rhetorical situation, you can begin to organize your ideas. During the planning stages, you need to decide how you will give pattern and order to your research paper. The importance of planning cannot be overemphasized. Readers will use your skeletal plan, which should appear in some form in the written research paper, to reconstruct your meaning. Many recent investigations into the reading process have shown that readers reconstruct meaning in writing by using organizational plans, that is, explicit directional signals left by the writer in his or her work.

There is no one right way to make order out of the mass of material you have gathered in your research. Some people find that just beginning to write helps them to "discover" a direction and a pattern. Others prefer to outline and to organize or sort their notes by categories. Some writers spread their notes in seemingly random piles across the desktop; others sort notecards neatly by topics. Eventually, regardless of the process, you want to be able to write a thesis statement that captures succinctly the main point you wish to make in your paper.

Your purpose for writing the paper and the rhetorical situation you have defined can give you some clues about how to organize your paper. If your purpose is to inform readers of something, ask yourself what organizational plan that might suggest. To be informative implies that you will need to provide background and definitions on the subject, perhaps describing how something works or how it is used. In Kauleen's case, she decided to begin with a discussion of the ancient Chinese philosophy of yin and yang upon which acupuncture is built. Next, she thought her readers would want to know about the needles, since her classmates seemed to have many questions about their uses, and finally to end the paper with some modern-day treatments based on acupuncture techniques.

Organizational Patterns

The patterns described in the list that follows are meant only to suggest possible ways of organizing a research paper. A project may combine several of those patterns, perhaps using one main pattern as an overall guide. Or, you might find you need a totally different pattern, such as those commonly used in research reports (abstract, problem statement, methods, results, discussion). But, your rhetorical situation, your intention as a writer, must be your ultimate guide. However, as human beings, we do have standard ways of making sense of our environments. The patterns described below reflect our habitual ways of organizing experience. Our readers will be looking for familiar patterns in our writing, so the more explicitly we signal those patterns, the more likely it is that the readers will understand what we have to say.

1. *Cause and effect.* Many research projects and/or reports seek to link phenomena through cause-and-effect relationships. For example, from a chemical experiment: "The cause of the chemical change was the new substance introduced into the compound; the effect of the experiment was the change in chemical structure." From political science:

"The cause of the incumbent's unsuccessful ad campaign was the negative image projected in his TV advertisements; the effect of the ad campaign was to unseat the incumbent."

Does your research topic lend itself to an organizational pattern based on causes or effects? One student, for example, writing about children's self-concept, decided that it was important to spend considerable time in her paper discussing the causes of low self-esteem in children. She also talked later in the paper about the effects that low self-esteem had on a child's success in school.

2. *Compare and contrast.* Many research projects seek to compare or contrast two or more ideas, issues, or events. In comparing, we look for likeness; in contrasting, for difference. For example, from history: "The events surrounding World War I and World War II are compared and contrasted in an effort to understand how they were alike and different." From psychology: "The case histories of two psychotic individuals are studied to find common threads."

Think about your research topic; do you find yourself comparing or contrasting two very similar or very different ideas? For example, a student writing about puberty rituals found it interesting to compare and contrast the ways in which different cultures marked entry to manhood.

3. *Classification and definition.* To make sense of our world, we classify and define ideas, issues, and events by their characteristic parts. When we define something, we describe what it is and perhaps what it is not. For example, from sociology: "A ghetto is defined as a section of an urban area heavily populated by a particular minority group. A slum is not the same as a ghetto because a slum may contain a mixture of minority groups, whereas a ghetto (which can be a slum) contains one predominant minority group."

Many research projects begin with definitions or classifications to help their readers understand complex topics. A student writing on computer crime, for example, began his paper by dividing up the types of computer crimes and defining the role of the computer in each of them: computer as object of crime, computer as site of crime, computer as instrument to create a crime, and computer as symbol for criminal deception.

4. *Question and answer.* In this pattern, a specific question is raised and probable answers to the question are presented. The question-and-answer pattern can exist by itself or as a part of another pattern, perhaps cause and effect, for example, from political science "What are the reasons for or causes behind President Johnson's decisions during the Vietnam War?"

Is there a fundamental question that your paper seeks to answer? If so, you can begin the paper by posing the question for your readers and then proceed to systematically answer it by providing details and evidence to support your position. A student writing on a literary topic framed the following question: "What are the major themes in Shakespeare's *Hamlet*?" To answer the question, she cited several examples from the text itself and reinforced her points by using expert opinions from secondary criticism of *Hamlet*.

5. *Problem and solution*. In this pattern, a particular problem is identified and solutions to the problem are posed. For example, from business: "The productivity of automobile workers in the United States has fallen considerably in the past two years." The researcher looks at the problem and proposes solutions to help raise productivity levels: "Solutions might include pay incentives, improved work environment, and exercise facilities for employees."

Perhaps your research topic lends itself to a problem/solution pattern. Your readers will need to know up-front what you consider the problem to be; then, they will expect to see alternative solutions, perhaps ending with what you consider to be the best solution. A student was researching the topic of remote sensing, which she defined as the "science of deriving information about the earth's surface from images acquired at a distance." In her reading about the topic, she uncovered the problem of the "human factor" in remote sensing: as a tool, it was only as good as its human interpreter. Her solution to this problem, as posed in her paper, was to minimize human errors by field checks of data.

6. *Narration and description*. Sometimes a narrative (story) or a description of a particular thing or event is included in a research paper. For example, from astronomy: "A new star is located in our galaxy. It is described in detail with reference to its size, shape, characteristics, location, and so on." Also, a narrative may be written to account for the star's probable origin and future development (based on the description).

You may find it important to describe something in detail or to tell a story of an event as a part of your research paper. Kauleen decided to open her paper with a compelling narrative of a man undergoing major surgery using acupuncture as the only anesthetic. In this way, she hoped to immediately grab the attention and interest of her readers.

7. *Process analysis*. Often, a particular process will be important in a research paper. Analysis of the process by which nuclear fission occurs is an example of a process analysis in physics. An example from political science would be the analysis of the election process in a democratic system.

Think about your research project; is there a process that it is important for your readers to understand? If so, you will want to spend considerable time analyzing the process. For example, a student writing about deterioration of air quality in major American cities decided that he needed to analyze for his readers the chemical processes by which auto emissions become "smog."

One final note about planning: write your tentative plans in your research notebook or computer file, but be sure to keep them flexible. In the actual process of writing your first draft, you may be led to new insights and discoveries. Do not cut off the discovery function of writing by rigidly sticking to a particular plan. Rather, be open to changing your plan to accommodate any new insight you might have along the way. When an architect is planning a building, he or she makes and discards several blueprints as the planning proceeds. Use your plans as blueprints—as guides only—not finished buildings encased in concrete.

✦ EXERCISES

1. For your research paper project, brainstorm possible organizational patterns based on those previously outlined. Choose two or three patterns and freewrite several paragraphs that discuss how those patterns might be used in your paper.

2. For one of the following writing assignments, write a thesis statement, informal outline, and one-paragraph summary of contents. Pay explicit attention to rhetorical context and to organization.

   A. A brochure on making the transition from high school to college written to an audience of high school students

   B. An editorial on academic cheating for the college newspaper

   C. A proposal for improving the food in the dorm cafeteria written to the coordinator of food services

3. Analyze the organizational patterns of the following student paragraphs. Identify the pattern that seems to dominate each paragraph and any other supporting patterns.

   A. When the rock star stepped on stage, he flashed a sexy smile at all the girls in the front row. He pranced to the music of their frantic screams, the muscles rippling on his bare torso. Slowly, excruciatingly, his left hand lifted the mike to his lips, his throat rumbling a low-pitched love phrase. He laughed as the girls fainted, exulting in his wild power over the female sex. Once again, he knew he was a god.

   B. The student who enrolls in a premedical program can look forward to a grueling four years. The primary reason for the tough course of study is that a premed student must be well versed in both sciences and liberal arts. In addition to obtaining a degree in a particular field of study, for example, psychology, the premed student must fulfill the medical school's prerequisite courses: chemistry (four semesters), physics (two semesters), biology (four semesters), and calculus (one semester). As well, the student must maintain a 3.5 grade point average to be considered by a medical school.

C. In Israel the cost of gasoline has gone to more than $3 a liter. High prices for fuel also pervade Europe and the Orient. But in places like Ecuador, the Arabian countries, and the United States, prices are less than half what they are in Israel. This difference in prices is not because Israel, Europe, and the Orient are incapable of marketing gasoline economically. Rather, places like Ecuador and the United States are capable of providing themselves with gasoline through their own transport systems while Israel, Europe, and the Orient are not. The price of commodities like gasoline, which require special transport, will continue to rise as transportation costs rise.

OUTLINING AND DRAFTING YOUR RESEARCH PAPER

Constructing an Outline or Plan

After you have done some preliminary planning, reread your notecards or research notebook, trying to define for yourself what your main point in your paper will be. Write one or two possible thesis statements that could be used to guide your writing. Kauleen wrote the following tentative thesis: "Acupuncture is an ancient Chinese remedy which is evolving into many modern day uses and cures."

As you review your notes and source materials, set aside any information that does not seem directly relevant to the main point you wish to make in the paper. Then, it might be helpful to sort your notes or notecards into related categories of information. Does the thesis you have written suggest any organizational pattern that might give you the skeleton of an outline? For example, if your thesis suggests a cause-and-effect pattern, you will probably need to discuss causes first, followed by effects. Kauleen's thesis suggested to her that she needed to first define acupuncture and describe how it works. Then, since she wanted to show how it has evolved into today's treatments, she realized that she would need a good portion of her paper to talk about its uses and its efficacy as a cure for certain medical problems.

Some writers like to flesh out that skeleton plan by incorporating major points and subpoints into an outline structure. Others prefer to begin writing and have the structure evolve more organically. You need not be overly concerned about formal structure at this point unless your teacher stipulates a particular outline format. An outline should be a guide to you when you write, and not a constraint that confines and limits your thinking. You may wish to change your organizational plan several times as you make new discoveries while writing. Here is Kauleen's informal outline:

```
Title: Is Your Ch'i in Balance?

Thesis: Acupuncture is an ancient Chinese
remedy, which is evolving into many modern day uses
and cures.
     I.  Introduction
     II.  How acupuncture works
             -ch'i
             -meridians
     III.  Needles
             -what made of
             -how far inserted
             -where inserted
     IV.  Anaesthesia
             -in China
             -in America
     V.  Treating drug addicts
             -kinds of drug addictions
             -treatment
             -how it works
```

Drafting Your Paper

Now you should be ready to begin seriously drafting the research paper itself, if you haven't yet done so. Remind yourself of your general understanding of the topic, of your starting question, and of the answer to that question as stated in your thesis. When writing your first draft, use concrete and simple language to explain in your own words your research conclusions. Ideally, you should type your draft on a computer or word processor to make revisions easier. But be certain to back up your computer files and save to a disk frequently so as not to lose any of your hard work.

Your Knowledge

Do not be overly concerned at this time about mechanics, usage, and spelling, but concentrate on communicating information and presenting that information in an orderly way. If you have prepared sufficiently, the actual writing of the paper becomes an important means of verifying for yourself the insights you have gained through your research.

As you write, it is best to put down your own understanding of your topic rather than relying heavily on your sources. Then, after you have written your draft, you can go back and add sources as support for your arguments. Your readers will want to know what *you* think about the subject. They don't want to read a string of quotes loosely joined by transitions. Studying the topic and reading the source materials should have provided you with a general understanding of your topic. Writing a preliminary thesis should have provided you with the main point you wish to make. Once you have drafted your paper, important data, facts, illustrations, and supporting evidence can be gleaned from your sources and added to your argument to give it authority and force.

Source Knowledge

As you begin to add source information, do not be too concerned about the formal details of documentation, which can be dealt with later, but do mark in the draft any ideas or words taken from your sources. Remember to place any word, phrase, or sentence you copy directly from a source in quotation marks and to note down the author and page reference for the quotation. Similarly, you must acknowledge paraphrases and restatements of ideas taken from a source even though you have cast them into your own words.

Common Knowledge

You need not document "common knowledge" on your topic. This term refers to knowledge that is generally known or accepted by educated people. If you can find information readily in general reference works such as encyclopedias or in the popular media (television, radio, newspapers, or magazines), that information is probably common knowledge and need not be documented.

In the model paper at the end of this chapter, it was not necessary for Kauleen to document the fact that acupuncture is an ancient Chinese medical procedure dating from around 2,500 BC based on a Chinese belief in a life force or energy flowing throughout the body; this information could be considered common knowledge because it is found in any general reference source. Well-proven historical facts and dates need not be documented. However, it is better to overdocument than to underdocument and be accused of plagiarizing. When in doubt, document.

REVISING YOUR RESEARCH PAPER

Important work still remains on your paper once you have completed a rough draft. You must revise the paper to make the most effective possible presentation of the research. Your readers expect you to be clear and correct in your presentation so that they are not distracted by confusing language or incorrect punctuation. Read your rough draft several times, both on the computer screen and on hard copy. Each time you read it, pay attention to a different aspect of the paper for possible revision and correction. At first, when reading your rough draft pay attention to the overall structure and style of the paper; the second time through, check grammar and punctuation; the third time, make sure source materials (paraphrases and quotes from sources) are incorporated smoothly and accurately into the text. Finally, consider formal details such as conventions of documentation, format, and presentation. After your paper has been typed and spell-checked, proofread it several times to catch and correct all typographical or transcription errors.

Revising for Structure and Style

The first time you read your draft, pay attention to the organizational structure and overall content of the paper. At this point, decide whether you need to make any major changes in the order of the ideas or whether you should alter the tone. Use the power of your word processing program, in particular its cut and paste functions, to accomplish quickly and easily these global changes. A helpful acronym to keep in mind as you revise for such large issues is EARS: *E*liminate, *A*dd, *R*earrange, and *S*ubstitute.

Do not be afraid to eliminate irrelevant material from your paper. Your teacher will prefer a paper that is tightly focused to one padded with irrelevant details. Conversely, if you discover a section of your paper that seems thin, do not hesitate to add more information: more evidence to support an idea, more explanation to clarify an idea, and so on. Be sure that the major sections of the paper are arranged in a logical order. If there seems to be any confusion, rearrange major sections. Finally, if you find an example or a piece of evidence that does not seem persuasive in the context of the paper, substitute a new example for the one you currently have.

Remember, your rough draft is exactly that—rough. It is important for you to read it critically now so that you can improve the overall presentation of your ideas. Share your draft with a friend, spouse, teacher, classmate, or coworker. Another reader can provide insights to your paper that may be very helpful to you as your revise. The following list of questions can guide both you and others as they read your draft:

1. Is my title creative and does it relate to the paper?
2. Is my introduction engaging and interesting? Does it make the reader want to read on?
3. Is my thesis clearly stated early in the paper so that the reader knows what to expect?
4. Is the organizational pattern of the paper clearly marked for the reader by subheadings or directional signals?
5. Are the various sections of the paper linked by good transitional words and phrases?
6. Have I used a variety of evidence to convey my points: examples, analyses, primary or secondary data, analogies, illustrations, narratives, descriptions?
7. Do the sections of the paper appear in a logical order or do I need to rearrange the parts? Does the logic of the argument seem clear?
8. Is each section of the paper supported with sufficient data and evidence from the sources and from my primary research? Are sources integrated smoothly into the flow of the paper? Can the reader tell where sources stop and my own writing begins?
9. Is my conclusion adequate? Does it return to the thesis and highlight the answer to the starting question that motivated the research?
10. Have I demonstrated a depth of analysis and complexity of thought concerning the topic such that readers will feel significantly taught by me?

Rework any troublesome aspects of the paper. If a particular section of the paper lacks sufficient evidence, go back to the library for some appropriate supporting material. If you are unsure about the tone of your paper, the clarity of the language, or the presentation of your ideas, ask for specific advice from other readers. Such outside readings of your work can sometimes provide the distance needed for an objective evaluation.

You may wish to try the technique of reverse outlining as a way of seeing any global structural problems in your draft. To reverse outline, number each paragraph in your draft. Then summarize in one sentence the essential content of each paragraph. In this way you may discover sections out of sequence or paragraphs on the same topic many pages apart. Or, if you are having difficulty summarizing a particular paragraph, you may find you have tried to cover too much information and need to divide a longer paragraph into a series of shorter, more focused paragraphs.

Improving Paragraphs

As previously suggested, you first look at the overall structure and content of your paper. Then begin to narrow the scope of your revising to individual paragraphs. Check to be sure that each paragraph has a single major focus and that the ideas within the paragraph are all related to that focus. Focusing your paragraphs in this way is a great aid to your reader. When this is done, a new paragraph indicates a change to a new idea or change in direction. Often, the first sentence of each paragraph serves as a transitional sentence, bridging the gap between the ideas in the two separate paragraphs. This is the time to check for transitions between paragraphs as well as paragraph focus. As you revise your paragraphs, ask yourself the following questions:

1. Does each paragraph relate to the overall point of my paper?
2. Does each new paragraph contain its own internal focus or coherence?
3. Does the first sentence of each paragraph offer a bridge or transition from the previous paragraph?
4. Is the language used in each paragraph concrete and clear? Are there unnecessary words or phrases that I should delete?
5. Is the tone of each paragraph objective? Do I sound interested and concerned about the subject but not overly emotional?

Improving Sentences

In continuing to narrow the scope of your revising, look at individual sentences within your paper. Revise any sentences that seem awkward or confusing. In general, the more simply and directly you state your ideas, the better. Do not use overly complex sentence structures—they will only confuse your reader. Any very long sentences may need to be broken down into shorter sentences. On the other hand, a series of short, choppy sentences may be more effective if rewritten as a single long sentence. Reading your draft aloud—to yourself or to someone else—can often help you to "hear" problematic sentences. Or perhaps your teacher can make additional suggestions about revising your sentence style.

Improving Words

Next, look at individual words in your paper with an eye toward spotting confusing vocabulary or unnecessary jargon. Define any terms that might be unfamiliar to a general reader and replace any jargon specific to a field or discipline with more common words.

The following passage from a student paper shows how the writer revised for structure and style:

> Sexual harassment not only affects the
> individual but also has a tremendous effect on
> the organization in which it occurs. [Employers
> are beginning to recognize ~~SH~~ this problem because it costs
> them ~~money and causes stressful situations in the~~
> ~~working environment~~ in terms of morale,
> productivity, and lost time.] ~~Business org. need~~
> ~~to admit that SH is a problem & then attempt to~~
> ~~do something about it.~~ If harassment keeps going
> on w/out anything being done about it, there will
> be a lack of trust between the employees and the
> employer.

move to end

Verbs are one part of speech that often cause writers problems. Performing these few simple editing tasks with the verbs in your research paper will vastly improve your own writing.[2]

Content Verbs versus Empty Verbs

The verb "to be" (is, was, were, am, are) asserts a state of being, telling us only that something exists. Because the "to be" verb in its various forms essentially has become empty of meaning, you should attempt to replace "to be" verbs with content verbs that do convey meaning.

EXAMPLES:

Original—with empty "be" verb

It is the custom for visitors to remove their shoes before entering a Japanese home.

Revision—with content verb

Visitors customarily remove their shoes before entering a Japanese home.

Original—with empty "be" verb

Many planes are twenty years old and will have passed their life expectancy of ten to fourteen years.

Revision—with content verb

Now twenty years old, many planes have long since passed their life expectancy of ten to fourteen years.

Action Verbs versus Nominalizations

Many writers slow down their readers by using complex nouns in their sentences instead of the more active verbs that those nouns come from. For example, *decision* is the noun form (nominalization) of the verb *to decide,* and *invasion* is the noun form of *to invade.* Somehow writers have gotten the erroneous impression that the use of nominalizations makes their writing sound more important or official. Changing your verbs into nouns, however, robs them of their power and motion, thus slowing down the reader's progress. Whenever possible, change nominalizations to action verbs.

EXAMPLES:

Original—Sentence with nominalization
This land has the appearance of being arid.

Revision—Sentence with action verb
This land appears arid.

Original—Sentence with nominalization
He finally came to his decision. He would run for office.

Revision—Sentence with action verb
He finally decided to run for office.

Active Voice versus Passive Voice

The passive voice of a verb can be used effectively in writing when we either do not know who the subject is or don't want the subject known, as in the following:

Passive: The Vietnamese countryside was bombed. [by whom?]
Active: The U.S. Air Force bombed the Vietnamese countryside.
Passive: The boys were asked to leave. [by whom?]
Active: The neighbors asked the boys to leave.

Although passive voice has a legitimate function, it is often overworked in writing. To keep the pace of your writing moving along and to provide your readers with often essential information, try to use the active voice whenever possible.

Editing for Grammar, Punctuation, and Spelling

Once you have revised the overall structure and style of your paper, you are ready to read the paper again, this time with an eye to grammar, punctuation, and spelling. It is important to present your ideas clearly, but it is equally important to present your ideas correctly. A reader will discount you as either ignorant or careless if your work is full of grammatical errors.

As you read your paper again, ask yourself the following questions:

1. Is the grammar of each sentence correct? Does each sentence contain subjects and predicates?
2. Do subjects and verbs agree?
3. Are pronouns clear and unambiguous in their reference?
4. Is the overall punctuation correct?
5. Have I punctuated and cited quotes and paraphrases correctly?
6. Are there any words that I need to look up in the dictionary, either for meaning or for spelling?
7. Have I used the active rather than the passive voice? Are my verbs vivid action words rather than empty "to be" verbs or nominals?
8. Have I varied sentence style and avoided repetition?
9. Does each sentence flow smoothly without being awkward, wordy, or confusing?
10. Is the format of my paper correct, including the title page, body of the text, endnotes, or bibliography page?

It would be helpful for you to refer to a recent grammar and usage handbook for questions of English grammar, punctuation, and syntax. (For information on punctuating direct quotations, see the section below on incorporating quoted material.) Use a dictionary to check the meaning of individual words and always run spell-check with each draft. Take the time now to look carefully for all problems in your writing. As always, errors in grammar, punctuation, syntax, and spelling detract from your message and make a negative impression on your reader. A paper full of grammatical or spelling errors signals to the reader that the authority of the writer, and hence the authority of the research, is questionable. The following passage from a student paper shows revising and editing to correct grammar, punctuation, and spelling:

He also noted that ~~these~~ *sexual harassment* victim~~s~~ often ~~felt~~ *feared* that their complaints would go unheard, and they would be blamed for wh*a*t happen*e*d, or they would be considered unprofessional. In addition, Renick found that SHed women had many of the same feelings as ~~those~~ *women* who had been raped. These ~~feelings~~ included *feeling* humiliated, cheap, embarrassed, and angry.

Rewriting Your Paper Using Word Processing

Using a computer word processing program to revise your research paper has many advantages. Using word processing, you can quickly and easily create a paper that is as attractive and free of distracting errors as possible. Some writers compose their research papers directly at the computer, perhaps using the research database they have already created in their computer research notebooks. Others type a rough draft into the computer for revising. Using word processing makes changing your paper easier, since it allows you to eliminate, add, rearrange, and substitute material, altering individual words, sentences, paragraphs, and even whole sections of the paper without having to recopy or retype.

Revising with Word Processing

Word processing allows you to move material in your paper from one location to another. Before doing so, however, be sure you have made a backup copy of your file so that you don't inadvertently lose part of your text. Once you have moved the material (typically using the cut and paste functions), be sure to read the revised version very carefully and make any changes needed to smoothly integrate the new material into the existing text. When revising for structure and style or to improve paragraphs, sentences, and words, you will find your word processing program's text manipulation features your greatest assets.

Editing with Word Processing

Word processing also makes editing for grammar, punctuation, and spelling easier. Most word processing programs now offer their users a spell-check feature, which is extremely helpful in identifying typographical errors. You should get in the habit of running spell-check several times as you are drafting your paper. Remember, though, that the spell-check feature does not identify words that you have inadvertently misused, such as homonyms: *there* for *their*, or *its* for *it's*, and so on. You still need to proofread very carefully yourself, even after using spell-check.

Another helpful tool for editing is your word processor's thesaurus. If you find you are overusing a particular word, you can use the thesaurus to supply alternatives. Or perhaps you find the verbs you have used are not as vivid and active as they could be; the thesaurus can suggest other verbs with similar meanings. Again, a note of caution: don't use a word suggested by a thesaurus that you don't know, because it might have connotations or slight variations in meaning that do not make sense in the particular context of your writing.

Grammar-Checking Software

Special software programs are now available that can help you edit and proofread your paper for selected stylistic or grammatical problems. For example, *Grammatik* and other similar programs will identify excessive use of inactive "to be" verbs, overuse of prepositions, vague words or jargon, and so on. However, the so-called grammar-checking programs currently available can be misleading to writers. The kinds of writing problems that such programs can check are very limited. For example, they are virtually useless at checking punctuation because they are not sophisticated enough to really analyze the underlying grammar of each sentence. Only you, the writer, can do that. So, if you use a grammar-check feature, be aware of what it can and cannot do.

Bibliography and Footnote Software

Many word processing programs currently on the market offer features to help you generate the footnotes, endnotes, or bibliography for your paper. I have found these features only marginally useful in my own writing, but I know some writers use them quite extensively. If you are using footnotes, having the word processing program automatically place them at the bottom of the appropriate page can be a big help. However, the documentation software is only as good as the information you give it, that is, you still need to type in to the computer all of the bibliographical information. The software then manipulates the information, placing it in the proper order and formatting it appropriately. You need to be aware that the documentation style built into the software may not be the same style as you need to use for your discipline. Again, you should be the final judge of what is the correct documentation format for your paper.

If you have access to computer word processing, you may want to investigate some of the software previously discussed that is designed to help you with your writing. But do not take a computer program's advice as gospel; you cannot count on a computer to know what is best for your own writing; only you can know that.

Incorporating Reference Materials

The earlier section on writing the rough draft suggested that you not worry about the smooth incorporation of quoted material until you began revising your paper. We have now reached the stage at which you should double-check all of the source material in your paper to be sure you have incorporated it smoothly and appropriately into the flow of your ideas. Your source material should be primarily in the form of paraphrases and summaries that you use to reinforce your own points. Even though they are written in your own words, both paraphrases and summaries still require documentation (identification of the source either through in-text citations or footnotes or endnotes). Putting source material into your own words greatly improves the flow of your paper, because the paraphrase style will blend with your own writing style and thus be consistent throughout.

You should use direct quotation very sparingly. Reading strings of direct quotations is extremely distracting; using excessive quotation creates a choppy, disjointed style. Furthermore, it leaves the impression that you as a writer know nothing and are relying totally on what others have said on your topic. The better alternative is to incorporate paraphrases and summaries of source material into your own ideas both grammatically and logically. At this time, check your paper to be sure you have documented all source material accurately and fairly. By following the documentation style outlined in one of the following chapters (Chapters 6, 7, 8, or 9), you will be able to produce a paper that is correctly and accurately documented for your chosen academic discipline. In general, remember to document both completely and consistently, staying with one particular documentation style.

Incorporating Direct Quotes

At times you may want to use direct quotes in addition to paraphrases and summaries. To incorporate direct quotes smoothly, observe the following general principles. However, it would be wise to also consult the style manual of your discipline for any minor variations in quotation style.

1. When your quotations are four lines in length or less, surround them with quotation marks and incorporate them into your text. When your quotations are longer than four lines, set them off from the rest of the text by indenting five spaces from the left and right margins and triple-spacing above and below them. You do not need to use quotation marks with such block quotes. (Note: In some disciplines, block quotes are customarily indented ten spaces from the left margin only and double-spaced throughout.) Follow the block quote with the punctuation found in the source. Then skip two spaces before the parenthetical citation. Do not include a period after the parentheses.

2. Introduce quotes using a verb tense that is consistent with the tense of the quote. (A woman of twenty admitted, "I really could not see how thin I was.")

3. Change a capital letter to a lower-case letter (or vice versa) within the quote if necessary. (She pours her time and attention into her children, whining at them to "eat more, drink more, sleep more.")

4. Use brackets for explanations or interpretations not in the original quote. ("Evidence reveals that boys are higher on conduct disorder [behavior directed toward the environment] than girls.")

5. Use ellipses (three spaced dots) to indicate that material has been omitted from the quote. It is not necessary to use ellipses for material omitted before the quote begins. ("Fifteen to twenty percent of anorexia victims die of direct starvation or related illnesses . . . [which] their weak, immuneless bodies cannot combat.")

6. Punctuate a direct quote as the original was punctuated. However, change the end punctuation to fit the context. (For example, a quotation that ends with a period may require a comma instead of the period when it is integrated into your own sentence.)

7. A period, or a comma if the sentence continues after the quote, goes inside the quotation marks. (Although Cathy tries to disguise "her innate evil nature, it reveals itself at the slightest loss of control, as when she has a little alcohol.") When the quote is followed with a parenthetical citation, omit the punctuation before the quotation mark and follow the parentheses with a period or comma: Cal has "recognized the evil in himself, [and] is ready to act for good" (Cooperman 88).

8. If an ellipsis occurs at the end of the quoted material, add a period before the dots. (Cathy is "more than Woman, who not only

succumbs to the Serpent, but becomes the serpent itself . . . as she triumphs over her victims. . . .")

9. Place question marks and exclamation points outside the quotation marks if the entire sentence is a question or an exclamation. (Has Sara read the article "Alienation in *East of Eden*"?)

10. Place question marks and exclamation points inside the quotation marks if only the quote itself is a question or exclamation. (Mary attended the lecture entitled "Is Cathy Really Eve?")

11. Use a colon to introduce a quote if the introductory material prior to the quote is long or if the quote itself is more than a sentence or two long.

```
Steinbeck puts it this way:

[long quote indented from margin]
```

12. Use a comma to introduce a short quote. (Steinbeck explains, "If Cathy were simply a monster, that would not bring her in the story.")

Formatting and Printing Using Computers

Besides helping you as a writer, word processing can also help you create a text that is professional in appearance. However, attention to format should be the last consideration of your writing process. Too often, writers using word processing spend excessive amounts of their time playing with the appearance of the text, varying the fonts, for example, rather than concentrating on content. Of course, in the end you must attend to both form and content if you want to communicate effectively with your readers.

Many word processing programs offer formatting features such as underlining, boldface, italics, and so on, with which you can vary the appearance of your text and highlight important information. Be certain, however, that you check with your instructor to ascertain his or her preferences for format style before varying the style too much. Your main goal should be to make your paper professional in appearance. Thus, an English Gothic typeface that prints in scrolling capital letters, for example, would not be appropriate for a research paper. Nor are margins that are justified (even) on the right of the page typically appropriate for a formal paper. It is best to be conservative and justify left margins only.

Proofreading

Once your paper has been typed to your teacher's specifications and you have run your word processing program's spell-check feature, you will still need to proofread carefully for any errors not caught by the computer. For example, spell-check cannot tell you if you have used "their" when you should have used "there." It is best to print out a clean copy of your paper after making all of your proofreading corrections. However, your teacher may not object to your making a few minor corrections on the paper, preferring that you correct any errors, even though this may necessitate some handwriting on the typed page, rather than leaving them uncorrected.

One helpful way to proofread for typing errors is to begin at the bottom of the page and read up one line at a time. In this way, you keep yourself from reading for meaning and look only at the form of the words. You can spot errors more easily when you are not actually reading the paper. If you are proofreading on a computer screen, you can use your search command to search for periods from the bottom of the text upwards. In this way, your computer's cursor will skip to the previous sentence, thus reminding you to read it independently.

Keep your dictionary handy and refer to it whenever you have any doubt about the appropriate use of a word. Use your grammar and usage handbook to double-check any last minute questions about grammar and punctuation. If you have access to grammar-check software, such as *Writer's Helper, Correct Grammar,* or *Grammatik,* it is sometimes helpful to run it on your paper, keeping in mind the cautions about such programs that were discussed previously.

It is impossible to overstress the importance of careful proofreading by you. Even if the paper was word processed or typed by a professional typist, you will probably find errors when proofreading. Since you are the paper's author, any errors are your responsibility, not the computer's or the typist's. It is a good idea to save early drafts of your paper even after the paper has been typed. Early drafts serve as a record of your thinking and your work on the paper. If you have taken care at every stage of the revision process, your paper will be one you can be justifiably proud of.

CONSIDERING FORMAL DETAILS

The formal details outlined in the paragraphs that follow incorporate some general principles in research writing. However, it would be wise to also consult the relevant style manual for your field to discover any minor variations from this format. The model papers in Part Two adhere to the formal conventions of their respective disciplines, so you may also use these as a resource.

Always type research papers or have them typed for you. Use a standard typeface or font and a fresh printer ribbon. It might be wise to ascertain whether or not your teacher prefers that papers not be printed on dot matrix printers. Sometimes these are light and difficult to read. If possible, print your final copy on a laser printer for a professional appearance and ease of reading. The paper should be a standard weight and size (8½ × 11 inches). If you do not have a self-correcting typewriter or a word processor, use Liquid Paper or correction tape to correct errors.

Spacing

Use only one side of the paper and double space all the way through, even for long quotes that are indented in the text (NOTE: Styles vary). Leave four blank lines between major sections, three or four between heading and section, and three or four above and below indented, long quotes (more than four lines of text). Also, double space the endnote page (if used) and references page. (If triple spacing is difficult in your word processing program, quadruple spacing will serve as well.)

Margins

Use a margin 1 to 1.5 inches wide on all sides of each sheet. Your word processing program allows you to set the margins appropriately. If you are typing your paper, use a typing guide (a sheet of paper that goes behind the sheet you are typing on and whose dark ruled lines show through), set the margins on your typewriter, or mark each sheet with a pencil dot one inch from the bottom so you will know when to stop typing on a page. Sophisticated word processing programs will help you format the pages appropriately. In particular, if you are using footnotes, these can be generated automatically by some word processing programs, which will leave the appropriate amount of space for footnotes on each page. If you are typing footnotes at the bottom of the page yourself, plan your bottom margins very carefully to allow room for the notes. Generally, endnotes are easier to type and perfectly acceptable in most cases.

Title

Ask your instructor whether you need a title page. If the answer is yes, find out what information should appear there. Generally, title pages contain three kinds of identifying information: the title of the paper, author identification, and course identification (including date). If you do not need a separate title page, put your name, date, assignment name, and any other identifying information on the upper right-hand corner of the first page. Center the title on the first page three or four lines below the identifying information or, if you use a separate title page, one inch from the top of the page. The title should not be underlined, surrounded by quotation marks, or typed in capital letters. Leave three or four lines between your title and the beginning of the text.

Numbering

Number each page starting with the first page of text after the title page. (Note: some styles omit the page number from page 1.) Place the numbers in the upper right-hand corners or centered at the bottom of the pages. Your word processing program allows you to automatically number your pages and to suppress numbering on any pages where they are not needed. For example, you typically don't need to number the endnote page and the references page. Rather, identify them with the appropriate heading centered one inch from the top of the page and followed by three or four blank lines. Some styles recommend headers along with the page numbers (for example, Hult - 2). Check your word processing manual for help in generating such automatic headers.

Indentation

Use uniform indentation for all paragraphs (five spaces is standard). Indent long quotes (more than four lines long) five spaces from both right and left margins or ten spaces from the left margin only. Indent the second and subsequent lines of the reference-list entries five spaces. Leave two spaces between each sentence and after a colon or semicolon. Divide words at the end of lines according to standard rules. Use your dictionary if you are unsure of where to divide a word.

The Abstract

An abstract is a very short summary of a paper, usually one tenth to one twentieth the length of the whole. The purpose of an abstract is to condense the paper into a few, succinct lines. Thus, the reader must be able to understand the essence of the paper from reading just the abstract, without actually reading the paper. Your abstract should cover the purpose of your paper as well as the major topics you discuss. To write an abstract, follow the same general procedure you used to write a summary paper. However, you will need to compress information into a few compact sentences. Even though the information in your abstract is necessarily densely packed, it should still be readable and understandable.

The Endnote Page

If your paper will have endnotes, type them on a separate page immediately after the text of your paper (and before the references page). Center the title, "Notes" or "Endnotes," one inch from the top of the page, and type it in capital and lower-case letters (not all capitals). Do not use quotation marks or underlining. Leave three or four blank lines between the title and the first line of your notes. Type the notes in consecutive order based on their appearance in the text. Indent the first line of the note five spaces from the left margin, type the superscript number, and leave a space before beginning the note. For any run-over lines of each note, return to the left margin. See Chapter 8 for the specific format of endnotes.

The References Page

Center the title "References," "Works Cited," or "Bibliography" and type it one inch from the top of the page in capital and lower-case letters (not all capitals). Do not use quotation marks or underlining. Leave three or four blank lines between the title and the first line of your references. The references themselves should be typed, double spaced, and listed in alphabetical order by the author's last name (or the title, if the author is not known). (Note: In the number system, references are listed consecutively as they appear in the text.) To make the alphabetical list, sort the bibliography cards (on which you have recorded the sources actually used in your research paper) into alphabetical order and transcribe the information in the proper form from the cards to your list. For the specific forms for references, see the appropriate chapter for your discipline (Chapters 6, 7, 8, or 9). The references page follows the last page of your paper or the endnote page (if included) and need not be numbered.

The Annotated Bibliography

The chapters in Part II of this book will guide you as you construct a list of references, also called a bibliography or a works cited page. However, in some cases it is helpful to provide your readers with more information about the sources you used in your research than is typically given in a bibliography. An annotated bibliography serves this purpose. To construct an annotated bibliography, you would first compile all of your references, alphabetize them, and format them according to the documentation style for your discipline. Then, following each bibliographical entry, you would state in a sentence or two the gist of the source you had read and its relevance to your paper. An annotated bibliography can help your readers to decide which of your sources they would like to read themselves. It should not be difficult for you to annotate (that is, provide brief glosses) for sources that you have used to write your paper. For an example of an annotated bibliography, see Kauleen's paper below.

The Appendix

Material that may not be appropriate to the body of your paper may be included in an appendix. You may use the appendix for collations of raw data, descriptions of primary research instruments, detailed instructions, and so on. The appendix is located after the bibliography or references page and is clearly labeled. If there is more than one appendix, label them Appendix A, Appendix B, and so on. When referring to the appendix in the paper itself, do so in parentheses: (For a detailed description of the questionnaire, see Appendix A.)

NOTES

1. I am indebted to Kauleen Kershisnik for the use of her research on acupuncture in this chapter.
2. I am grateful to Dr. Rebecca Wheeler for these sentence editing ideas.

Is Your Ch'i in Balance?   Title page
includes title,
Kauleen Kershisnik   student

Research Paper

for

Research Writing   course
identification
English 201

November 19, 1992   date

Chen Chien was diagnosed with a severe case of tuberculosis, so severe that his left lung and one rib had to be removed. The operation took place in Hun Shan Hospital in Shanghai. Chen was lying face down on the operating table while the doctors cut through skin, bone, and muscle to get to his lung. The doctors removed the lung with care and watched as the right lung began to work harder and harder to take on the work of two lungs. While the doctors were watching, Chen spoke out that he would like something to eat. The nurses assisted him with some fruit slices. Chen remained conscious throughout the entire operation, never showing any sign of pain or discomfort. No chemical anesthesia was administered during the operation, only acupuncture. Doctors had placed a single acupuncture needle into Chen's shoulder, which blocked the pain of the entire operation (Duke 2-3).

American medicine at times may not provide adequate medical care. Many people have wasted time and money running from one doctor to another just to be disappointed. Treatment by acupuncture

Opening anecdote to gain reader's attention

MLA citation style— author's last name plus page number (no comma)

1

may be helpful in cases where conventional medicine is inconvenient or
ineffective. Sometimes conventional methods have serious disadvantages: such as
when a patient becomes bed-ridden or
experiences an allergic reaction to a
commonly-used drug. Acupuncture in many
cases is a good, or sometimes the only,
alternative (Marcus 18). If acupuncture
is used correctly, there seems to be little or no risk involved, and it may even
effect a cure in a case that would not
have been cured with conventional American medicine. Even though acupuncture is

Thesis
sentence

not completely accepted in America, it is
becoming more and more acceptable, and
people should realize that they do have
the option for acupuncture in certain
cases.

Historical
background

Acupuncture has been a Chinese medical procedure since around 2,500 B.C. It
is based on a Chinese belief of a life
force or energy flowing throughout the
body. This energy is called ch'i, and
"the Chinese consider good health to be a
state of energy balance within the human
body" (Manaka 31). The ch'i is divided
into two separate forces—the Yin and the

2

Yang. The Yin, the female principle, is passive and dark and is represented by the earth; the Yang, the male principle, is active and light and is represented by the heavens. The forces of Yin and Yang act in the human body as they do throughout the natural universe as a whole. Disease or physical disharmony is caused by an imbalance or undue preponderance of one of these two forces in the body, and the goal of Chinese medicine is to bring the Yin and the Yang back into balance with each other, thus restoring the per-

Provide title son to health ("Acupuncture,"
to
distinguish Britannica). Any imbalance of Yin and
two
sources Yang obstructs the flow of ch'i. Ch'i is said to flow through twelve pathways, or meridians, throughout the body. Acupuncture is necessary to even out the Yin and Yang when they get out of balance. Acupuncturists place needles along these meridians in over a hundred places on the body. Each point is associated with a certain organ within the body. The idea of a needle being poked into the skin seems very painful, but in all actuality the pain is no greater than a "mosquito bite and draws no blood" (Langone 70).

3

As one might suspect, there is no scientific evidence to support the idea of ch'i flowing through meridians. These meridians have never been seen under any microscope, but still have been effective in curing many people. "To the American public, acupuncture sounds like either a bizarre torture or a miracle cure-all; it has been labeled hoax, black magic, faith-healing, psychological trick" (Duke, cover). None of which is true. Duke says that acupuncture is based on a complete medical system which focuses on a single principle: man is a part of nature. Nature is precise, therefore, man is precise. Nature is predictable, therefore, man is predictable. Any disruption results in illness, and the work of an acupuncturist can restore that order and cure the illness.

Doctors use many different kinds of needles for their acupuncture procedures. Needles have varying shapes, diameters, and lengths and are made out of different materials. Early needles were made out of stone, flint, quartz, bamboo, and bones (Nightingale 70). Due to new advances in technology, needles have evolved into

4

gold, silver, and most commonly stainless
steel. Depending on the reason for
acupuncture, the needles are inserted
.1-.4 inches deep, and sometimes they are
inserted up to 10 inches deep ("Acupuncture," <u>Britannica</u>). Some needles are
inserted straight into the skin, others
are inserted at an angle to the skin, and
some even parallel to the skin (Nightingale 74). These needles are then
"twisted, twirled, or connected to a low-
voltage alternating current for the
duration of its use" ("Acupuncture," <u>Bri-
tannica</u>). Acupuncturists use all of these
varying procedures to accomplish the best
results for their individual patients.

The needles used in acupuncture
should be sterilized after each use. Needles should be "cleansed with surgical
spirit or dilute antiseptic," then auto-
claved and stored in a closed container
until used (Nightingale 73). Without
proper sterilization, diseases such as
Hepatitis B and HIV can be spread. The
spread of HIV is not very common, but
there is at least one reported case. A
boy who had never had sex, blood transfu-
sions, tattoos, or used intravenous drugs

was diagnosed with the HIV virus. He had
undergone some acupuncture treatment for
an earlier injury, and this was suspected
as the only method of transmission. There
have also been cases of Hepatitis B, but
only when careless doctors didn't properly sterilize their needles (Mettetal et
al. 250). The spread of diseases can easily be avoided with proper sterilization.
When choosing a doctor, one should be
cautious of sanitary procedures, regardless of what kind of doctor.

For several authors, use *et al.*, Latin for "and others"

Before a doctor performs acupuncture, he or she conducts an ordinary
check-up similar to the one a family
practitioner would use to evaluate an
illness. Other than that fact, acupuncture is handled much differently than any
other kind of treatment. The doctor takes
more time to deal with the patient one on
one. A patient and doctor develop an actual relationship that is rare in America
due to busy schedules and the mere fact
that the more patients each doctor sees,
the more money. According to Langone,
people should be cautious when choosing
any doctor. Some doctors realize that you

6

are willing to try something new and will
take advantage of it. Beware of doctors
who promise to cure everything. Acupuncture can't cure cancer, mental retar-
dation, multiple sclerosis, or many other
diseases (Langone 72). These precautions
should be taken in any situation, not
only in acupuncture. There are doctors in
every field of medicine who make false
diagnoses and are dangerous to the safety
of their patients.

The story in the beginning is an
example of acupuncture being used as an
anesthetic. As with Chen, patients may be
wide awake, reading, eating, drinking and
talking during many serious operations.
These patients feel no pain and the only
anesthesia used is acupuncture needles
placed into the skin. "Authorities on
pain believe that acupuncture somehow
sends signals to the brain that compete
with or eliminate pain signals that ordinarily would accompany surgery"
("Acupuncture," <u>Fishbein's</u> 42). American
doctors are still very skeptical about
this procedure. In the past, some American doctors have visited China and

witnessed several successful operations
where acupuncture was used. Their skepti-
cism may even lead some doctors to
believe that the operations have been
staged (Duke 4). However, new evidence
indicates that acupuncture releases pain-
killing endorphins, which are strong
chemicals that block pain signals to the
brain (Langone 70). These endorphins
might be what enables a person to undergo
surgery without feeling any pain.

Using acupuncture as an anesthesia
has two main advantages. First, the
recovery process is facilitated because
the dangers and postoperative effects of
general anesthetics are completely
avoided. The patient only has to recover
from surgery, not from the associated
illness brought on by the potent drugs
needed to put patients to sleep (Duke 3).
The second advantage is the cost. An
individual's medical costs are greatly
reduced by using acupuncture anesthesia.
"Anesthesia, a doctor and assistant in
the operating room, and expensive life-
sign monitoring equipment comprise up to
twenty percent of the cost of an opera-

8

tion" (Duke 28). The use of acupuncture would also lessen the amount of time spent in the hospital by "thirty percent." And in the long run, the money saved may benefit society with lower insurance rates (Duke 28).

Americans have adapted the use of acupuncture in curing drug addicts. In 1990, Baltimore opened Maryland's first municipally funded acupuncture treatment program whose primary function was to treat crack and cocaine abusers, but they also allow alcoholics and addicts of other drugs to participate. They have found their combined treatment of acupuncture and behavioral counseling to be very effective. The acupuncture lessens or eliminates the symptoms of withdrawal and makes a patient more receptive to counseling, education, and support. Needles are placed in the ear, which is said to relieve anxiety, giving the patient a sense of well-being and relaxation ("Baltimore" 436). Especially in the case of alcoholics, acupuncture is not necessarily a cure, but it does seem to reduce the urge to drink. This at

When no author is given, use first word of article title in quotation marks.

9

least is a step in the right direction,
and, with added counseling, may even be a
cure ("Acupuncture," RN 113).

Veterinary medicine has also adapted
the use of acupuncture in treating animals. John Nicol is a vet that practices
acupuncture on animals to relieve pain.
He has saved dogs that had back problems,
muscle diseases, and arthritis. Nicol has
also used acupuncture treatment on cows
as an anesthesia during minor surgery.
The success of this treatment is impres-
sive to people who don't believe in
acupuncture because an animal's reaction
to the treatment can't be staged or mis-
read. The animal reacts only by sensing
the pain or cure, which has nothing to do
with the desire to be cured (Birke
34-36).

Acupuncture is used for the treatment of many more pains, illnesses, and
diseases than mentioned so far. Some
examples are nervous hypertension, weight
problems, asthma, various kinds of
arthritis, menstrual problems, deafness,
emphysema, and insomnia (Duke 22). Of
course the success of acupuncture varies
with the illness being treated, but

10

nonetheless acupuncture is a fairly safe and effective treatment in many cases.

As mentioned at the outset of this paper, acupuncture sometimes is the most effective cure available, and may even be a patient's only alternative when conventional medicine has proven ineffective. Knowing something about acupuncture, how it works, and the risks associated with it, should give a person a better understanding of what to expect. Being more educated about the subject makes people more educated about their choices. Acupuncture is an available choice, and patients should consider all of their options to decide, in consultation with their doctors, what will be best for them.

11

Annotated Bibliography

References
use MLA
style.
Annotations
are included
to describe
the source
for the
reader.

"Acupuncture." Fishbein's <u>Illustrated</u>

<u>Medical and Health Encyclopedia.</u>

1978 ed. Good source of background

information. Concentrated on an

introduction, then provided

specifics about anesthesia. Shows

pictures of acupuncture being per-

formed.

"Acupuncture." <u>The New Encyclopedia Bri-</u>

<u>tannica</u>. 1992 ed. Not a specialized

source, but provides some good back-

ground information. Tells the theory

of how acupuncture works.

"Acupuncture Boom Punctured." <u>Nature</u> 318

(1985): 222. A real short article

with some general information about

anesthesia, its acceptance and uses.

"Acupuncture for Craniofacial Pain."

<u>Geriatrics</u> 40 (1985): 36. From a

scholarly source, this article shows

how acupuncture can be an alterna-

tive to surgery for certain

problems.

"Acupuncture May Offer Hope for Alco-

holics. <u>RN</u> 53 (1990): 113. Specific

information on acupuncture being

used on "skid row" alcoholics. Some
statistics.

"Baltimore Tries Treating Substance Abuse
with Acupuncture." <u>Public Health
Reports</u> 105 (1990): 436. Scholarly
source reporting on a clinic in Baltimore that uses acupuncture to
treat people with drug addictions.

Birke, Lynda. "An Open Mind in the Veterinary Surgery." <u>New Scientist</u> 115
(1987): 34-36. This article summarized the use of acupuncture on
pets, some of which is somewhat
experimental. Also, talks some on
acupuncture used on humans.

Duke, Michael. <u>Acupuncture.</u> New York:
Pyramid Communications, 1972. The
source is somewhat outdated, but
this was one of the few books that
were available to me. Lots of general information on all aspects of
acupuncture, background and specific.

Langone, John. "Acupuncture: New Respect
for an Ancient Remedy." <u>Discover</u> 5
(1984): 70-73. Talks about America's
acceptance of acupuncture and how

much acupuncture has evolved. Some
specifics on certain procedures.

Manaka, Yoshio and Ian A. Urquhart. <u>The
Layman's Guide to Acupuncture.</u> New
York: John Weatherhill, 1973. The
source is somewhat outdated, but
provides lots of general information
on all aspects of acupuncture.

Marcus, Paul. <u>Acupuncture: A Patient's
Guide.</u> New York: Thorson's Publishers, 1985. General information on
all aspects of acupuncture.

Mettetal, John, Carl Rouzioux, and David
Vittecoq. "Acute HIV Infection After
Acupuncture Treatment." <u>The New England Journal of Medicine</u> 320 (1989):
250–251. The idea of the HIV virus
being spread by acupuncture is confirmed by a case reported in this
journal.

Nightingale, Michael. <u>The Healing Power of
Acupuncture.</u> New York: Javelin Books,
1986. Lots of general information on
all aspects of acupuncture.

6

♦ ♦ ♦

Writing a Review Paper in Science and Technology

INTRODUCTION

As discussed in Chapter 1, sciences in general attempt to explain phenomena in the natural and physical world. Since scientists rely on current technology as tools to help them in their work, technology itself has become a branch of science. Scientific researchers must have knowledge of the current research being conducted by others in their fields. They must also have knowledge of the technologies needed to conduct that research. Although the experimental method is at the heart of scientific research, library research is also important. It is in the scientific journals and reviews that scientists report their findings for scrutiny and replication by other researchers. You need to become familiar with the library tools used by scientists so you can gain access to the current thinking in their fields.

Two major types of papers typically written in science and technology are discussed here: the research report and the review paper. The research report is a formal report of original (primary) research. The purpose of a scientific or technological research report is to describe clearly and understandably a particular researcher's findings and conclusions. The report may be argumentative or persuasive in tone—arguing in favor of a particular research method or result, for example. Or the report may be interpretive, explaining or interpreting a particular research finding with an attempt to draw conclusions or make recommendations. The review paper, on the other hand, presents a synthesis of existing work on a particular, defined scientific topic rather than presenting original findings.

In this chapter we focus on writing the scientific review rather than the research report. In the scientific review paper, you analyze for your readers the present state of knowledge in an ongoing field of research. Your contribution, then, is in the way you interpret, organize, and present the complex information, thus making it easily accessible to the reader. In the scientific review paper, you argue a particular position with support from the literature and review the topic through paraphrase and summary as objectively as you can, but you don't introduce any new primary data. Several library research principles and skills are important for you as you investigate the topic you have chosen to review. These include:

1. A familiarity with library research tools, including databases, bibliographies, and indexes used in science and technology.
2. The ability to understand and evaluate information and data from a variety of sources.
3. The ability to paraphrase and summarize information and data in your own words.
4. The ability to synthesize the information and data gathered into an organized presentation.
5. The ability to employ the formal conventions of scientific review papers.

A GUIDE TO THE SCIENTIFIC REVIEW PAPER

To begin your review paper, first determine a topic and narrow it to a manageable, researchable size. If you are taking a science course now, your textbook is a good place to begin looking for research ideas. Check the table of contents in your textbook and in any references that may be listed. Another source of ideas is current scientific journals. Todd Quarnberg, whose research serves as the model for this chapter, became interested in the subject of immunity when he read about it in a biology class. As a premed student, he was already interested in both science and medicine. Be sure you select a topic that will hold your interest and attention, preferably a topic that you already know something about, so that you will be an informed and objective reviewer.

Preparation

Gather the necessary materials for your research project: a notebook or notecards. Todd decided to use a file on a computer disk as a computerized research notebook (see p. 59 for a discussion of using a computer in this way). Make a schedule that gives you several weeks to conduct your library research and several weeks to write a draft and final copy of your review paper. If you foresee that your research project will contain primary research data, make sure you allow yourself sufficient time to gather that data. Careful planning at the outset of such a major project ensures that you have enough time to carry out the research necessary to write an informed review.

Developing a Search Strategy

Todd had formulated some general impressions about the human immune system through reading for his classes. He wanted to discover the current thinking in the life sciences about the immune system's defenses against disease. His library search, then, began with a look at general background sources in life sciences and moved to more specific works on immunity. The following is an outline of Todd's search strategy (your particular search may differ somewhat from this outline):

Todd's Search Strategy

1. Look up immunology in background sources from the reference area of the library, including *Handbook of Microbiology* and *Dictionary of Immunology*.
2. Look up reviews on the subject using *Current Contents: Life Sciences*.
3. Use the library online catalog to find books and documents on immunology; be sure to check appropriate terminology in the LCSH. Begin to narrow and focus search.
4. Use databases and print indexes and abstracts for access to scientific journal articles: the *Biological Index*, the *Index Medicus*. Search by subject headings from LCSH and by key words.

The Library Reference Area

Many students begin their research at the library catalog; however, you may find it more profitable to begin with the general sources in the reference area of your library. In a scientific review, it is usually important to obtain the most current library information. Since books take years to write and sometimes years to produce, even the most recent editions of books can contain information that is three or four years old. The most recent information is probably in journals (in print or online), which generally publish papers one or two years after the studies are conducted and the paper written.

The reference area of your library provides you with valuable background and contextualizing information on your topic. Plus, the reference area typically contains the tools, such as indexes and computers, that give you access to a variety of other materials. Reference materials are usually arranged by Library of Congress call numbers, which are grouped by subject area. If you cannot easily discover on your own how your reference area is organized, do not hesitate to ask your reference librarian for help.

To illustrate the use of a library search strategy in the sciences and technology, we will follow the search steps above using Todd's research on immunity as a model for your own search.

✦ EXERCISE

Outline your own search strategy, beginning with general and working to specific sources. Draw up a research time schedule.

General Sources

By reading general information about your topic, you can put it into a context and start focusing your search—narrowing your topic to a manageable size. Also, in reading general and specialized encyclopedias and dictionaries, you will learn what is considered common knowledge on the topic. Depending on your particular topic, you may be reading general encyclopedias, such as *Britannica,* and specialized encyclopedias, such as the *McGraw-Hill Encyclopedia of Science and Technology.* The general sources commonly found in the reference area are listed in Chapter 2; specialized sources for science and technology are at the end of this chapter on pages 223–227. Todd used the following background sources, which he listed in his computerized research notebook at the beginning of his working bibliography:

```
Dictionary of Immunology, 3rd ed. W. J. Herbert, et

     al., eds. Oxford: Blackwell Scientific; 1985.

Encyclopedia of Immunology. Ivan M. Roitt and Peter

     J. Delves, eds. New York: Academic; 1992.

Van Nostrand's Scientific Encyclopedia. 7th ed. New

     York: Van Nostrand Reinhold; 1989.
```

At the end of each source, such as the encyclopedia previously mentioned, you usually find a list of bibliographic citations and references. This reference list can be an important place to locate key sources and reports written about your topic. List any promising references on your working bibliography, because later they may lead you to valuable information. It is not necessary for you to look up each entry on your working bibliography at this time. In the specialized immunology encyclopedia, Todd found and listed the following references:

```
Abramoff, P. Biology of the immune response. New

    York: McGraw-Hill; 1970.

Chandra, R. K., ed. Nutrition and immunity. New York:

    Alan R. Liss; 1988.
```

✦ EXERCISE

Find and read background sources relevant to your topic to obtain general information. See Chapter 2 for a list of general sources and the end of this chapter for a list of sources specific to sciences and technology.

Focusing Your Search

After you have read several background sources about your topic, you are ready to narrow the subject of your review. Todd, for example, decided to report on the current state of knowledge regarding host-bacterial interactions within human beings. Todd developed the following starting questions to guide his research: "How does the human body protect itself from bacterial invasion? What is the virulence factor in bacteria that causes disease?" These starting questions provided Todd with a direction for his research.

✦ EXERCISE

Define for yourself just what topic you are trying to review and what specifically within that topic you will cover in your review paper. Then write a starting question that you intend to investigate in your research.

Reviews

For many scientific review papers, reviews and reports of research that have already been written on the topic are useful. Scientists customarily publish reviews of current scientific studies to help other scientists keep abreast of the field. Even though you are writing a scientific review yourself, it might be helpful to see what others have to say on the subject before you begin. You may need to update somewhat any review you find by reading the most current sources in the field.

Reviews of research and research reports can also provide you with reference lists from which to build your working bibliography. Generally, scientific disciplines publish annual reviews in a particular journal within the field. In the library online catalog, look up the field, for example, chemistry, and find the annual review journal. If your library carries the *Index to Scientific Reviews,* you can locate relevant reviews there as well. If you have difficulty finding reviews from a particular field, do not hesitate to ask your reference librarian for assistance.

Another useful tool for finding current articles and reviews is the *Current Contents* journal, which indexes articles and reviews by discipline. The following are some examples of *Current Contents* journals relevant in the sciences:

Current Contents: Life Sciences
Current Contents: Physical, Chemical, Earth Sciences
Current Contents: Engineering and Technology
Current Contents: Agriculture, Biology, and Environmental Sciences

The *Current Contents* journals are particularly useful because they allow easy and quick access to current articles and reviews written on a particular subject. *Current Contents* publish weekly issues, which include the tables of contents from the latest journals in a particular discipline. The journals are indexed by key title words and by authors. In our library, the *Current Contents* journals are provided in a computerized database; they are also available in print. By typing the keywords human immunity and bacteria into the computer while searching the database for *Current Contents: Life Sciences,* Todd discovered the following recent articles, which he listed in his working bibliography:

Structural basis for antigen-antibody recognition, by

Robert Huber. Science 233 August 15, 1986

p. 702-703.

The T cell and its receptor, by Philippa Marrack and

John Kappler. Scientific American 254 February,

1986 p. 34-46.

✦ EXERCISE

Locate and read reviews of research available on your topic. See the end of this chapter for a list of sources and databases used in the sciences and technology.

The Library Catalog

At this point in your search you will want to use the library online catalog. First, use the catalog to help you track down the book sources you may have already listed on your working bibliography from background sources. Once in the database that lists your library's book holdings, you will indicate that you want the computer to search by title (e.g., t=Nutrition and Immunity). If this book is available in your library, it will be listed, along with its call number to help you locate the book.

The most important and powerful use for the online catalog is its cross-referencing function: using the subject headings and keywords to locate additional titles on the same or related topics. You want to instruct the computer to search for books on your subject (for example, s=immunity) or by keyword or combinations of keywords (for example, k=immunity and human host). (For more information on using the online catalog, see Chapter 2.)

Todd used the LCSH list to discover headings under which his topic might be listed. He found the following headings to be useful: Antigen-Antibody Reactions; Antigens; Immune Response Regulation; Cellular Immunity. Using these headings in the online catalog, Todd found the following titles:

Bellanti, J. A. Immunology II. Philadelphia: W. B.
    Saunders; 1978.

Golub, E. S. Immunology: A synthesis. Boston: Sinauer
    Associates; 1987.

Kiyono, H. Molecular aspects of immune response and
    infectious diseases. New York: Raven; 1990.

Klurfeld, D. M. Nutrition and immunity. New York:
    Plenum; 1993.

Youmans, G. P. The biologic and clinical basis of
    infectious disease. 3d ed. Philadelphia: W. B.
    Saunders; 1985.

◆ **EXERCISE**

Use the library online catalog's subject and keyword searching
to find additional books and materials on your topic. Use the
LCSH list to find the appropriate subject headings under which
sources for your topic are listed.

Indexes and Abstracts

Once you have gathered a substantial amount of information on
your subject and have located several key references and books, you are
in a position to expand your bibliography by gathering additional articles found in professional journals and periodicals. Helping you find
articles on your subject is the principal function of subject indexes, citation indexes, and abstracts. These referencing tools are generally
found either online or in print.

Computerized Indexes and Abstracts

Most modern libraries rely heavily on computer databases to
help patrons search for professional journal articles. Our library, for example, contains databases of all the indexes produced by the W. W. Wilson company; these databases can be searched by individuals via
computer. Our screen initially shows a menu of possible databases to
search: one for general periodicals; one for professional literature in
the sciences, agriculture, and engineering; one for professional literature in the arts and humanities; and one for professional literature in
the social sciences. After selecting the appropriate database for your
topic, you can search the database using the subject headings you
found while searching for books, or you can use keywords and combinations of keywords.

Other databases may be available in your library through computers that make use of compact disks (CD-ROMs). These databases
usually index specialized professional articles. Our library, for example, currently offers patrons CD-ROM databases to search for articles in
the areas of business, agriculture, education, medicine, psychology,
natural resources, and wildlife. At the end of this chapter is a listing of
indexes and abstracts that indicates which are likely to be available
through computerized database searching. Check with your library to
find out whether any of these indexes via computer are available to
you. Searching in this way is far more efficient and thorough than
searching through print media. (NOTE: Many of these databases are indexed using "controlled vocabularies" other than the LCSH. Be sure to
check for a "thesaurus" or listing of subject headings for each database
you use. For more information on computerized searching, see Chapter 2, pp. 34–44.)

Print Indexes

The subject indexes, such as *General Science Index* or *Applied Science and Technology Index,* list articles published in a given year by subject and author. By using these indexes, you can search for citations to journal articles written on your topic. You should usually start with the most recent volume of the index and work your way back, looking up your topic in several volumes of the index.

The second type of print index you may need to use in your library search is the citation index. Through the use of the citation index, you can begin with a particular researcher's name and work your way forward to other researchers who have listed (cited) that researcher in their subsequent work. Citation indexes are relatively comprehensive listings of such citations. The key sources listed in other reference works are the cited sources in the citation index. Typically, you will know the names of key researchers on your topic after a thorough search of the encyclopedias and reviews of research. Then you can follow up by searching each volume of the citation index for citations to these key sources that have appeared since the original publication of the key source. In this fashion, you will quickly build your working bibliography.

The most important citation index for the sciences is the *Science Citation Index.* Todd, for example, knew that J. A. Bellanti was a major researcher on immunology, because he had written several textbooks on the subject. Todd looked up the name of the key source, J. A. Bellanti, in the most recent citation volume of the *Science Citation Index.* He found Bellanti's 1978 book, *Immunology II,* listed as a cited source (meaning that authors had used his work in subsequent research). Under Bellanti's name were listed the researchers who had used his work as a basis for their own (that is, the citing sources). Todd added the following source to his working bibliography as found in the citation index:

```
Zhaorei, G. J Infec Dis 158 160 88
```

Listed first is the name of the author who cited Bellanti's work; then comes the abbreviated title of the journal, followed by publication data—volume number, page number, year. To find the full title of the journal, you must look at the abbreviations list at the front of the source volume. In this case, the abbreviation refers to the *Journal of Infectious Diseases.*

It may take you some time to become familiar with how the citation indexes work, but doing so will be well worth the effort. These indexes are a major tool in the sciences. When using the citation index, you may find that the complete title of the citing source is omitted, so it may be difficult to know whether the article will turn out to be relevant to your search or not. By looking up the author's name in the source index for the same year, you may find a more complete listing. You should review each article later to determine its importance to your search.

A third important type of indexing service is abstracts. Todd found *Biological Abstracts* to be useful in his search. Abstracts go one step further than indexes by providing you with a short summary of the article, which can help you sort through your references for those that are the most appropriate for your own search. Other abstracts for the sciences are listed in Chapter 2. Some abstracts may be available on computers: *Psychology Abstracts,* for example, is available in a CD-ROM database called Psychlit. Check with your librarian to find out which abstracts in your library may be searchable via computer. (NOTE: Even when using abstracts, it is important to be careful not to plagiarize. If you use information from an abstract, it needs to be cited. See page 201 for information on citing electronic abstracts.)

✦ EXERCISE

Use subject and citation indexes to find titles of articles related to your topic, using both subject headings and keywords to search. Do not limit your search to print media only; also search any relevant databases by subject and keyword. For a complete list of indexes and abstracts in the sciences and technology, see pages 225–227 later in this chapter.

Evaluation

Once you have located a book or an article, immediately evaluate it for its relevance or usefulness in your search. It is not unusual for a book or article with a very promising title to turn out to be something totally different from what you expected to find. Or you may discover a controversy in the field that you were not aware of prior to your search. As you review your sources, continually sort through and discard any that are not relevant. If, after an initial screening, a book looks as though it could be useful to you, check the book out at the circulation desk. In the case of articles, either photocopy them for later use or take notes from them in the library, since they are generally noncirculating materials and cannot be checked out.

✦ EXERCISE

In your research notebook, evaluate each article and book to be used in your research paper. Follow the source evaluation guidelines in Chapter 3 on pp. 80–81.

Taking Notes

As you begin to take notes on the sources, remember to record complete bibliographic information so that you will not need to look up a particular source again. If you are using a research notebook (whether on paper or in a computer file), complete information must be kept on each source you use in your research, including author(s), title, and publication data. Taking care at this stage will benefit you when you get to the actual writing stage.

If you are taking notes in your research notebook or in a computer file, take care to identify each source as you are writing down your notes. Put into quotation marks any information or wording taken directly from the source, and at the end of the source information, mark down the exact page number on which you found the material and whether you paraphrased or quoted the author.

If you are using notecards, for each source on your working bibliography that you locate in the library, make a bibliography card. On the bibliography card, write the library call number in the upper left-hand corner and the control number of the source in the upper right-hand corner. Enter complete bibliographical information on the card: author, title, and publication data (see Documentation in Science and Technology later in this chapter for examples of science citations). On your notecards, write the corresponding control number in the upper right-hand corner of the card and title the card.

ORGANIZING AND WRITING THE SCIENTIFIC REVIEW PAPER

A major task in writing a scientific review is organizing the material you have gathered. It is your job to make sense of the information you found in your library search. Remember, you are trying to make the information accessible to your readers as well as objective and comprehensive. When Todd began to narrow his topic, he decided to focus on the process by which the human body recognizes foreign cells and destroys them. As he thought through the rhetorical situation, he decided that he wanted to convey to a lay audience his own fascination with the human body's ability to carry out processes that prevent disease. (For more information on rhetorical situation, see Chapter 5 pp. 137–140.)

After completing his library research, Todd articulated an answer to his starting question in the form of a thesis statement: "Throughout my research on host-bacterial interactions, I have found that it is the level of host immunity that is the key issue in the acquisition of and recovery from infectious disease." This thesis statement provided Todd with an overall focus to his paper: he would describe the processes by which the human body wards off disease and the host deficiencies that would allow bacterial infection a "window of opportunity."

In order to understand the process of disease prevention, Todd decided to first discuss the disease-producing organisms and their mechanisms of spread; then he would discuss the defense mechanisms mounted by the human body against the invasion of disease. This organizational plan made the information easily available to the reader. He divided each subsection with descriptive headings to further help the reader discern his organizational plan. Scientific reviews often are subdivided in this way to allow the reader easy access to the information.

✦ EXERCISE

Write a thesis statement and sketch a preliminary organizational plan for your research paper. Refer to Chapter 5 (pp. 140–144) for help with organization.

Arranging the Materials

Once Todd had decided on the thesis statement and organizational plan, he grouped related information in his computerized research notebook, using the cut and paste functions of his word processor, under the headings he had decided on in planning his paper. Because all his information was stored in his own words in his computer research notebook, it was an easy matter to move blocks of material in the notebook using the block move (cut and paste) commands; furthermore, he didn't need to worry about plagiarizing any of the sources because he had already been very careful to summarize and paraphrase while taking notes. (Be sure to make a backup file of your notebook before beginning to manipulate the information in this way.)

Todd moved to the end of the computer file any information that did not seem to fit into the paper, such as information he had gathered on the specific diseases. This material was not relevant to his particular thesis statement. To make a unified, coherent presentation of your research, you must discard any information that is irrelevant. With his preliminary plan set, Todd wrote a more detailed outline to guide him in writing the paper:

        Outline
        Introduction
        Classification of disease-producing organisms
            Extracellular

Facultative intracellular
Obligate intracellular
Transmission of microbes
Multiplication and spread of bacteria
Lethal dose 50
Spread of infection throughout the body
Direct extension
Hematogenous spread
Lymphatic spread
Attachment of bacteria to epithelial surfaces
External defense mechanisms
Skin
Respiratory tract
Alimentary tract
Genitourinary tract
Eye
Inflammatory response
Internal defense mechanisms
Humoral
Cell-mediated immunity
Conclusion
David the bubble boy
Immunodeficiencies

✦ EXERCISE

Sort your notecards by their titles, number related ideas in your research notebook, or block related information together in a computer file. Write an informal outline of your research paper, using your thesis statement and organizational plan as a guide. Begin writing the first draft of your research paper. (See Chapter 5 for additional guidance.)

Writing the First Draft: Verification

After you have completed your outline, you are ready to write the first draft of your research paper. Remember, you are writing in order to review for your readers the current state of thinking on a particular scientific topic. Remind yourself at this time of the general understanding you had of your topic and of your answer to the question you posed as you began researching. When writing your first draft, use concrete and simple language to explain as objectively as you can the current thinking on your topic. Your outline will guide the writing of this first draft. Any word, phrase, or sentence you copy directly from a source must be placed in quotation marks, followed by the last name of the author, the date the source was published, and the page number (in parentheses):

```
The body's T cells "are responsible for the

ability of vertebrate animals to recognize that

antigens, or foreign materials, have invaded

their bodies" (Marrack and Kappler 1988, p. 36).
```

(Note: In the number system, sources are identified by a superscript number or a number in parentheses immediately following the sources instead of the author's name, date, and page number in parentheses. See The Number System later in this chapter.)

Similarly, paraphrases and restatements of ideas taken from a source should be given documentation even though you have recast them in your own words:

```
Microbes can easily enter the blood from the

lymphatics and spread infection throughout the

body (Wyss 1971).
```

Remember: you do not need to document common knowledge on your topic (see pp. 147–148 for a discussion of common knowledge).

For general information on planning, writing, and revising your scientific review paper, refer to Chapter 5. Use the following information on documentation in the sciences and technology to cite sources in the correct form. The sample review paper at the end of this chapter serves as a model of a scientific review conducted on a limited, accessible topic.

DOCUMENTATION IN SCIENCE AND TECHNOLOGY

There is no uniform system of citation in the sciences and technology, but all disciplines follow either a journal style or a style guide; therefore, some general principles apply to most scientific disciplines. The sciences use in-text citation and list the works cited at the end of the text. The recency of the source is important, so the year of publication is stressed in the citation. Entire journal articles rather than specific pages may be cited, and direct quotes are seldom used.

Internal Citation

In the sciences, authors are cited within the text itself by means of either the author/year system or the number system.

The Author/Year System

The author/year system is widely used in the sciences and has been adopted (with variations) by the social sciences and business. It is a fairly easy system for the reader to use. The following principles should be observed:

1. When an author's journal article in general is cited, the source material is followed by the last name of the author and the date of the source article in parentheses:

   ```
   The T cell plays a key role in immunology

   (Marrack and Kappler 1988).
   ```

2. If the source material is paraphrased or directly quoted, the page numbers should be included:

   ```
   Analysis indicates that "binding does not change

   the structure of interacting units" (Davis 1987,

   p. 134).
   ```

3. If the author's name is used in introducing the source material, only the date is necessary:

   ```
   According to Davis (1987) scientists are on the

   verge of discovering the secrets of antibodies.
   ```

4. Multiple sources may be cited:

   ```
   Recent research indicates that antibodies may

   also bind to microbes and prevent their

   attachment to epithelial surfaces (Bellanti 1985;

   Getzoff 1987; Geyson 1987).
   ```

5. When citing a work with multiple authors, use et al. ("and others"):

The earlier work suggested other substance
involvement in fish fertilization (Henkert et
al. 1978).

6. When citing a work with two authors, join them with *and*:

Similar observations have been made in sea
urchins (Shumomura and Johnson 1976).

7. Information obtained from another work cited within the first
work should appear as follows:

Such a factor is apparently not present in
unactivated sturgeon (Chulitskai 1977, cited by
Meyerhof and Masui 1980).

8. When the same author has written two or more publications in
the same year, designate them with an *a, b,* and so on following
the year:

Some of the earliest responses of eggs to sperm-
egg interaction are electrical (Nuccitelli 1980a).

The Number System

The number system is also used in the sciences and technology.
Here a number is assigned to each source listed on the references page.
To cite the source within the text, one simply lists the number of that
source, either in parentheses or as a raised superscript:

Temperature plays a major role in the rate of
gastric juice secretion (3).

Temperature plays a major role in the rate of
gastric juice secretion.[3]

You can cite multiple sources easily with this system:

Recent studies (3,5,8) show that antibodies may
also bind to microbes and prevent their
attachment to epithelial surfaces.

Recent studies[3,5,8] show that antibodies may also bind to microbes to prevent their attachment to epithelial surfaces.

Content Notes

Some scientific papers might require notes that explain something about the text itself rather than refer to a particular source being cited. These content notes are listed either as footnotes or endnotes rather than internal citations. For the proper form of footnotes and endnotes, see Chapter 8.

The Reference List

The reference list, found at the end of your research paper, contains all the sources actually used in the paper. The title of this page is "References," "Works Cited," or "Literature Cited." The purpose of the reference list is to help readers find the materials you used in writing your paper. Therefore, you must give complete, accurate information here. The following principles are generally accepted for the reference list in the sciences and technology:

1. On the references or work-cited page, references are arranged in alphabetical order and may be numbered. (Note: The numbering system may proceed consecutively, i.e., in the order in which the sources appear in the text.)
2. Authors are listed by surnames and initials.
3. Generally the first word only of a title is capitalized, the title of an article is not enclosed in quotation marks, and the title of a book is not underlined.
4. Names of journals are often abbreviated.
5. The volume and page number system often resembles that found in the indexes (for example, 19:330–360). Sometimes the volume number is in boldface type, indicated by a wavy line in manuscript: **16,** or 16.
6. The year of publication appears either immediately after the author's name or at the close of an entry, depending upon the particular journal's publication style.

BOOK

Golub, E. S. 1987. Immunology: A synthesis.

    Boston: Sinaur Associates.

ARTICLE

Milleen, J. K. 1986. Verifying security. ACM

    Computing Surveys 16:350-354.

or

Milleen, J. K. Verifying security. ACM Computing

    Surveys 16:350-354; 1986.

7. If the same author has published two or more works in the same year, indicate this with a lower case a and b: 1984a, 1984b.
8. Author/year system: The first word of the entry is typed at the left margin. Subsequent lines of the same entry are indented five spaces. Generally, the entire reference list is double spaced. Number system: The numbers are typed at the left margin. The first line of each entry is typed two spaces after the number. Subsequent lines are even with the first line.

If you are writing a paper for a specific discipline, it is important for you to find out which documentation form your instructor prefers. Some style guides that will help you:

The ACS Style Guide: A Manual for Authors and Editors. Janet S. Dodds, ed. Washington, D.C.: American Chemical Society, 1986.

Council of Biology Editors Style Manual. 5th ed. Council of Biology Editors, 1983.

Geowriting: A Guide to Writing, Editing, and Printing in Earth Science. 3rd ed. American Geological Institute, 1979.

Style Manual: For Guidance in the Preparation of Papers for Journals Published by the American Institute of Physics. 3rd ed. New York: American Institute of Physics, 1978.

(NOTE: some scientific journals follow the APA style as outlined by the *Publications Manual of the American Psychological Association.* See pp. 250–256.)

The model references in the accompanying table are based on the form used in many science journals. They follow the style found in the *Council of Biology Editors Style Manual* (CBE). (A few of the model references are taken directly from CBE.) For further examples, refer to one of the manuals listed in the previous paragraph. (Please note the position of the date in CBE style. Alternatively, many science journals place the date immediately after the author's name.)

MODEL REFERENCES: NATURAL AND PHYSICAL SCIENCE (CBE)

Type of Reference

BOOKS

1. One author

   Campbell, R. C. Statistics for biologists. 2d ed.

   London and New York: Cambridge Univ. Press;

   1974.

2. Two or more authors

   Snedecor, G. W.; Cochran, W. G. Statistical

   methods. 6th ed. Ames, IA: The Iowa State

   Univ. Press; 1967.

3. Two or more books by the same author (list chronologically, or use a and b if published in the same year)

   Parker, D. B. Crime and computer security.

   Encyclopedia of computer engineering. New

   York: Van Nostrand Reinhold; 1983a.

   Parker, D. B. Fighting computer crime. New York:

   Scribner's; 1983b.

4. Book with an editor

   Buchanan, R. E.; Gibbons, N. E., editors.

   Bergey's manual of determinative

   bacteriology. 8th ed. Baltimore: Williams

   and Wilkins; 1974.

5. Section, selected pages, or a chapter in a book

   Jones, J. B.; Beck, J. F. Asymmetrical syntheses

   and resolutions using enzymes. Jones, J. B.;

   Sih, C. J.; Perlman, D. eds. Applications of

biochemical systems in organic chemistry.
New York: Wiley; 1976: pp. 107-401.

6. Book with a corporate author

American Society for Testing and Materials.
Standard for metric practice, ANSI/ASTME
370-376. Philadelphia: American Society for
Testing and Materials; 1976.

7. Work known by title

American men and women of science. 13th ed.
Jacques Cattell Press, ed. New York: Bowker;
1976. 6 vol.

8. All volumes in a multivolume work

Colowick, S. P.; Kaplan, N. O. Methods in
enzymology. New York: Academic Press;
1955-1963. 6 vol.

ARTICLES

1. Journal article (one author)

Solokov, R. Endangered pisces: The Great Lakes
whitefish is exploited by both lampreys and
humans. Nat. Hist. 90:92-96; 1981.

2. Journal article (two or more authors)

Berry, D. J.; Chang, T. Y. Further
characterization of a Chinese hamster ovary
cell mutant defective. Biochemistry
21:573-580; 1982.

3. Article on discontinuous pages

Balack, J. A; Dobbins, W. O. III. Maldigestion
and malabsorption: Making up for lost

```
nutrients. Geriatrics 29:157-160, 163-167;
    1974.
```

4. Article with no identified author

```
Anonymous. Frustrated hamsters run on their
    wheels. N. Sci. 91:407; 1981.
```
[Note: May also be listed by title only]

5. Newspaper article (signed)

```
Shaffer, R. A. Advances in chemistry are starting
    to unlock the mysteries in the brain. The
    Wall Street Journal. 1977 Aug. 12; 1
    (col. 1), 10 (col. 1).
```

6. Newspaper article (unsigned)

```
Puffin, a rare seabird returns to where many were
    killed. The New York Times. 1977 Sept. 6;
    Sect. C: 28.
```

7. Magazine article

```
Starr, D. Students who tap the Universe.
    Omni. 1989 May; 66-72.
```

TECHNICAL REPORTS

1. Individual author

```
Brill R. C. The TAXIR primer. Occasional paper—
    Institute of Arctic and Alpine
    Research. 1971; 71p. Available from: Univ.
    of Colorado, Boulder, CO.
```

2. Corporate author

```
World Health Organization. WHO Expert Committee
    on Filariasis: 3d report. WHO Tech Rep. Ser
    542; 1974. 54p.
```

3. Government document

U.S. Congress, House of Representatives. The
    international narcotics control community. A
    report on the 27th session of the
    U. N. Commission on Narcotics to the Select
    Committee on Narcotics Abuse and Control.
    Ninety-fifth Congress, first session. 1977
    Feb. 37p. Available from: U.S. Government
    Printing Office. Washington, DC: SCNAC-95-1-
    10.

OTHER SOURCES

1. Motion picture

Rapid frozen section techniques [Motion Picture].
    U.S. Public Health Service. Washington DC:
    National Medical Audiovisual Center and
    National Audiovisual Center; 1966. 6 min.;
    sd; color; super 8 mm; loop film in
    cartridge; magnetic sound track.

2. Dissertation or thesis (unpublished)

Dotson, R. D. Transients in a cochlear model.
    Stanford, CA: Stanford Univ.; 1974. 219p.
    Dissertation.

3. Letters and interviews

Darwin, C. [Letters to Sir J. Hooker]. Located
    at: Archives, Royal Botanical Gardens, Kew,
    England.

Quarnberg, T. [Interview with Dr. Andy Anderson,
    Professor of Biology, Utah State
    University]. 1988 April 25.

4. Unpublished paper presented at conference

   Lewis, F. M.; Ablow, C. M. Pyrogas from biomass.
   Paper presented to Conference on capturing
   the sun through bioconversion. Washington,
   DC; 1976. Available from: Stanford Research
   Institute, Menlo Park, CA.

5. Reference work

   Handbook of psychopharmacology. Section I: basic
   neuropharmacology. Iverson, L. L.; Iverson,
   S. D.; Snyder, S. H., eds. New York: Plenum
   Press; 1975. 6 vol.

6. Abstract on CD-ROM

   Rodriguez, A. M. 1991. Multicultural education:
   Some considerations for a university setting
   [CD-ROM]. Abstract from: SilverPlatter's
   ERIC Item: ED337094.

7. Online abstract

   Lawrence, O. J. 1984. Pitfalls in electronic
   writing land. [Online]. English Education,
   16.2; 94-100. Abstract from: Dialog file:
   ERIC Item: EJ297923.

8. Online journal article

   Herz, J. C. 1995, April. Surfing on the internet:
   A nethead's adventures online. [Online
   serial]. Urban Desires, 1.3. Available
   Internet: www/desires.com/ud.html.

9. Electronic Correspondence, such as e-mail messages and conversations via bulletin boards and electronic discussion groups, are

typically cited as personal communication in the text. In-text information to include:

author, date, subject of the message
name of the listserv, bulletin board, or e-mail discussion group
available from: e-mail address

Note: Do not cite electronic correspondence without the author's permission. (For further information on citing electronic information, see Li, X.; Crane, N. B. Electronic style: A guide to citing electronic information. Westport and London: Meckler; 1993.)

EXERCISES AND RESEARCH PROJECT

Complete the exercises outlined in this chapter as you research a limited scientific or technological topic and write a scientific review paper. The three exercises that follow will give you additional practice using skills associated with science research projects.

1. For each entry on your reference list, write a three- or four-sentence annotation that describes the content of that source.

2. Write a "review of the literature" report that summarizes in three to four pages the major ideas found in your sources. In your review, try to avoid using direct quotes or copying words used in the articles. Often, a literature review, which lists and comments on the works done to date in a particular area of scientific investigation, is a component of a larger scientific paper. The review of the literature often proceeds in chronological order based on the publication date of the source and thus may differ from the scientific review paper, which is typically organized around concepts or other categories.

3. When you have finished writing your paper, write an abstract (approximately 100 words long) of your paper in which you summarize the major points in your review (see Chapter 5 for a discussion of how to write abstracts).

SAMPLE SCIENTIFIC REVIEW: SCIENCE FORMAT (CBE)

Host-Bacterial Interactions in Humans

Todd Quarnberg

Term Paper

for

Animal Biology

Biology 127

May 11, 1993

Outline

I. Introduction 3

II. Classification of disease-producing organisms 4

III. Transmission of microbes 5

IV. Multiplication and spread of bacteria 6

V. Spread of infection throughout the body 8

VI. Attachment of bacteria to epithelial surfaces 9

VII. External defense mechanisms 9

VIII. Inflammatory response 11

IX. Internal defense mechanisms 12

    A. Humoral immunity 13

    B. Cell-mediated immunity 15

    C. Phagocytosis 16

X. Case Studies 17

Host-Bacterial Interactions

I. Introduction

The most important factor in the acquisition and eradication of human disease is the health and immunity of the host. In times past, the wrath of God was blamed for disease caused by living microorganisms. Sick people were either put to death or lived a life of ostracism and ridicule (Quarnberg 1988). Throughout my research on host-bacterial interactions, I have found that it is the level of host immunity that is the key issue in the acquisition of and recovery from infectious disease. Virulence factors of the microbes are of secondary importance. All pathogenic microbes are opportunists, but some require more severe and obvious host deficiencies to cause disease. When suppression of host defenses takes place, a particular microbe will enter this window of opportunity. Its presence at an opportune moment and the ability of the microbe to survive and multiply in the

4

host are of vital importance in causing

disease. Pathogenic microbes must also be

able to resist host defense mechanisms

for a period sufficient to reach the num-

bers required to produce disease.

II. Classification of

Disease-Producing Organisms

Researchers have identified three

different classifications of disease-pro-

ducing microorganisms. First are

extracellular parasites, which produce

infection by multiplying primarily out-

side phagocytic cells (blood cells that

ingest and destroy foreign bacteria).

Such parasites produce disease if they

avoid the human defense mechanisms. Sec-

ond are facultative intracellular

parasites, which may be destroyed by

phagocytic cells, but are resistant to

intracellular killing by them. Last are

the obligate intracellular parasites,

which cannot multiply unless they are

within cells (Youmans et al. 1986). All

humans have microbes that normally live

5

in or on our bodies; this population of
organisms is called our normal flora, or
indigenous microbiota. The normal flora
are becoming a more frequent cause of
human illness by taking advantage of
deficiencies in host defenses. Decreases
in host resistance can allow the normal
flora to invade and establish disease.
Knowledge of the different organisms present at various body sites may give a
clue to the type of infection that might
occur following injury at these sites. It
also is clear that the normal flora are
important in stimulating the immune system. For example, germ-free mice lack
good immune systems because they lack
stimulation of their immune systems; thus
pathogens are free to spread throughout
their bodies (Sommers 1986).

III. Transmission of Microbes

Researchers have identified several
different modes of transmission of disease and pathogens. Man is the major
reservoir for human disease, and cough-

6

ing, sneezing, touching, and intimate
contact are ways the transmission of
microbes can occur. In our time, overcrowding in day-care centers, hospitals,
and so on also increases disease transmission. Disease in developed countries
has been on the increase because of the
overcrowded conditions (Youmans et
al. 1986).

IV. Multiplication and Spread of Bacteria

Bacteria multiply by dividing into
two daughter cells in a process known as
binary fission. Their growth is exponen-
tial (1, 2, 4, 8, 16, and so on), with an
average twenty- to thirty-minute doubling
time. Scientists have demonstrated that
animals infected with highly virulent
bacteria will die or show signs of infection only when a certain bacterial
population has been reached in the
infected animal. It follows that the
larger the dose of the infecting agent,
the quicker death or signs of disease
will occur. It also follows that a

7

smaller infecting dose will usually
result in a longer incubation period.

It is possible to measure the number
of bacteria necessary to produce disease
in an experimental animal. Lethal dose 50
(LD 50) is the number or dose of bacteria
that when injected into experimental animals eventually causes 50% of the
population to die. The LD 50 is useful in
comparing relative virulence of bacterial
strains and the relative susceptibility
of experimental animals. Observation of
natural human infections indicates that
certain bacteria are more virulent than
others and that humans vary in their susceptibility. People infected with the
same strain of the same bacterium either
die from infection or recover. Consider
it a race between two opposing forces,
the most important factor in eradicating
a disease being the ability to mount a
specific immune response in time, which
may be anywhere from five to ten days. It
is also possible for a person to develop
an immune response before enough bacteria
are present to actually cause disease.

8

This is called an inapparent or subclini-
cal infection (Youmans et al. 1986). When
an infected host recovers from an infection caused by an extracellular parasite,
usually all the bacteria are killed. In
some infections caused by facultative
intracellular parasites, some of the
microbes may survive and become dormant.
They can become active again when resistance has been lowered.

V. Spread of Infection
Throughout the Body

Depending on the effectiveness of
host defenses, an infection may remain
localized or spread throughout the body.
There are three ways infection may
spread. First is direct extension to
neighboring tissues. Second is direct
entry into a blood vessel (hematogenous
spread). And third is spread by the lymphatic system (lymphatic spread), with
the latter as the most common method.
Microbes can easily enter the blood from
the lymphatics and spread infection
throughout the body (Wyss 1971).

9

VI. Attachment of Bacteria to
Epithelial Surfaces

Some bacteria are directly deposited
inside human tissue by traumatic entry.
Other bacteria must first attach to
epithelial (protective) tissue to cause
infection and disease. The respiratory
tract is the most common route of invasion, and the bacteria use small hairlike
projections (pili) to attach to a specific binding site on host cells. Normal
flora microbes may help to prevent colonization of respiratory tract surfaces by
covering up specific attachment sites
required by pathogenic microbes. Flora
are also in competition with pathogens
for nutrients. Some normal flora organisms even produce inhibitory products to
kill pathogens and limit disease (Quarnberg 1988).

VII. External Defense Mechanisms

The body has several external
defense mechanisms to limit disease and
infection from entering the body. The

10

skin represents a mechanical barrier to the entry of microbes. Infection through the skin takes place only when the skin has been damaged. The skin has normal flora that help maintain an acid pH to prevent colonization by pathogens. Sebaceous glands in the skin also produce a bactericide to kill invading microorganisms (Golub 1987). Human bites have the potential of causing deep infections because of the high bacterial counts from the mouth (Wise 1987).

The respiratory tract has several defense mechanisms to limit invasion. Nasal hairs and normal flora in the upper respiratory tract help prevent colonization. Phagocytic cells in the alveoli of the lung destroy and remove small infectious particles that could potentially cause damage and infection to the lung (Youmans et al. 1986). The alimentary tract (digestive system) also has several defensive mechanisms. Normal flora of the mouth and large intestine help to prevent colonization by pathogens. And the highly acidic pH of the stomach kills most

11

microbes as they pass through the digestive system.

In the genitourinary tract, the pro-
static fluid in males contains
bactericidal substances. The frequent
flushing action of urine also helps to
control microbial populations in the ure-
thra. The normal flora in the female
vagina consists primarily of lactobacilli
that break down glycogen (a polysaccha-
ride) to form acid. The acidic pH
prevents colonization by most pathogens
(Youmans et al. 1986).

The eye limits microbial growth by
the flushing action of tears. Tears also
contain lysozyme, which plays a considerable role in resistance to infection by
destroying the cell walls of some bacteria (Youmans et al. 1986).

VIII. Inflammatory Response

The body also has a specific defense
mechanism called inflammation, which is a
protective response of the tissues of the
body to irritation and injury. It is

12

characterized by several events. First,
blood flow changes. The blood vessels
dilate and allow an increased blood flow
to the site of injury, which causes red-
ness and heat. Increased permeability of
blood vessels, caused by the chemical
histamine, allows fluid to escape into
the tissues (Serafin 1987), causing the
swelling and pain. Inflammation, because
of its combination of effects, is usually
protective against infection.

IX. Internal Defense Mechanisms

The human body also has internal
defense mechanisms. These are the body's
defenses that react against specific
microbes. Extracellular parasites are
the most susceptible to serum antibody
produced by the body's humoral (fluid-
producing) response. Facultative and
obligate intracellular parasites are more
susceptible to cell-mediated immunity.
The body also has a third internal
defense mechanism, called phagocytosis,
which is a nonimmune defense.

13

A. Humoral Immunity

In humoral immunity, lymphocytes, which are a portion of the white blood cells, are processed into B-cells either in the bone marrow or in the lymph nodes along the intestinal tract. Antibodies are produced when B-cells are stimulated by a foreign substance called an antigen. The antigen (on an invading microbe) is presented to a B-cell by a macrophage and binds with receptors on the surface of the B-cell. The specific B-cell becomes activated by the antigen and rapidly divides to form a large group of cells. This mechanism, in which B-cells are stimulated, is known as clonal selection (Davis 1986). It is a mechanism of anti-body production. The activated cells of this clone will carry out two functions: some become plasma cells and actively secrete antibody for days and die, while others become memory cells, which live for years and respond more rapidly and forcefully should the same antigen appear at a future time (Golub 1987).

14

There are two ways immunity to
infection may be obtained by antibodies,
either actively or passively. Active
immunity is the production of specific
antibody in response to the presence of a
microbe or its products. Active immunity
may be obtained by direct infection of
the disease or by vaccination. Passive
immunity occurs when protective antibodies are transferred from an actively
immunized animal to a nonimmunized one. A
good example of passive immunity is antibodies that are transferred from mother
to fetus across the placenta. Colostrum,
which is the mother's first milk, is rich
in antibodies and can also passively
transfer immunity to a child

Antibodies have several functions to
aid the body in the fight with infection.
One function is toxin neutralization.
Some poisons produced by bacteria can be
neutralized by antibodies. Antibodies are
also able to attach to microbes and pro-
mote phagocytosis by aiding in the
process of attachment. They may also bind
to microbes and prevent their attachment
to epithelial surfaces, thus not allowing

15

them to establish and cause disease (Bellanti 1985; Getzoff 1987; Geyson 1987).

B. Cell-Mediated Immunity

Intracellular parasites are more
susceptible to cell-mediated immunity
(CMI). CMI is the result of thymus-
derived lymphocytes (T-cells) and
macrophages (Silberner 1986). When activated, these cells are very effective at
attacking facultative and obligate intracellular parasites. An antigen (an
invading microbe) is presented to the T-
cells in the lymphoid tissue by a
macrophage. That specific T-cell becomes
activated and rapidly divides to form
effector cells. Some effector cells are
cytotoxic T-cells that migrate to the
site of invasion and destroy foreign
cells on contact. Some effector cells are
delayed hypersensitivity T-cells that
migrate to the site of invasion and produce lymphokines, which are a type of
bactericidal. In certain types of infection, macrophages accumulate in large
numbers at the site of infection. This
response is called a granulomatous

16

response and may lead to formation of a
nodule or swelling in the tissue (Bass
1985; Bellanti 1985).

C. Phagocytosis

Phagocytosis (destruction of bacteria by phagocytic blood cells) is a
nonimmune internal defense mechanism.
Phagocytosis is usually carried out by
cells called neutrophils and macrophages.
Neutrophils are the most important and
are produced in the bone marrow. They
survive only a few days and contain
enzymes and antimicrobial substances.
Macrophages are found in the tissues and
may live for weeks or months. Neutrophils
and macrophages marginate on the walls of
blood vessels adjacent to a site of
inflammation. They undergo diapedesis and
squeeze between endothelial cells (cells
that line blood vessels) to enter damaged
tissue. The phagocytic process can be
divided into two stages. The first is
attachment of a phagocyte to a pathogenic
microbe. However, if a bacterium has a
capsule, it interferes with attachment.
Ingestion follows attachment, and the

17

microbe is exposed to the digestive
enzymes and substances contained within
the phagocyte (Bellanti 1985; Golub 1987;
Langman 1989).

X. Case Studies

Most of us don't spend much time
thinking about the immune system, and
that's because it usually functions well.
Not so for David, the boy who spent
twelve years in a germ-free plastic bubble. David was born with SCID (severe
combined immunodeficiency disease) and
couldn't produce the cells that are
needed to protect the body from disease-
producing organisms. A treated bone
marrow transplant was given by his sister, but unfortunately, it was infected
and caused him to develop cancer. The
infection hadn't caused this difficulty
in his sister because she already had a
functioning immune system when she was
exposed to the cancer. A well-functioning
immune system permits us to live in a
world that is filled with all sorts of
disease-causing agents (Mader 1988).

18

No other system on earth is able to repair itself and automatically fight off disease as efficiently as the human body. The study of immunity is really the study of host-bacterial interactions. The outcomes depend on factors that allow one or the other to win the battle. It's up to you and your body to win the fight. The most common type of immune malfunction is caused by aberrations in lifestyle: physical overexertion, malnutrition, stress, alcohol, and drugs, all of which lower your resistance and allow pathogens to invade your body (Miller 1986; Klerfeld 1993). The immune system preserves our existence, but we must do our part to not allow disease that "window of opportunity."

19

References

Bass, A. B. Unlocking the secrets of
    immunity. Technology Review.
    8:62-65; 1985.

Bellanti, J. A. Immunology II.
    Philadelphia: W. B. Saunders; 1985.

Davis, L. Unlocking secrets of antibody
    binding. Science News. 130:134; 1986.

Getzoff, E. D. Mechanisms of antibody
    binding to a protein. Science.
    235:1191-1197; 1987.

Geyson, H. M. Chemistry of antibody
    binding to a protein. Science.
    235:1184-1191; 1987.

Golub, E. S. Immunology: A synthesis.
    Boston: Sinauer Associates; 1987.

Herscowitz, H. Cell-mediated immune
    reactions. 2d ed. Philadelphia: W.
    B. Saunders; 1985.

Klerfeld, D. M., editor. Human nutrition:
    A comprehensive treatise, Vol 8,
    Nutrition and immunology. New York:
    Plenum Press; 1993.

Langman, R. E. The immune system. New
    York: Academic Press; 1989.

Mader, S. S. Human biology. Dubuque, IA:
    Wm. C. Brown; 1988.

20

Miller, J. A. Keeping a step ahead of
    immunity. Science News. 129:162;
    1986.

Quarnberg, T. [Interview with Dr. Andy
    Anderson, Professor of Biology, Utah
    State University]. 1988 April 25.

Serafin, W. E. Current concepts:
    Mediators of immediate
    hypersensitivity reactions. New
    England Journal of Medicine.
    130:30-35; 1987.

Silberner, J. Second T-cell receptor
    found. Science News. 130:36; 1986.

Sommers, H. Indigenous microbiota.
    Youmans, G. P. et al., eds. The
    biological and clinical basis of
    infectious disease. 3d ed.
    Philadelphia: W. B. Saunders; 1986:
    pp. 110-145.

Wise, H. Man bites man. Hippocratic.
    100:93; 1987.

Wyss, O. Microorganisms and man. New
    York: John Wiley and Sons; 1971.

Youmans, G. P. et al. The biological and
    clinical basis of infectious
    disease. 3d ed. Philadelphia: W. B.
    Saunders; 1986.

DISCIPLINE-SPECIFIC RESOURCES FOR SCIENCE AND TECHNOLOGY

General Sources and Guides to Literature

Guide to Sources for Agricultural and Biological Research. J. Blanchard and L. Farrell. Los Angeles: University of California Press, 1981.

Information Sources in Agriculture and Horticulture, 2nd ed. G. P. Lilley. UK: H. Zell, 1992.

Information Sources in Engineering. 2nd ed. L. Anthony, ed. UK: H. Zell, 1985.

Information Sources in Physics. 2nd ed. D. Shaw. UK: H. Zell, 1985.

Information Sources in the Life Sciences. 4th ed. H. V. Wyatt, ed. UK: H. Zell, 1992.

Information Sources in the Medical Sciences. 4th ed. L. T. Morton and S. Godbolt, eds. UK: Bowker-Saur, 1992. A useful reference guide for all medical fields.

Information Sources in Science and Technology. C. D. Hurt. Littleton, CO: Libraries Unlimited, 1988. A general reference guide for the sciences.

Reference Sources in Science and Technology. E. J. Lamsworth. Metuchen, NJ: Scarecrow, 1972.

Science and Engineering Sourcebook. Cass R. Lewart. Littleton, CO: Libraries Unlimited, 1982. Lists and annotates reference works in various scientific fields.

Chambers Dictionary of Earth Science. Peter Walker, ed. Edinburgh: W. & R. Chambers, 1992. Concise source for definitions of terms.

Dictionary of Chemistry. Sybil P. Parker, ed. New York: McGraw-Hill, 1985.

Dictionary of Artificial Intelligence and Robotics. Jerry Rosenberg. New York: Wiley, 1986.

Dictionary of the Biological Sciences. P. Gray. Melbourne, FL: Krieger, 1982.

Dictionary of Computing. 3rd ed. New York: Oxford University Press, 1991. Lists over 4,000 terms used in computing and associated fields of electronics, mathematics, and logic.

Dictionary of Geology and Geophysics. D. F. Lapidus. New York: Facts on File Publications, 1987. Defines many terms in the context of modern geological theories.

Dictionary of Electrical and Electronic Engineering. New York: McGraw-Hill, 1985. Very comprehensive guide to terms.

Dictionary of Inventions and Discoveries. 2nd ed. E. F. Carter. New York: Crane Russak, 1976. Catalogs and describes major scientific inventions and discoveries.

Dictionary of Physics. New York: McGraw-Hill, 1986. Comprehensive dictionary of terms.

Glossary of Chemical Terms. 2nd ed. C. A. Hampel and G. G. Hawley. New York: Van Nostrand Reinhold, 1982. Helpful definitions.

McGraw-Hill Dictionary of Earth Sciences. 3rd ed. New York: McGraw-Hill, 1984. Helpful definitions.

McGraw-Hill Dictionary of Scientific and Technical Terms. 4th ed. New York: Mc-
Graw-Hill, 1989. Provides clear definitions of terminology.
A Modern Dictionary of Geography. 2nd ed. J. Small and M. Witherick. Baltimore:
Edward Arnold, 1989. Provides definitions of terms that are accessible to
college students.

Handbooks, Atlases, and Almanacs

Handbook of Chemistry and Physics. 58th ed. Cleveland: Chemical Rubber,
1913–present. Provides facts and data on chemistry and physics.
Materials Handbook. 13th ed. G. S. Brady. New York: McGraw-Hill, 1991. De-
scribes nature and properties of commercially available materials.
Medical and Health Information Directory: Organizations, Agencies, and Institutions.
7th ed. Detroit: Gale, 1994. Comprehensive guidebook.
Physician's Handbook. 21st ed. M. A. Krupp et al. E. Norwalk, CT: Appleton and
Lange, 1986. Useful, quick reference book for all medical questions.
Standard Handbook for Civil Engineers. 3rd ed. F. S. Merritt, ed. New York: Mc-
Graw-Hill, 1983. Provides basic information in an easy reference format.
Standard Handbook for Electrical Engineers. 12th ed. D. G. Fink and H. W. Beaty,
eds. New York: McGraw-Hill, 1987. Provides basic information in an easy
reference format.

Encyclopedias

The Astronomy Encyclopedia. P. Moore, ed. Stafford, England: Mitchell Beagley,
1989. Illustrated.
Cambridge Encyclopedia of Earth Sciences. D. G. Smith, ed. Cambridge, England:
Cambridge University Press, 1982. Short articles of interest to geologists,
geographers, and so on.
Cambridge Encyclopedia of Life Sciences. A. Friday and D. S. Ingram, eds. Cam-
bridge, England: Cambridge University Press, 1985. Short articles of in-
terest to biologists, zoologists, and others.
Classification and Synopsis of Living Organisms. S. P. Parker, ed. New York: Mc-
Graw-Hill, 1982. Invaluable reference tool for life sciences.
The Encyclopedia of Astronomy and Astrophysics. Maran, ed. New York: Van Nos-
trand Reinhold, 1991. Concise summaries of information geared for a
nontechnical audience.
The Encyclopedia of Bioethics. W. Reich, ed. New York: Macmillan, 1982.
Encyclopedia of Computer Science and Engineering, revised ed. A. Ralston, ed. New
York: Van Nostrand Reinhold, 1992. Provides concise information in the
fields of computer science and engineering.
Encyclopedia of Computer Science and Technology. J. Belzer, ed. New York: Dekker,
1990. Short articles on subjects in computer science.
Encyclopedia of Physical Science and Technology. 15 vols. R. A. Meyers, ed. Or-
lando: Academic Press, 1987. A comprehensive encyclopedia on the status of knowledge across the entire field of physical science and related
technologies.
The Encyclopedia of Physics. R. G. Lerner and G. L. Trigg, eds. Reading, MA: Ad-
dison-Wesley, 1980. Provides background information on major principles and problems in physics.

Grzimek's Animal Life Encyclopedia. B. Grzimek, ed. New York: Van Nostrand Reinhold, 1972-present. Provides an overview of the animal kingdom, with illustrations.

Grzimek's Encyclopedia of Mammals. B. Grzimek, ed. New York: MacGraw-Hill, 1990. Provides general information on the study of mammals.

McGraw-Hill Encyclopedia of Energy. 2nd ed. New York: McGraw-Hill, 1980. Short articles about all fields of energy.

McGraw-Hill Encyclopedia of Environmental Science. 2nd ed. S. P. Parker, ed. New York: McGraw-Hill, 1980. Provides information on the earth's resources and how they have been used.

McGraw-Hill Encyclopedia of Science and Technology. 15 vols. 7th ed. New York: McGraw-Hill, 1992. Provides concise, current background information on scientific and technical topics; an excellent place to begin a science research project, since the articles are not written for specialists.

McGraw-Hill Yearbook of Science and Technology. New York: McGraw-Hill, annual. Updates the encyclopedia (listed above) every year. Consult the yearbook for the most recent developments in a particular field.

Van Nostrand's Scientific Encyclopedia. 7th ed. New York: Van Nostrand Reinhold, 1988. Provides concise background information on a variety of scientific disciplines.

VNR Concise Encyclopedia of Mathematics. W. Gellert et al., eds. New York: Van Nostrand Reinhold, 1989. Short articles on all areas of mathematics.

VNR Encyclopedia of Chemistry. 4th ed. D. M. Considine, ed. New York: Van Nostrand Reinhold, 1984. Short articles on all areas of chemistry.

Biographies

American Men and Women of Science. 16th ed. J. Cattell, ed. New York: Bowker, 1986. Provides information on living, active scientists in the fields of economics, sociology, political science, statistics, psychology, geography, and anthropology.

Dictionary of Scientific Biography. New York: Scribner's, 1970-1981. Provides information on scientists from classical to modern times. Covers only scientists who are no longer living.

National Academy of Sciences, Biographical Memoirs. Washington, D.C.: National Academy of Sciences, 1877-present. Provides information on American scientists.

Who's Who in Science in Europe. 5th ed. Detroit: Gale, 1984.

Indexes and Abstracts

AEROSPACE

Aerospace Medicine and Biology
*International Aerospace Abstracts
*Scientific and Technical Aerospace Reports
*U.S. Government Reports, Announcements and Index (NTIS)

AGRICULTURE

*Agricola
*Agricultural Engineering Abstracts
Agritrop
*Agronomy Abstracts
*Bibliography of Agriculture
*Biological and Agricultural Index

* = computer searching available

FAO Documentation, Government
    Documents Index
Farm and Garden Index
*Fertilizer Abstracts
*Field Crop Abstracts
*Herbage Abstracts
*Seed Abstracts
*Soils and Fertilizers
*World Agricultural Economics and
    Rural Sociology Abstracts

ANIMAL SCIENCE

*Animal Behavior Abstracts
*Animal Breeding Abstracts
Bibliography of Reproduction
*Dairy Science Abstracts
*Index Veterinarius
*Veterinary Bulletin

ASTRONOMY

*Astronomy and Astrophysics
    Abstracts
*Meteorological and Geoastrophysical
    Abstracts

BIOLOGY, BOTANY, ENTOMOLOGY, AND ZOOLOGY

Asher's Guide to Botanical
    Periodicals
*Biological Abstracts
*Biological and Agricultural Index
Botanical Abstracts
Biology Digest
Current Advances in Plant Science
*Entomology Abstracts
*Genetics Abstracts
*Horticultural Abstracts
International Abstracts of Biological
    Science
*Plant Breeding Abstracts
*Review of Applied Entomology
*Review of Medical and Veterinary
    Entomology
Review of Plant Pathology
*Soils and Fertilizers
Torrey Botanical Club Bulletin
*Virology Abstracts
*Weed Abstracts

*Zoological Record

CHEMISTRY

Analytical Abstracts
*Chemical Abstracts

COMPUTERS AND ROBOTICS

*Artificial Intelligence Abstracts
*CAD/CAM Abstracts Index
*Computer Abstracts
*Computer and Control Abstracts
Computing Reviews
Data Processing Digest
*Electrical and Electronic Abstracts
*Microcomputer Index
Robomatix Reporter

ENERGY AND PHYSICS

Energy Abstracts for Policy Analysis
*Energy Information Abstracts
*Energy Research Abstracts
INS Atomindex
Nuclear Science Abstracts
*Physics Abstracts

ENGINEERING

Agricultural Engineering Abstracts
Applied Mechanical Reviews
Civil Engineering Hydraulics
    Abstracts
*Electrical and Electronics Abstracts
*Engineering Index
International Aerospace Abstracts
*ISMEC Bulletin (mechanical
    engineering)

ENVIRONMENT AND ECOLOGY

Abstracts on Health Effects of Envi-
    ronmental Pollutants
Air Pollution Abstracts
Current Advances in Ecological
    Sciences
Ecological Abstracts
Ecology Abstracts
*Environment Abstracts
*Environment Index
Environment Information Access

*Environmental Periodicals Bibliography
*Pollution Abstracts
*Selected Water Resource Abstracts
*Water Resources Abstracts

FOOD SCIENCE AND NUTRITION

*Food Science and Technology Abstracts
*Foods Adlibra
*Nutrition Abstracts and Reviews
Nutrition Planning

FORESTRY

Fire Technology Abstracts
*Forestry Abstracts

GEOGRAPHY, GEOLOGY, AND MINING

*Bibliography and Index of Geology
*Bibliography of North American Geology
Current Geographical Publications
Deep Sea Research Part B
*GEO Abstracts
*Geographical Abstracts
Geophysical Abstracts
*Meteorological and Geoastrophysical Abstracts
*Oceanic Abstracts
Population Index

MATHEMATICS AND STATISTICS

*American Statistics Index
Current Mathematical Publications
Demographic Yearbook
*Mathematical Reviews
Statistical Abstract of the United States
Statistical Reference Index
Statistical Theory and Method Abstracts
Statistical Yearbook

MEDICINE, NURSING, AND ALLIED HEALTH FIELDS

AIDS Bibliography
*Ageline

Bibliography of Reproduction
*Cumulated Index Medicus
*Cumulative Index to Nursing and Allied Health Literature
Endocrinology Index
*International Nursing Index
*Medline Clinical Collection

MEDOC

*Physical Fitness/Sports Medicine
Virology Abstracts

SCIENCE—GENERAL

*Applied Science and Technology Index
Current Bibliographic Directory of the Arts and Sciences
*General Science Index
Index to Scientific and Technical Proceedings
*Science Citation Index

TEXTILES

Clothing and Textile Arts Index
Clothing Index
Textile Technology Digest
World Textile Abstracts

VETERINARY SCIENCE

*Index Veterinarius
*Veterinary Bulletin

WILDLIFE AND FISHERIES

*Aquatic Science and Fisheries Abstracts
Commerical Fisheries Abstracts
Fisheries Review
Marine Fisheries Abstracts
Ocean Abstracts
Sport Fishery Abstracts
Wildlife Abstracts
Wildlife Research
Wildlife Reviews
World Fisheries Abstracts

7
♦ ♦ ♦

Writing a Research Paper in Social Science

INTRODUCTION

The social sciences have as their goal the systematic study of human behavior and human societies. For this reason, it is particularly important for social science research to include primary research (for example, interviews, surveys, and questionnaires) in which field research is conducted and reported. You need to know in general how social scientists proceed when gathering information on a particular subject or issue, using both primary and secondary sources.

Social science researchers must have knowledge of current research being conducted by others in their field. That is why library work, using secondary sources, is also important. In the social science journals, researchers report their findings for scrutiny and replication by other researchers. As you become familiar with the tools used by social scientists to gain access to current research, several research principles and skills will be important to you. These skills include:

1. A familiarity with primary research techniques used by social scientists.
2. A familiarity with library research tools used by social scientists, including databases, bibliographies, and indexes.
3. The ability to synthesize and evaluate data and opinions from a variety of primary and secondary sources.
4. The ability to develop a thesis consistent with the evidence found in primary and secondary sources.

5. The ability to organize and write a paper that effectively presents and supports your thesis.
6. The ability to employ the formal conventions of research papers in the social sciences.

A GUIDE TO THE SOCIAL SCIENCE RESEARCH PROCESS

Your first task is to choose a topic or research problem to investigate. If you are taking a social science course such as psychology or sociology, your textbook is a good place to start looking for research ideas. Remember that the inquiry process generally begins with a perceived incongruity, problem, or question. Perhaps something you read in your textbook or in a popular magazine such as *Psychology Today* will raise a question in your mind, or perhaps a particular issue will seem interesting or intriguing to you. In any case, you need to find a topic that will hold your interest and attention, a topic on which you are willing to spend considerable time and energy. Kristen Shipman, whose research will serve as the model for this chapter, chose the topic of childhood schizophrenia because of a general interest in psychology and a particular interest in the impact of psychological problems on families.

Preparation

You need to gather the materials for your research, including a research notebook or index cards (if you plan to use them); then make a schedule that allows sufficient time for your research. Your interest in the topic will get you started, but you will still need to think about the problem you have posed for yourself and begin to propose ways to investigate it. For example, Kristen began with the topic of childhood schizophrenia and its effects on the family. She wanted to find out about the psychological condition of schizophrenia as it occurred in children. Kristen, a frequent computer user, decided to develop a computer research notebook rather than take notes on index cards or in a notebook. She set up a database file on a computer disk to serve as the repository for information collected during the research. Her first entries in the research notebook file were her topic idea and starting research questions. Then she outlined for herself a search strategy, as described in this chapter.

Developing a Search Strategy

Through her reading in an introductory psychology course, Kristen had formulated some general impressions about mental illness. Her library search proceeded from a general look at the psychological disorder schizophrenia to specific sources dealing with childhood schizophrenia. An outline of Kristen's search strategy is presented in the next paragraph (your particular search may differ somewhat from this outline but should begin with general reference sources and proceed to more specialized sources):

Kristen's Search Strategy

1. Encyclopedias, dictionaries, and textbooks for general background information including the *Encyclopedia of Psychology* and the *Encyclopedic Dictionary of Psychology.*
2. Library's computerized online catalog for a subject search on childhood schizophrenia, using headings from the LCSH.
3. A database search of WSOC, the social science database, in addition to print subject indexes for access to magazine and journal articles on childhood schizophrenia.
4. Abstracts of scholarly sources from *Psychological Abstracts* using PsychLit on CD-ROM.

To illustrate the use of a library search strategy in the social sciences, we will follow Kristen's research on childhood schizophrenia so that you may use it as a model for your own research.

✦ EXERCISE

Outline your own search strategy, beginning with general and working to specialized sources. You will also probably wish to proceed in reverse chronology, that is, beginning with the most recent sources and working your way back in time. Include any primary research (such as interviews or questionnaires) you might wish to use in your project. Draw up a research time schedule.

General Sources

Reading general information on your subject enables you to put it into context. It helps you focus your search and refine your starting questions. Reading specialized encyclopedias and dictionaries also helps you define what is considered common knowledge on your subject. Depending on your particular subject, you may be reading general encyclopedias, such as *Americana,* and specialized encyclopedias, such as *The Encyclopedia of Psychology.* The disciplinary sources commonly used in the social sciences are listed at the end of this chapter on pp. 277–280. It would be useful for you to review that section of the chapter now.

Kristen used the following general sources (among others), which she listed in her computer notebook file along with brief summaries of each background source:

Davidoff, L. Childhood psychosis. Encyclopedia of

Psychology, 1984 ed.

This source includes a list of the characteristics of childhood psychosis and discusses the signs of a schizophrenic child, which occur between the ages of thirty months to twelve years. The author provides lists of signs and symptoms, discusses varying causes, and outlines the treatments available for the schizophrenic patient, which differ from patient to patient and doctor to doctor.

Schizophrenia. The Encyclopedic Dictionary of

Psychology, 1983 ed.

This source provides an overview of schizophrenia. It states that schizophrenia can influence all aspects of the personality. Some of the symptoms are delusions, hallucinations, thought disorder, and disturbances of mood and behavior. Genetic predisposition seems to be the strongest contributing factor to the onset of schizophrenia. However, other factors such as social class, social deprivation, and migration also contribute. It is also evident that physical and social stresses may lead to the onset or relapse of the disease.

At the end of each general source, such as the encyclopedia articles previously mentioned, you will usually find a list of bibliographic sources. This reference list can be an important place to locate key sources and studies on your topic. List the promising references in your research notebook or computer file at the beginning of your working bibliography; they may lead you to valuable information. It is not necessary for you to look up each entry on your working bibliography at this time. In the specialized encyclopedia, Kristen found and listed the following references:

Wing, J. K. (1978). Schizophrenia: A new

synthesis. London: Academic Press.

American Psychiatric Association (1980).

Diagnostic and statistical manual III.

✦ EXERCISE

Find and read background sources relevant to your topic to obtain general information (see Chapter 2 [pp. 29–33] for a list of general sources and pp. 277–280 for a list of discipline-specific sources used in the social sciences).

Focusing Your Search

After you have read several general background sources about your subject, you are ready to define starting questions to help you focus your search. The questions must be realistic so that you are able to complete your research given the information and time available to you. These questions are critical to the success of your research paper. Make sure that they are neither trivial nor overly ambitious but allow you sufficient scope for research. As mentioned earlier, your interest in a topic is the impetus for your choice. Generally, as with most research, the starting questions are motivated by a problematical event or an incongruity you perceive about your topic. As you were reading the encyclopedias and general background sources, you may have noted some important idea or question that could serve as a focus for your research. There is no one right question, nor is there one right way to discover a question, but it should be something that interests and intrigues you, and it should be supportable by evidence you can discover in your research. And certainly, as you read, your thinking on a topic will evolve as well.

Kristen, for example, began with the question, "How does childhood schizophrenia differ from adult schizophrenia?" She wished to find out what caused it, what its symptoms were, and how it could be treated. But most of all, she was interested in the following question: "How does childhood schizophrenia affect the families of afflicted children?"

✦ EXERCISE

Define for yourself starting questions to guide your research. Use these questions as a place to begin—your research direction may change as you actually find and read your sources.

The Library Catalog

After finding and reading general background sources, Kristen decided to use the library online catalog next for a subject search. Using the LCSH list, Kristen discovered the terminology that would give her access to information from the catalog. Some of the headings included the following:

Schizophrenia in children
Child psychopathology
Psychoses in children

By typing each of these subject headings into the computerized catalog, Kristen was able to search the library's collection of books and government documents for relevant information. Among the books and documents located through the catalog were the following, which Kristen listed on her working bibliography:

Despert, J. (1968). <u>Schizophrenia in children</u>.

New York: Robert Brunner.

Goldfarb, W. (1961). <u>Childhood schizophrenia</u>.

Cambridge, MA: Harvard University Press.

Torrey, F. (1983). <u>Surviving schizophrenia</u>. New

York: Harper & Row.

✦ EXERCISE

Using your library's card catalog or computerized online catalog, locate relevant books and government documents. Be sure to check the LCSH for the appropriate subject headings for your topic.

Subject Indexes

Once you have gathered a substantial amount of information on your subject and noted several key references and authors, you are in a position to expand your working bibliography by gathering more-specialized information from magazine and journal articles. Providing access to such information is the principle function of the subject indexes.

The subject indexes, such as the *Social Sciences Index*, list articles published in a given year on a particular subject. These indexes may be available to you either online through a computer or in print.

An online subject search works much like the search of the online book catalog, that is, you type in the subject headings and the computer searches its database for magazine and journal articles indexed under that subject heading. Kristen found current magazine sources on her topic by using the online *Reader's Guide* database for a subject search. Be aware, though, that magazine sources may not be acceptable for scholarly topics in advanced courses. She used the same headings and subheadings found in the LCSH to search the database and found the following sources:

MacDonald, A. (1982, Winter). Schizophrenia: The

solitary nightmare. Highwire Magazine,

pp. 37-39.

Stephens, R. (1984, June). Adam: A child's

courageous battle against mental illness.

Family Circle, pp. 98-102.

When using the print indexes, you typically start with the most recent volume and work your way back, looking up your subject in several volumes of the index. Depending on the nature of your search, you may either be looking for very recent information in the index or for historical information from a particular time period. In the *Social Sciences Index*, Kristen found the following sources:

Allen, J. (1985). Development of schizophrenia.

Menninger Perspective, 2, 8-11.

Kulick, E. (1985). Treatment of schizophrenia.

Menninger Perspective, 2, 12-14.

For many searches in the social sciences, you will want to use the citation indexes. The most important citation index for the social sciences is the *Social Sciences Citation Index, 1972–present*. Since Kristen was more interested in general information on childhood schizophrenia than in specific research studies on the topic, she did not use the citation indexes. However, you may wish to consult the citation index for your own research.

The citation index is a comprehensive listing of citations to subsequent works. The key sources you have found listed in other works are the cited sources in the citation index. Typically, you will know the names of key researchers on your topic and the titles of their works after your thorough search of background materials. Now you can follow up on key researchers by searching each volume of the citation index for citations to those key sources that have appeared since the original source was published.

For example, a student who was researching the subject of anorexia nervosa knew that H. Bruch was a major researcher in the field because Bruch had written the summary article in one of the specialized encyclopedias and because Bruch's name was listed in the online catalog as the author of several books and studies on anorexia. For these reasons, the student could assume that Bruch's work would be a key source used by many other researchers interested in the same topic. Therefore, she looked up H. Bruch in the most recent volume of the *Social Sciences Citation Index*. In the citation volume of the index, she found Hilda Bruch listed as a cited source (meaning that other authors had used her work in subsequent research). Under Bruch's name were listed all the researchers who had used her work as a basis for their own (that is, the citing sources). Bruch is the *cited* source in Bruch, H. 73 EATING DISORDERS. The following are some of the *citing* sources:

Dietz, W. NUTR RES Vol 3, Pg 43, Yr 83
Garner, D. INT J EAT D Vol 2, Pg 18, Yr 83

Complete information on each of these citing sources can be found in the companion source volume of the citation index. It may take you some time to become familiar with how the citation indexes work, but it will be well worth the effort. These indexes are a major tool for forward searching in the social sciences, that is, reaching from a known source published on a particular date to unknown related sources that subsequently use and cite that work.

✦ EXERCISE

Use subject and citation indexes to find titles of magazine and journal articles related to your topic (see pp. 279–280 for a list by discipline of indexes used in the social sciences).

Abstracts

In addition to subject indexes, abstracts are a useful tool for locating and sorting journal articles; like subject indexes, abstracts may be available to you either in print or online. The abstracts take indexing a step further by providing you with a brief summary (abstract) of the source listed. The abstract can help you decide whether the source is really relevant to your research. However, you should be aware that abstracts are typically more selective rather than comprehensive and, therefore, may not list as many articles as the indexes do.

Kristen used *Psychological Abstracts*, available to her through a CD-ROM database called PsychLit, to locate and read about more scholarly journal articles on childhood schizophrenia. Searching the database by subject, Kristen found the following source:

> History of developmental disorder, prevalence rate of childhood schizophrenia, 2–12 yr olds

The computer listed for Kristen the complete article citation information as well as an abstract that summarized the article's contents. She found that the article, published in the *Journal of the American Academy of Child and Adolescent Psychiatry,* recounted a study of children in North Dakota to determine the prevalence of childhood schizophrenia in the state. After reading the abstract, Kristen determined that the article was not relevant to her search.

✦ EXERCISE

Use abstracts to locate new articles or to read about articles you have already listed on your working bibliography. Note any promising sources on your working bibliography. (Abstracts are listed by discipline area with indexes at the end of this chapter on pp. 279–280.)

Primary Research

As a last step in your research, you may wish to conduct some primary research to reinforce the information gathered in your library search. (Primary research projects are discussed in detail in Chapter 4.) Some possible primary research projects might include interviews, observations, case studies, or questionnaires, depending on the nature of your research topic.

✦ EXERCISE

Conduct any primary research connected to your research project. Analyze your results and determine the best method of displaying them, whether in a graph, table, or discussion section in your paper.

Evaluation

It is important that you read and evaluate carefully each source located in your library search. (See Chapter 3, pp. 80–81 for some evaluation suggestions.) It is not unusual for a book or article with a promising title to turn out to be something totally different from what you expected to find. You must continually sort through sources and discard any that are not relevant or useful to your search. If, after an initial screening, a book still looks useful, check it out at the circulation desk. In the case of articles, either photocopy them for later use or take notes from them in the library, since they generally are noncirculating materials and cannot be checked out. If your library does not carry a source you are interested in, ask the circulation librarian about the possibility of an interlibrary loan.

✦ EXERCISE

In your research notebook, evaluate each article and book to be used in your research paper. Follow the source evaluation guidelines in Chapter 3 on pages 80–81.

Taking Notes

As you begin to take notes on the sources, remember to record complete bibliographic information so that you will not need to look up a particular source again.

If you are taking notes in your research notebook, identify each source carefully. Put into quotation marks any information taken directly from the source and write down the exact page number on which the note was found at the end of the note itself. Also identify paraphrased or quoted material. Taking care at this stage is beneficial when you reach the actual writing stage of your research paper.

If you are using notecards, make a bibliography card for each source on your working bibliography that you locate in the library. On the bibliography card, write the complete library call number in the upper left-hand corner and the control number of the source in the upper right-hand corner. Enter complete bibliographical information on the card: author, title, and publication data (see Documentation in the Social Sciences, in this chapter, for examples of social science citations). Write the corresponding control number in the upper right-hand corner of the card and title the card.

Illumination

Since you are actively seeking the answer to the starting question you posed at the beginning of your search, continually "talk to yourself" while researching. Try to understand and interpret the source information as you go, synthesizing data from numerous authors and sources, taking what is relevant and discarding what is not. This is where your research notebook can be of particular value to you. Take the time to write down your own thoughts and comments as you go; note for yourself those sources and ideas that you find particularly important or revealing. Think about your topic consciously but also allow yourself enough time to let your ideas brew in your subconscious mind. It is during this stage in your research that you are seeking the answer to your starting question. Gradually, you arrive at a tentative answer, a hypothesis or thesis that satisfactorily explains the question's answer as you see it. Or you may modify or completely change the hypothesis or thesis in light of what you ultimately find in your research.

This is the illumination stage of the inquiry process, wherein you begin to "see the light," that is, the answer to your question. Perhaps your answer is that there is no definitive answer, and that would be all right too. In such a case, you would provide the most likely hypotheses and argue the relative merits of each. At any rate, you would present your understanding of the subject in a thesis statement that explained the data you gathered. In your thesis, then, state your opinion, articulating what you believe based on the evidence you have gathered.

For example, Kristen first asked a question; then, through preparation and research, she came to a better understanding of her topic, stated in the form of a thesis statement:

> *Starting question:* How does childhood schizophrenia affect the families of afflicted children?
>
> *Thesis statement:* Childhood schizophrenia is not only frightening to the children, but also may be devastating emotionally, socially, and financially to their families.

✦ EXERCISE

Write a thesis statement that articulates the tentative conclusion you have reached through your research. In your thesis, state your preliminary answer to the starting question posed at the beginning of your research. But, keep an open mind; you may find that as you actually begin drafting your paper, you may arrive at new insights.

Verification

Once you have defined a thesis statement for yourself, you will have a place to begin your actual written presentation of the research. As you write, however, you may find that the thesis statement needs to be revised in some way. The actual writing of the research paper may help you see things in new ways or discover meanings you had not thought of before you began writing. Actually writing down your ideas in a systematic fashion is an important way of verifying the research you have done. As you try to articulate in writing the understanding you have gained of your topic, you may find that there are gaps in your knowledge that you need to fill by further research, or you may find that the thesis you have articulated really does not seem to explain the research findings adequately. In either case, you need to go back to both your primary and secondary sources for further information and more thought. On the other hand, you may find that your writing has clarified your ideas, thereby verifying them both for you and your potential readers.

ORGANIZING AND WRITING THE SOCIAL SCIENCE RESEARCH PAPER

When thinking through her rhetorical situation for this research paper (purpose, persona, audience, subject matter; see pages 137–140), Kristen decided that she wanted to be largely informative to a general audience, helping the reader to come to a better understanding of the causes and treatments of childhood schizophrenia. She also wanted to include a discussion of the effects of this devastating disease on both the child and the family.

Her thesis statement helped her to articulate her intentions in the paper and, at the same time, implied an organizational plan: the causes and treatments for childhood schizophrenia followed by a discussion of its effects on both the child and the family.

Other possible organizational plans that may have been suggested, depending on your own intentions as a writer:

chronological: ("Historically, treatment of childhood schizophrenics has varied from institutionalization to family therapy")

comparison and contrast: ("Childhood schizophrenia is different from other childhood psychoses in its severity and response to treatment")

process ("The disorder childhood schizophrenia progresses from a mild behavior disturbance in early childhood to a full-blown psychosis in adulthood")

example ("Mental illness strikes children as well as adults. Some examples of childhood mental illness are autism and childhood schizophrenia")

These are only examples of the possible organizational plans that you might wish to use. It is important that you pay attention to planning at this stage in your project or the extensive materials you have gathered may seem overwhelming. It is your job to make order out of the chaos.

Organizing Your Materials

Sort your notecards or organize your research notebook by related topic areas. Group information on topics together. You may wish to write brief summaries of information found in your notebook to help you understand the ideas contained in each source. Using the thesis as a guide, you are now arranging information into a logical order. The actual sorting process you use depends on the project itself. However, the main idea is to group and categorize your information.

Since Kristen had saved all her notebook information in a computer file on disk, it was a relatively easy matter for her to block related information and to move it, using her word processing block move command, to the appropriate section in the paper. (Before manipulating your notebook in this way, be sure to make a backup file.)

Planning and Outlining

Now you are ready to plan and outline your research paper. Your thesis statement may help you to come up with main headings for your outline. The subpoints on your outline are the supporting points that you wish to discuss in your paper. Look through the categories you have used to sort your notes. These may make good outline headings. Carefully think through the main points you wish to cover in your paper. Consider the needs of your readers and their expectations when deciding what information to include in your paper.

Do not be overly concerned about formal outline structure. An outline should be a guide to planning and not a constraint that confines and limits your thinking. However, an informal outline is an important organizational device that can help you to construct a logically developed, unified, and coherent research paper. Your own outline will be based on the material you have discovered in your library search and in your primary research. It will describe in an organized way all the material you wish to include in your paper.

Many writers go back and forth between their outlines and their actual papers, thus in effect revising and refining their outlines as they write. Others prefer to have fairly comprehensive outlines before beginning to write. Kristen wrote the following informal outline when she was actually writing the paper. The form of the outline changed several times as she wrote and thought about the paper.

Informal Outline
I. Introduction
II. Description and Definition of Schizophrenia
  A. Definition and diagnosis of childhood schizophrenia
  B. Symptoms
  C. Study comparing schizophrenic and normal children
  D. Case study of Adam
III. Development and Treatment
  A. Key factors in the development of schizophrenia
    1. Biochemical abnormality
    2. Early disabilities in adapting
    3. Family difficulties
    4. Drug use
    5. Maladaptive personality
    6. Shattering of self-esteem
  B. The first stage of treatment
    1. Patient realizes disease
    2. Outcomes
  C. Goals of treatment
  D. Treatments available
IV. Schizophrenia and the family
  A. Blame, anger, depression
  B. Financial burden
V. Conclusion

✦ EXERCISE

Think through your rhetorical situation: Who is the audience for your paper and what do you wish them to learn by reading it? Arrange your source material, decide on a preliminary organizational plan, and construct an outline to guide your writing of the first draft of your research paper. Refer to Chapter 5 for help with organization pp. 140–144.

Writing the First Draft

After you have completed your informal outline, you are ready to write the first draft of your research paper. Remember, your objective is to present to your readers the answer you have discovered to the starting question. Remind yourself at this time of the question that initially motivated your search. When writing your first draft, use concrete and simple language to explain your thesis and the supporting evidence you gathered in your research as objectively as you can. Your thesis statement and your outline will guide the writing of this first draft. You should remain flexible as you write and be open to any fresh insights you may have along the way.

As you are writing the first draft, it is important to make a note of which material comes from which sources. Do not be concerned at this point about the formal details of documentation; you can deal with that later. But do mark for yourself in the draft any ideas or words taken from your sources. Place any word or words you copy from a source in quotation marks, and after the quote write down the last name and the date of publication of the source and the page number of the quoted material (in parentheses). For example,

> "First, there are a wide range of outcomes, all the way from excellent to poor. Second, recovery, like the illness itself, has many facets" (Allen, 1985, p. 11).

Similarly, document paraphrases and restatements of ideas taken from a source even though you have recast them in your own words:

> The children may also become confused by their surrounding environment (Davidoff, 1984, p. 204).

However, you need not document common knowledge (see pp. 147–148). That is, if three or more general sources (such as encyclopedias) agree on a certain idea, it is probably in the domain of common knowledge: anyone familiar with the topic would accept or agree to the idea, and so it does not need to be attributed to any one author.

When you are not quoting or paraphrasing from a specific page in a source, it is sufficient to include simply the author's name (or names, where there is more than one author) and the publication date:

> Noshpitz's work was written to help us better understand childhood schizophrenia (Noshpitz, 1979).

When you are quoting an author referred to by the source you have read, you need to acknowledge that original author in your own text. For example, if Johnson's study is referred to and discussed in Bruch, in the text you should say:

Johnson's study (cited in Bruch, 1973,

p. 89) shows that . . .

[Only Bruch needs to appear on your references page.]

For general information on planning, writing, and revising your social science research paper, refer to Chapter 5. Use the following information on documentation in the social sciences to make your citations. The model paper below illustrates the writing and documentation styles commonly used in the social sciences.

MANUSCRIPT PREPARATION (APA STYLE)

The *Publication Manual of the American Psychological Association* describes in great detail the types of articles typically written in the social sciences and the manuscript format of those articles. The major parts of a manuscript are the title page, abstract, introduction, body, references page, and appendix. I will briefly describe each section here, but please refer to the APA manual for a more detailed discussion. The sample paper beginning on p. 257 follows the APA style for manuscript preparation, so you may use it as a model for your own paper.

Title Page

Write a title that summarizes the main idea of the paper as simply (yet as completely) as you can. Do not use a clever or cute title, but rather, summarize the main idea of your paper in an informative title that could stand alone. Kristen's title "Childhood Schizophrenia: A Family Problem" sums up quite well the main idea of her paper. You will also need to compress your title into a manuscript page header, usually the first two or three words of your title, that will serve to identify each page of your paper. Identify the title page with the manuscript page header and page number 1 in the upper right-hand corner of the page.

The title page should also present identifying information on the author (called the byline) and the course (when the paper is submitted as part of a course requirement). The title, author information, and course information should be centered on the page and evenly spaced. A running head should be listed at the top of the title page, flush left in all capital letters, one line below the manuscript page header and page number (see Kristen's title page on p. 257).

Abstract

The second page of your paper will include an abstract that briefly summarizes the essential content (about 100 words long). The APA manual points out that an abstract should be accurate, self-contained, concise and specific, nonevaluative, coherent, and readable. By reading your abstract, the reader should get a clear sense of the information covered by your paper. The abstract is typed in a one-paragraph block on its own page with no paragraph indentations (see Kristen's abstract on p. 258).

Text

Begin typing the text of your paper on a new page. Type the title, centered, in lower- and upper-case letters. Double space after the title. The text of your research paper begins on page 3 (which is listed along with the manuscript page header in the upper right-hand corner).

Introduction

The text of your paper should open with an introduction that makes a commitment to the reader about what is to come in the paper. A good introduction should lead the reader into the paper and usually concludes with your thesis statement. There is no need to label the introduction; just begin it immediately after your title.

Body

The body of your paper should flow logically and follow the organization set up by your outline. You may wish to divide your paper visually by using headings and subheadings. Such headings can help your reader to visually ascertain the importance of topics within your paper and their relationship to other topics covered. Your headings function much as an outline would, that is, they provide your reader with a sense of your paper's organizational structure.

The APA manual describes five levels of headings and subheadings. However, they suggest using just one or two levels for short papers such as your research paper. For one level of headings, center your headings in the middle of the page (double spaced above and below), using lower- and uppercase letters. For two levels of headings, use the centered headings (lower- and uppercase) for the main headings and use side headings (flush with the left margin), underlined, for the sub-headings:

Research Methods   *Main heading*

Procedures   *Subheading*

See the sample student paper beginning on p. 257 for an example of using one level of headings.

References Page

The references page is a listing of all the articles and books you refer to in the body of your paper. Your reference to source information in your paper helps support your own ideas and conclusions by relating them to other authors' ideas and conclusions. Each author you cite in the text of your paper (in-text citations) must appear on your reference list; similarly, each reference on your list must be cited in your text at some point. That is, do not list any sources you used for background reading but did not cite in the paper itself. These sources will be listed on your working bibliography, however, so your teacher will know the extent and breadth of your reading on the topic.

The reference list begins on a new page. Type the word References in upper- and lower-case letters, centered at the top of the page. Double space the entire references page.

The APA format for references on the references page is provided in the section on Documentation in Social Science. If you have a source that is not modeled shown there, refer to the APA manual for the appropriate style.

Appendix

Sometimes additional information is included in an appendix to a paper. If you have conducted some primary research in connection with your project, the data you collected may be presented in an appendix, for example. However, you should include an appendix only if it will help your reader understand or evaluate something that you have discussed or presented in your paper.

DOCUMENTATION IN SOCIAL SCIENCE: THE AUTHOR/DATE STYLE (APA)

In the social sciences, the author/date method of documentation is standard. This format is outlined in *The Publication Manual of the American Psychological Association*, 4th ed., Washington, D.C.: American Psychological Association, 1994. The citations are included in the text and thus help the reader identify authorities and the dates of the research immediately. This form of documentation is particularly useful when you are citing books and articles but are not quoting or paraphrasing from them.

Internal Citation

At the appropriate place in the text, you will give the author's name, followed by a comma, a space, and the year of publication:

> The therapist's goals sometimes cannot be
> reached because of the complex and diverse wants
> and needs of the child and his family (Allen,
> 1985).

As an alternative that prevents monotony and improves readability, you can give the author's name in the text occasionally, supplying only the year in parentheses:

> As Allen (1985) points out, the therapist's
> goals may conflict with the needs and wants of
> the patient and his family.

When continuing to cite the same study within a paragraph, it is not necessary to keep repeating the date, as long as there are no other studies by authors with the same name with which it could be confused:

> In a study on childhood schizophrenia, Smith
> (1988) found . . . Smith also describes . . .

For paraphrases and direct quotations, follow the date with a page number:

> "Recovery, like the illness itself, has many
> facets" (Allen, 1985, p. 11).

If your source has two authors, list the surnames of both authors:

> Schizophrenic patients are often children of
> high intelligence (Woodman & Groen, 1987,
> chap. 3).

If your source has more than two authors, list all authors the first time a reference occurs; in subsequent citations, use the first author's name with "et al." (abbreviation for Latin et alii, "and others"):

First citation:

(Garfinkle, Garner, Schwartz, & Thompson, 1980)

Subsequent citation:

(Garfinkle et al., 1980)

If there is no author's name, use either the title or an abbreviated form of the title. Place the title in quotation marks. Use underline for the title of a periodical, book, brochure, or report:

> ("Schizophrenia in children," 1981)
>
> <u>College Bound Seniors</u> (1979)

If you have two articles with the same title, list the source as well to distinguish them:

> ("Schizophrenia," <u>The Encyclopedic</u>
> <u>Dictionary of Psychology</u>, 1983)
>
> ("Schizophrenia," <u>The Encyclopedia of</u>
> <u>Psychology</u>, 1984).

If you have two authors with the same last name, use first initials:

> (M. Woodman, 1979) . . . (J. Woodman, 1981)

If you have two or more works by the same author published in the same year, identify them on the reference list with lowercase letters in parentheses: (a), (b). In the text, use the following format:

```
(Bruch, 1973a) . . . (Bruch, 1973b)
```

If you wish to cite several articles within the same parentheses, arrange the authors' names alphabetically and use a semicolon to separate the entries:

```
Several studies (Bruce, 1980; Garfinkle et

al., 1980; Woodman & Groen, 1987) show the

effects of childhood schizophrenia on the family.
```

For personal correspondence, letters, memos, lecture notes, e-mail, electronic bulletin boards, and so on, list only in the text itself, but not on the references page. Provide initials, surname of correspondent, plus the type of correspondence and date.

```
H. J. Miller (letter to author, April, 1979)
```

The Reference List in APA Style

The reference list, at the end of the research paper, contains all the sources actually used in the paper. When you use this documentation style, it is titled "References" or "Works Cited." The purpose of the reference list is to help readers find the materials you used in writing your paper. You must give complete and accurate information so that others may find the works. The following principles are generally accepted in documenting social science works, although many social science journals and fields have their own particular method of documenting. These guidelines have been adopted by the American Psychological Association (APA) in their style manual:

1. Present the author's surname and initials, followed by the date (in parentheses), the title, and the publication information.
2. The publication information required is place and name of publisher and date for books; date, volume and issue number, and page numbers for articles.
3. Place periods after the three main divisions: author, title, and publication information. Within these divisions, use commas to separate information.

4. Use capital letters for the first word only of a book or article title or following a colon in a subtitle. [For names of journals, capitalize all first letters.]
5. Underline titles of books, journals, magazines, and newspapers. Also underline volume numbers in journal references to indicate italics.

The accompanying model references and the term paper that follows both use the APA documentation format (and a few of the models) as found in the 1994 edition of *The Publication Manual of the American Psychological Association*. For additional examples and further information on documentation in the social sciences, consult the APA manual.

MODEL REFERENCES: SOCIAL SCIENCE (APA)

Type of Reference

BOOKS

1. One author

   Torrey, F. (1983). <u>Surviving schizophrenia</u>. New

   York: Harper & Row.

2. Two or more authors

   Minuchin, S., Rosman, B., & Baker, L. (1978).

   <u>Psychosomatic families: Anorexia nervosa in</u>

   <u>context</u>. Cambridge, MA: Harvard University

   Press.

3. Two or more books by the same author

   Bruch, H. (1973). <u>Eating disorders: Obesity,</u>

   <u>anorexia nervosa, and the person within</u>. New

   York: Basic Books.

   Bruch, H. (1978). <u>The golden cage: The enigma of</u>

   <u>anorexia nervosa</u>. Cambridge, MA: Harvard

   University Press.

[Note: References are in chronological order.]

4. Book with editor(s)

Hartman, F. (Ed.). (1973). <u>World in crisis</u>:

    <u>Readings in international relations</u> (4th

    ed.). New York: Macmillan.

5. Essay, chapter, or section of an edited work

Cherns, A. (1982). Social research and its

    diffusion. In B. Appleby (Ed.), <u>Papers on</u>

    <u>social science utilisation</u> (pp. 316–326).

    Loughborough University of Technology:

    Centre for Utilisation of Social Science

    Research.

6. Encyclopedia entry

(signed)

Davidoff, L. (1984). Childhood psychosis. In the

    <u>Encyclopedia of psychology</u> (Vol. 10,

    pp. 156–157). New York: J. Wiley & Sons.

(unsigned)

Schizophrenia. (1983). In <u>The encyclopedic</u>

    <u>dictionary of psychology</u> (Vol. 8,

    pp. 501–502). Cambridge, MA: MIT Press.

7. Corporate author

American Psychiatric Association. (1980).

    <u>Diagnostic and statistical manual of mental</u>

    <u>disorders</u> (3d ed.). Washington, DC: Author.

[Note: The word *Author* here indicates that the author and publisher are the same.]

ARTICLES

1. Journal article (one author)

    Allen, J. (1985). Development of schizophrenia.
    <u>Menninger Perspective</u>, <u>2</u>, 8–11.

2. Journal article (two authors)

    Steinhausen, H., & Glenville, K. (1983). Follow-
    up studies of anorexia nervosa: A review of
    research findings. <u>Psychological Medicine</u>,
    <u>13</u>(2), 239–245.

3. Journal article (several authors)

    Garfinkle, P., Garner, D., Schwartz, D., &
    Thompson, M. (1980). Cultural expectations
    of thinness in women. <u>Psychological Reports</u>,
    <u>13</u>, 483–491.

4. Magazine article (discontinuous pages, monthly)

    Miller, G. (1969, December). On turning
    psychology over to the unwashed. <u>Psychology
    Today</u>, pp. 53–54, 66–74.

5. Magazine article (no known author, weekly)

    The blood business. (1972, September 7). <u>Time</u>,
    pp. 47–48.

6. Newspaper article

    Eight APA journals initiate controversial blind
    reviewing. (1972, June). <u>APA Monitor</u>, p. 1.

7. Newspaper article (discontinuous pages)

    Lublin, J. S. (1980, December 5). On idle: The
    unemployed shun much mundane work, at least
    for awhile. <u>The Wall Street Journal</u>,
    pp. A1, A25.

TECHNICAL REPORTS

1. Individual author

Gottfredson, L. S. (1980). How valid are occupational reinforcer pattern scores? (Report No. CSOS-R-292). Baltimore, MD: Johns Hopkins University, Center for Social Organization of Schools (ERIC Document Reproduction Service No. ED 182 465).

2. Corporate author

Life Insurance Marketing and Research Association. (1978). Profit and the AIB in United States ordinary companies (Research Rep. No. 1978-6). Hartford, CT: Author.

3. Government document

National Institute of Mental Health. (1982). Television and behavior: Ten years of scientific progress and implications in the eighties (DHHS Publication No. ADM 821195). Washington, DC: U.S. Government Printing Office.

OTHER SOURCES

1. Film or videotape

Maas, J. B. (Producer), & Gluck, D. H. (Director). (1979). Deeper into hypnosis [Film]. Englewood Cliffs, NJ: Prentice-Hall.

2. Abstracted or unpublished dissertation or thesis (in Dissertation Abstracts)

Foster-Havercamp, M. E. (1982). An analysis of the relationship between preservice teacher training and directed teacher performance

(Doctoral dissertation, University of
Chicago, 1981). <u>Dissertation Abstracts
International</u>, <u>42</u>, 4409A.

Pendar, J. E. (1982). Undergraduate psychology
majors: Factors influencing decision about
college, curriculum and career. <u>Dissertation
Abstracts International</u>, <u>42</u>, 4370A-4371A.
(University Microfilms No. 82-06, 181)

3. Unpublished manuscript

Cameron, S. E. (1981). <u>Educational level as a
predictor of success</u>. Unpublished
manuscript.

[Note: You can cite university affiliation for such works.]

Unpublished data

Locke, C. (1983). [Survey of college women at
Texas Tech University]. Unpublished raw
data.

4. Review of book or film

Carmody, T. P. (1982). A new look at medicine
from the social perspective [Review of film
<u>Social contexts of health, illness, and
patient care</u>]. <u>Contemporary Psychology</u>, <u>27</u>,
208-209.

5. Interview
(published)

Newman, P. (1982, January). [Interview with
William Epstein, editor of <u>JEP: Human
Perception and Performance</u>]. <u>APA Monitor</u>,
pp. 7, 39.

(unpublished)

Hult, C. (1984, March). [Interview with Dr. Lauro
    Cavazos, President, Texas Tech University].

6. Personal correspondence
Do not list on reference page. See in-text citation in sample on
p. 249.

7. Paper presented at conference

Brewer, J. (1979, October). <u>Energy, information,</u>
    <u>and the control of heart rate</u>. Paper
    presented at the Society for
    Psychophysiological Research, Cincinnati,
    OH.

8. Television program

Miller, R. (Producer). (1982, May 21). <u>Problems</u>
    <u>of freedom</u>. New York: NBC-TV.

9. Electronic information:
Online abstract:

Meyer, A. S., & Boch, K. (1992). The tip-of-the-
    tongue phenomenon: Blocking or partial
    activation? [Online]. <u>Memory & Cognition</u>,
    <u>20</u>, 715–716. Abstract from: DIALOG File:
    PsychINFO Item: 80–16351

CD-ROM abstract:

Meyer, A. S., & Boch, K. (1992). The tip-of-the-
    tongue phenomenon: Blocking or partial
    activation? [CD-ROM]. <u>Memory & Cognition</u>,
    <u>20</u>, 715–716. Abstract from: SilverPlatter
    File: PsychLIT Item: 80–16351

Online journal article:

Herz, J. C. (1995, April). Surfing on the
    internet: A nethead's adventures online.

```
[Online serial]. Urban Desires, 1.3.

Available Internet: www/desires.com/ud.html.
```

Electronic Correspondence, such as e-mail messages and conversations via bulletin boards and electronic discussion groups are typically cited as personal communication in the text. In-text information to include:

author, date, subject of message;
name of the listserv, bulletin board, or e-mail discussion group available from: e-mail address.

[See also Li, X., & Crane, N. B. (1993). <u>A guide to citing electronic information</u>. Westport: Meckler.]

EXERCISES AND RESEARCH PROJECT

Follow the procedures outlined in this chapter to research a limited social science topic and write a social science research paper. The four exercises that follow give you additional practice in skills associated with research projects.

1. For each entry on your research paper bibliography, write a three- or four-sentence annotation describing the contents of that source.

2. Write a "review of the literature" report that summarizes in three to four pages the major ideas found in your sources. Often, a literature review, which lists and comments on the works done to date in a particular area, will be a component of a larger social science paper.

3. Write a report that details a primary research project and summarizes your findings. Use tables or graphs where possible to illustrate your results.

4. After you have completed your research paper, write an abstract of about 100 words that succinctly summarizes what your paper is about. An abstract should accurately reflect the scope and organization of your paper.

SAMPLE RESEARCH PAPER: SOCIAL SCIENCE FORMAT (APA)

Childhood Schizophrenia: A Family Problem

Kristen Shipman

Utah State University

Psychology 201-15

Professor John Nash

May 18, 1989

Childhood Schizophrenia 2

Abstract

Childhood schizophrenia, a mental disorder characterized by the falling away of the processes of reasoning and thought, is one of the most common forms of mental illness. Its origin has been linked to biochemical abnormalities in afflicted individuals. However, although the link is inherited, the disease does not always emerge but rather seems to be triggered in susceptible individuals by life stresses. The treatments for childhood schizophrenia vary from drug therapy to family therapy and psychotherapy. Childhood schizophrenia is not only frightening to the children it afflicts but also may be devastating emotionally, socially, and financially to the families of these children.

Childhood Schizophrenia 3

Childhood Schizophrenia: A Family Problem

In our society today we are becoming
more concerned about mental health and
mental disease. As new findings arise, we
become more aware of the facts concerning
mental illness and are able to dispel
many of the myths and misconceptions surrounding mental disorders. To add to this
awareness we must first understand mental
health. Good mental health is defined as
"the ability to keep it all together, or
to maintain one's balance in the face of
life's myriad challenges" (Allen, 1985,
p. 8). It is normal and quite healthy to
feel stress, anxiety, and anger. These
feelings need to be expressed and dealt
with in order to develop a healthy mental
outlook. However, the inability to
respond to problems and to grow from them
is very often associated with severe mental disorders such as schizophrenia.

Nearly one percent of the people in
the world today are fighting the frightening, and often misunderstood, disease
of schizophrenia. Schizophrenia is one of

the most common forms of mental illness
and yet one with many unanswered questions (MacDonald, 1982, p. 37). This
disease comes in many forms—all with
varying characteristics. One of these
forms that has recently been diagnosed is
childhood schizophrenia (Despert, 1968,
p. 1). This horrifying disease is not
only frightening to the children but is
also devastating emotionally, socially,
and financially to the families of these
children.

Description and Definition of Childhood Schizophrenia

Childhood schizophrenia is a mental
disorder that is characterized by the
falling away of the processes of reasoning and thought. The schizophrenic speaks
in irrational sentences or word clumps
that are confusing to a listener but completely coherent to the schizophrenic.
Thus, a child cannot be diagnosed for the
disease until his speech has developed
sufficiently for him to speak in three-
or four-word sentences (Noshpitz, 1979,

Childhood Schizophrenia 5

p. 15). This disease affects every aspect
of the child's personality ("Schizophrenia," *The Encyclopedic Dictionary of
Psychology*, 1983). He becomes socially
withdrawn, has trouble making friends,
and may experience auditory hallucinations, which may cause fantasizing with
paranoid thinking. Although the schizophrenic child may throw tantrums, he is
not always violent or hostile (Stephens,
1984).

The symptoms of a schizophrenic
child may not appear until 30 months to
12 years of age. It is in between this
time that caregivers notice the symptoms
of repetitive behavior, language difficulties, inability of the child to focus
his attention, and poor coordination and
balance skills. The child may also become
confused by his surrounding environment
(Davidoff, 1984, p. 204).

A study was undertaken to compare
schizophrenic and normal children in the
areas of physical development and behavior. The research found no difference in
physical characteristics between the two
groups but large differences in behavior.

Childhood Schizophrenia 6

Schizophrenic children scored far lower
in abstract and conceptual abilities, and
their speech was impaired by their confusion over time, space, person, and their
own bodies. This all leads to the children's inability to conceptualize their
personal identities (Goldfarb, 1961,
p. 118).

In an article by Reney Stephens
(1984), the true story is told of a young
child and his family battling the child's
schizophrenia. The child, Adam, a
healthy, full-term baby, was born into a
partially disrupted family. His mother
was very loving and caring, but his
father was a self-centered alcoholic who
resented his son.

The first sign of trouble started at
age two when Adam became overly active.
He couldn't sit still and ran instead of
walked everywhere he went. Much of his
behavior was repetitive and monotonous.
When his mother became pregnant with
another child, Adam became demanding and
dominated much of her time. Adam's mother
felt guilty that whatever Adam's problem

Childhood Schizophrenia 7

was, it was being exaggerated by her
pregnancy. There was also another side of
Adam. Around adults he was pleasant and
content. He would sing and dance for the
adults and they all loved him, but around
children he was withdrawn. The teachers
at school found him to be above average
in intelligence, but he was unable to
make friends. He would play near the
other children for a while, then frighten
them away with a sudden screaming fit or
a physical attack.

After the baby was born, Adam became
more demanding, more active, and more
hostile. When around the baby, Adam would
treat her kindly one minute and with hos-
tility the next. The family was scared
and did not know how to control their
son. After several consultations with
different doctors, one doctor found Adam
to be schizophrenic. The doctor suggested
the family admit Adam to the hospital for
around-the-clock care. The family struggled with the decision and finally, with
much reluctance, chose to admit him. At
the hospital, Adam was treated without

the use of medication. Using a combination of structured activity and
one-on-one play therapy, the therapists
were able to bring Adam back to the real
world. After one year of treatment, Adam
was finally gaining better control of
himself and learning to express anger in
a more appropriate manner. In 1984, two
years after the beginning of treatment,
Adam was still in the hospital. The family was encouraged by the progress of
their son and felt, because of his
tremendous courage and fighting quality,
that he had a chance of recovery
(Stephens, 1984, pp. 98-101).

Development and Treatment of
Childhood Schizophrenia

The development of schizophrenia is
both complex and diverse. Dr. Jon Allen,
a staff psychologist for the Menninger
Foundation, lists the basic factors that
contribute to the development of severe
schizophrenia (Allen, 1985). Many of
these factors are combined in varying
degrees in each individual patient.

Childhood Schizophrenia 9

One of the clearest factors in the development of schizophrenia is a bio-chemical abnormality that seems to have a genetic link. Although this link is inherited, one only has a potential to develop the disease, and it may not emerge unless the stresses of life are too much for the individual to cope with.

Early disabilities in adapting and family difficulties are also factors that may contribute to this disorder. The inability of both the parents and the young child to respond in an appropriate manner to one another's needs may result in poor caretaking. This early caretaking is what forms the basis for later development, and without it, the child doesn't learn early coping skills. Family difficulties such as marital problems or poor parenting abilities also influence the development of the susceptible child and can possibly lead to the development of schizophrenia.

Another factor pointed out by Dr. Allen is the prominent use of drugs in our culture today. Drug abuse can be frightening for anyone, but for an indi-

vidual with a genetic link to schizophrenia, the effects of drug use may
trigger the disorder.

A combination of factors seem to
intertwine to bring on the most severe
developmental schizophrenic symptoms:
maladaptive personality, shattering of
self-esteem, and the loss of reality. The
potential schizophrenic may develop a
protective wall that won't allow him to
learn and grow from the realities of
life, thus producing a maladaptive personality. This personality prevents the
individual from coping with separation or
loss and the trials of reality. From this
inability, the individual feels a complete shattering of self esteem. In an
attempt to adjust to the stresses of his
life, the schizophrenic blames his failures on external factors instead of taking the responsibility for his own
actions. A vicious cycle is created for
the patient, who does not gain the ability to conquer obstacles and becomes more
inept at dealing with reality.

At some point during the course of
the disease, the schizophrenic or his

Childhood Schizophrenia 11

family recognizes that he has a serious
problem. It is at this stage that treatment is most critical, because the
therapist must challenge the patient to
face the horrifying realities of the disease. This step takes considerable
courage and determination on the part of
the patient and his family. Once the
patient has received treatment, his
recovery is uncertain for two major reasons, as pointed out by Allen (1985):
"First, there is a wide range of outcomes, all the way from excellent to
poor. Second, recovery, like the illness
itself has many facets" (p. 11). Because
of these factors and the nature of the
disease, it is difficult to predict the
extent of recovery.

The goal in the treatment of schizophrenia is to have an ongoing treatment
program that gradually introduces the patient to a less restrictive outpatient
therapy. Another goal of treatment is to
release the patient with a greater awareness than that which he had prior to the
disease. These ideal goals of the therapist sometimes cannot be reached because

Childhood Schizophrenia 12

of the complex and diverse needs and wants of the patient and his family (Allen, 1985).

Although there are no curative treatment programs available for the long-term schizophrenic, a considerable number of options are accessible to reduce and alleviate some of the suffering of the individual and his family. These treatments include drug treatment, individual psychotherapy, and family therapy. Drug treatment uses many antipsychotic drugs such as Thorazine. Thorazine was the first antipsychotic drug to be used and, although controversial, revolutionized the treatment of schizophrenia by allowing more patients to lead happier and more productive lives outside of hospitals. Individual and family therapy is usually used in conjunction with drug treatment. In individual therapy the doctor focuses on the needs and feelings of the patient. The doctor provides support and guidance for the patient to be able to understand reality. Family therapy is usually led by

Childhood Schizophrenia 13

a social worker who studies the family to
find cues, such as a genetic link or
internal family difficulties, that may be
adding to the patient's problems. After
identifying these factors, the social
worker educates the family on how to
adjust their lifestyles to help their
family member adjust (Kulick, 1985).

A Family Problem

When one member of a family becomes
afflicted with schizophrenia, so does the
whole family. Normal family problems are
magnified and many new problems are
added. For example, one of the most
pressing problems is where the schizophrenic should live. Often when the
family decides to send the patient to a
hospital, the family is tormented by
feelings of blame, shame, anger, and
depression. Parents often blame themselves for their child's illness and feel
for one reason or another that they have
not done right by their child. This, of
course, is irrational thinking on the

Childhood Schizophrenia 14

part of the parents, because schizophrenia is a biological disease of the brain
and cannot be caused exclusively by
external factors.

If families believe that they, in
some way, have caused the child to have
schizophrenia, they become ashamed and
try to hide the child and will deny his
illness to friends and neighbors. The
child in turn feels more isolated than
ever, reacts angrily toward the family,
and does not try to control his bizarre
behavior.

It is quite natural for parents to
show anger toward the child for becoming
schizophrenic and to show anger toward
God for creating disorders such as this.
When the anger is not openly expressed
but rather is held inside, it causes
depression. It is then necessary to
resolve the responsibility of who is to
blame for the disease. Why is there anger
surrounding the disease? Why should anyone feel shame because of the disease?
When these questions are answered for the
family members, they can begin to be
relieved of the impact caused by them

Childhood Schizophrenia 15

(Torrey, 1983). Many families of schizophrenic children have literally had their
life savings wiped out by the tremendous
expenses incurred because of this disease. The majority of people carry
medical insurance that will cover short-
term psychiatric hospitalization, but for
long-term care in a rehabilitative facil-
ity, the expenses are so prohibitive that
only the very wealthy can afford them
(Torrcy, 1983). Tn rare instances there
has been help from local school districts
for treatment of special children
(Stephens, 1984).

Conclusion

Tremendous strides have been made in
the treatment of childhood schizophrenia;
however, much more still remains to be
done. Although there is no cure for the
disease, there is encouraging hope as
researchers come closer to finding a
cause. Most psychiatrists and physicians
are now recognizing more of the symptoms
of childhood schizophrenia at an earlier
stage, and therefore, they are much more

able to begin early treatment. The earlier the disease is diagnosed, the better
chance the child has of having the devastating symptoms of the illness
alleviated.

Childhood Schizophrenia 17

References

(Annotated)

Allen, J. (1985). Development of schizophrenia. <u>Menninger Perspective</u>, <u>2</u>,
   8-11.
   In this article, Dr. Jon Allen discusses seven of the developmental
   factors of schizophrenia. This gives
   general information that is easy to
   understand. The article also discusses treatment procedures and
   their implications for patients and
   their families.
Davidoff, L. (1984). Childhood psychosis.
   In the <u>Encyclopedia of psychology</u>
   (Vol 10, pp. 156-157). New York: J.
   Wiley & Sons.
   This source deals directly with the
   symptoms, the causes, and the treatments of childhood schizophrenia. It
   gives lists of signs and symptoms,
   discusses varying causes, and outlines the treatments available for
   the schizophrenic patient.
Despert, J. (1968). <u>Schizophrenia in
   children</u>. New York: Robert Brunner.

Childhood Schizophrenia 18

This book has many useful items directly relating to childhood schizophrenia. The contents are clearly labeled, which is useful in locating specific items, such as statistics and facts relating to the disease.

Goldfarb, W. (1961). <u>Childhood schizo-phrenia</u>. Cambridge, MA: Harvard University Press.

This source is a compiled book of extensive research on childhood schizophrenia. It contains very specific information. It is helpful for citing research comparing normal children and schizophrenic children in the areas of physical and behavioral abilities.

Kulick, E. (1985). Treatment of schizophrenia. <u>Menninger Perspective</u>, <u>2</u>, 12-14.

This article deals directly with the differing treatments of schizophrenia, such as somatic treatment, individual psychotherapy, and family therapy. It gives insight into the use of these treatments and how they

Childhood Schizophrenia 19

affect the patients.

MacDonald, A. (1982, Winter). Schizophrenia: The solitary nightmare.
Highwire Magazine, pp. 37–38.
This article is excellent for general facts and information relating
to schizophrenia. The article is
written in an easy-to-understand
form and thus is useful for a general definition of schizophrenia and
some specific statistics.

Noshpitz, J. (1979). Basic handbook of
child psychiatry (Vol. 2). New York:
Basic Books.
This handbook gives a variety of
information on childhood schizophrenia. It deals specifically with the
signs and symptoms of the disorder
and the criteria involved for diag-
nosing it.

Schizophrenia. (1983). In the Encyclopedic dictionary of psychology (Vol.8,
pp. 502–503). Cambridge, MA: MIT
Press.
This source states that schizophrenia influences all aspects of the
personality. It also lists delu-

Childhood Schizophrenia 20

sions, hallucinations, thought dis-

orders, and disturbances in mood and

behavior as symptoms of the disease.

Stephens, R. (1984, March). Adam: A

child's courageous battle against

mental illness. <u>Family Circle</u>,

pp. 98-102.

This article describes a true story

of a schizophrenic child and his

family. From the story you get a

feel for the pain and confusion the

family experiences with their son.

Torrey, F. (1983). <u>Surviving schizophre-</u>

<u>nia</u>. New York: Harper & Row.

This book deals with problems that

the family of a schizophrenic faces.

It discusses the feelings of anger,

shame, blame, and depression, all

caused by external forces such as

where the schizophrenic should live,

how to pay for his bills, and what

to tell the neighbors.

DISCIPLINE-SPECIFIC RESOURCES
FOR SOCIAL SCIENCE

General Sources and Guides to Literature

The Annual Register: A Record of World Events. H. G. Hodson, ed. Detroit: Gale, 1980–present. For any given year, a record is kept of major events happening in the world.

A Bibliographical Guide to Education. New York Public Library staff editors. New York: G. K. Hall, 1985. A guide to sources for education topics.

Family Facts at Your Fingertips. C. A. Thacher. Salt Lake City, UT: Hawkes, 1987. Useful, up-to-date statistics about families.

Guide to Library Research in Psychology. J. E. Bell. Dubuque, IA: Wm. C. Brown, 1971. A useful source for undergraduate research in psychology.

Guide to Library Sources in Political Science: American Government. C. A. Vose. San Antonio, TX: American Political, 1975. A useful source for undergraduate research in American government and politics.

Information Sources in Education and Work. K. Dibden and J. Tomlinson, eds. Stoneham, MA: Butterworth, 1981.

Information Sources in Politics and Political Science: A Survey Worldwide. D. Englefield and G. Drewry, eds. Stoneham, MA: Butterworth, 1984.

Information Sources of Political Science. 4th ed. F. Holler. Santa Barbara, CA: ABC-Clio, 1986. Lists and annotates reference sources, including specific areas of political science.

The Literature of Political Science: A Guide for Students, Librarians, and Teachers. C. Brock. New York: Bowker, 1969.

The Student Anthropologist's Handbook. C. Frantz. Cambridge, MA: Schenkman, 1972. A guide to the discipline, including research materials.

The Student Sociologist's Handbook. 4th ed. P. Bart and L. Frankel. New York: Random House, 1986. Useful source for undergraduate research in sociology.

Study of International Relations: A Guide to Information Sources. R. Pfaltzgraff, Jr., ed. Detroit: Gale, 1977. A guide for students of international politics.

Dictionaries and Almanacs

Almanac of American History. A. M. Schlesinger, Jr., ed. New York: G. P. Putnam's, 1983. Provides facts and data on American history.

Almanac of American Politics, 1990. M. Barone, G. Ujifusa, ed. Washington, D.C.: National Journal. Provides facts and data on American politics for each year—updated annually.

Congressional Quarterly Almanac. Washington, D.C.: Congressional Quarterly, 1945–present. Summarizes the yearly activities of Congress, including voting records and major legislation.

Dictionary of American History, rev. ed. Martin et al., eds. New York: Rowman, 1990. Defines terms and discusses briefly subjects of interest in American history.

Dictionary of Anthropology. C. Winick. Totowa, NJ: Littlefield, 1977. Provides information on anthropological topics.

Dictionary of Behavioral Sciences, 2nd ed. B. Wolman, ed. New York: Van Nostrand Reinhold, 1989. Provides simple and concise definitions of terms in psychology and related fields.

Dictionary of Education. D. Rowntree. New York: B&N Imports, 1982. Concise definitions of terminology in education.

Dictionary of Political Thought. Roger Scrutin. New York: Hill & Wang, 1984.

Dictionary of Psychology, 2nd ed. J. Chaplin. New York: Viking, 1985. Provides concise definitions of psychological terms.

Handbooks

Handbook of Developmental Psychology. B. Wolman, ed. Englewood Cliffs, NJ: Prentice-Hall, 1982. Guide to issues and information in human development.

Handbook of Educational Technology: A Practical Guide for Teachers, 2nd ed. F. Percival and H. Ellington. New York: Nichols, 1988. Guide to terms in educational technology.

Historian's Handbook: A Key to the Study of Writing of History, 2nd ed. W. Gray et al. New York: Houghton Mifflin, 1991. Useful guide for undergraduates in history.

International Yearbook of Education. Lanham, MD: Bernan-Unipub, annual. 1979–present. Each year, a new topic in education is covered; for example, the 1984 yearbook theme was "Education for Life."

Political Handbook of the World. 1982–present (annual). A. S. Banker et al., eds. Binghamton, NY: CSA. Summaries of world political events.

United States Government Manual. Washington, D.C.: U.S. Government Printing Office, 1934–present. Provides current information on all aspects of the federal government.

Encyclopedia

Encyclopedia of Educational Research. M. Alkin, ed. New York: Macmillan, 1992. Excellent summaries of research in education.

Encyclopedia of Human Development and Education. R. Thomas, ed. New York: Pergamon, 1990. Contains terms, theories, and information on topics related to development and education.

Encyclopedia of Policy Studies. Nagel (Public Administration and Public Policy Services). New York: Dekker, 1983. Contains information about public policy issues.

Encyclopedia of Psychology. R. Corsini. New York: Wiley, 1984. Provides an overview of important terms and concepts in psychology.

Encyclopedia of Social Work. 18th ed. A. Minahan, ed. New York: National Association of Social Workers, 1965–present. Provides general information on a variety of topics related to social work. Includes both articles and biographies.

Encyclopedia of Sociology. Borgata and Borgata. New York: Macmillan, 1991. Describes terms, concepts, major ideas, major theorists in sociology.

International Encyclopedia of Education. Husen and Postlethwaite. New York: Pergamon, 1985. Provides background information on topics related to higher education (education beyond high school).

International Encyclopedia of Politics and Law. Published by Archives Publishers. New York: State Mutual Book and Periodicals Services, 1987.

International Encyclopedia of Psychiatry, Psychology, Psychoanalysis, and Neurology. 12 vols. B. B. Wolman, ed. New York: Van Nostrand Reinhold, 1977. Provides concise information on psychology and related fields.

International Encyclopedia of the Social Sciences. 8 vols. plus supplements. D. L. Sills, ed. New York: Macmillan, 1977. Provides analyses of current topics and issues in the social sciences. Includes a biographical supplement published in 1979.

Man, Myth, and Magic. R. Cavendish, ed. New York: Marshall Cavendish, 1983. An illustrated encyclopedia of mythology, religion, and the unknown.

Biographies

Biographical Dictionary of American Educators. 3 vols. J. F. Ohles, ed. Westport, CT: Greenwood, 1978.

Biographical Dictionary of Modern Peace Leaders. H. Jacobsen et al., eds. Westport, CT: Greenwood, 1985. Provides concise biographies about important figures in the peace movement around the world.

Biographical Dictionary of Psychology. L. Zasne. Westport, CT: Greenwood, 1984. Provides concise biographies about important psychologists.

Statesman's Yearbook. New York: St. Martin's, 1975–present. Provides concise information about important political leaders in any given year.

Who's Who in American Politics. 10th ed. Compiled by J. Cattell. New York: Bowker, 1985 plus annual updates. Discusses important figures in American politics each year.

See also Biographies (pp. 30–31), and Encyclopedias, p. 30.

Indexes and Abstracts

ANTHROPOLOGY

Abstracts in Anthropology

ASIAN STUDIES

Bibliography of Asian Studies
*Public Affairs Information Services Bulletin (PAIS)

BLACK STUDIES

Black Index: Afro-Americans in Selected Periodicals
Index to Periodical Articles by and about Negroes

CRIME

Abstracts on Criminology and Penology
Criminology and Penology Abstracts

EDUCATION

Child Development Abstracts and Bibliography
*Current Index to Journals in Education
Deaf, Speech, Hearing Abstracts
Educational Administration Abstracts
*Education Index

* = Computer searching available

*ERIC on Disc
*Exceptional Child Education
    Resources
Physical Education Index
Physical Fitness/Sports Medicine
*Resources in Education
*Resources in Vocational Education
State Education Journal Index

FAMILY STUDIES

Inventory of Marriage and Family
    Literature
Sage Family Studies Abstracts

LAW

Current Law Index
Index to Legal Periodicals

LIBRARY SCIENCE

*Library and Information Science Ab-
    stracts
*Library Literature
Library Science Abstracts
Library Technology Report

POLITICAL SCIENCE

ABC Political Science
Combined Retrospective Index to
    Journals in Political Science
Congressional Quarterly Weekly
    Reports
International Political Science
    Abstracts
*Public Affairs Information Service
    Bulletin

PSYCHOLOGY

*Psychological Abstracts

SOCIAL SCIENCES—GENERAL

Consumer's Index
*Public Affairs Information Service
*Social Science Citation Index
*Social Science Index

SOCIOLOGY AND SOCIAL WORK

Combined Retrospective Index to
    Journals in Sociology
Index to Current Urban Documents
Rehabilitation Literature
Social Work Research and Abstracts
*Sociological Abstracts
Women's Studies Abstracts
*World Agricultural Economics and
    Rural Sociology Abstracts

TRANSPORTATION

Highway Research Abstracts
Highway Safety Literature
Transportation Research Abstracts

UNITED NATIONS

Specialized Agency Catalogs
United Nations Documents Index

**U.S. CONGRESS AND U.S. GOVERN-
MENT**

*American Statistics Index (ASI)
CIS Annual Index to Congressional
    Publications of Legislative
    Histories
CIS U.S. Congressional Committee
    Prints Index
Commerce Clearing House Congres-
    sional Index
*Congressional Information Service
Congressional Quarterly Almanac
Index to U.S. Government Periodicals
*Monthly Catalog of U.S. Government
    Publications
*U.S. Government Reports, An-
    nouncements and Index (NTIS)

8

✦ ✦ ✦

Writing a Research Paper
in the Humanities

INTRODUCTION

In many research projects in the humanities, the researcher must read a primary text carefully and interpret it. Such a research task, performed frequently by working scholars in the humanities, requires a thorough reading of the text, a systematic search for information written about the text, extensive preparation time, and a knowledge of formal conventions in the field. The same principles and skills you have learned in the earlier chapters apply when you use a primary text. These skills include:

1. The ability to read the primary text carefully and critically.
2. A familiarity with bibliographic indexes and other library resources relating to humanities.
3. The ability to synthesize and evaluate information and opinions from a variety of secondary sources.
4. The ability to develop a thesis consistent with the evidence found in both the primary and secondary sources.
5. The ability to organize and write a paper that effectively presents and supports your thesis.
6. The ability to employ the formal conventions of research papers in the humanities.

REPORTS AND RESEARCH PAPERS

Some of the writing you will be expected to do in the humanities is report writing, in which you report on the current consensus within the field on a particular topic or issue. In report writing, you research only in the sense of finding out what others have said on a topic. Usually, reports are written on non-controversial subjects in which the writer can discover the facts easily and present them without the need to interpret their significance. Such a report is also sometimes called a "review of the literature."

For example, in a history class, you might be asked to write a report on early colonial life in Plymouth, Massachusetts. As a reporter, you would look up relevant, authoritative history resources written about colonial New England and write down what those sources say about life in Plymouth.

In contrast, a research paper does more than report the facts or widely held beliefs on a particular topic. A research paper is necessarily more evaluative than a report, because it interprets the available evidence. Often, a research paper is written about a subject or topic that has sparked controversy in the field. A controversial issue is evident when scholars in the field do not agree on interpretations or when the range of known facts is great enough to allow differing opinions. A question such as "Were colonists at Plymouth significantly helped or hindered by local Native American tribes?" would allow the researcher to locate and interpret a wide range of known facts. The researcher would investigate a question that other scholars in the field had grappled with. For example, current mythology has the colonists of Plymouth sitting down to Thanksgiving dinner with benevolent Native Americans. The researcher would ask, "Is this picture based on facts? Or were the colonists really constantly on guard against attacks by Native Americans?" Some writers today portray the colonial settlers as the aggressors, indiscriminately killing tribe members to satisfy their own need for land and food. Which is the true picture? What facts do we actually have? What is a reasonable interpretation of the relationship between colonial settlers and Native American tribes based on those known facts?

The questions posed above are typical of the kinds of problems often researched in the humanities. There is room for differences of opinion, provided those opinions are supported by, and consistent with, the known facts on the subject. The researcher arrives at a thesis through lengthy preparation and investigation. Then the researcher verifies that thesis by constructing a persuasive argument woven from and supported by the known facts. Such a thesis is a reasonable answer to the question, an answer that fits the known facts and helps to explain them.

In your work for this chapter, you will be expected to write a research paper, not a report paper. In other words, you need to go beyond reporting the known facts to interpretation of those facts, to formulate your own interpretation, your own thesis. The examples in this chapter are taken from a research project in an English class in which the students were asked to interpret a literary text critically. Such a research project assumes more than reporting; the student must read the primary text carefully and formulate his or her own impressions of its "meaning." The research itself mainly involves comparing those impressions to other interpretations made by scholars in the field.

A GUIDE TO THE HUMANITIES
RESEARCH PROCESS

First, choose a literary text (novel, play, short story, or poem) that seems to you to be significant in some way. Often in your college classes these texts are assigned reading, since your instructor already is aware of which literary texts are considered significant by others in the field. Sally Batten, whose research will serve as the model for this chapter, chose John Steinbeck's novel *East of Eden.*

Before beginning your research, obtain a notebook and notecards (if you wish to use them. Some students prefer to keep all their information together in one research notebook). You may use the notecards to record the notes you take while reading the primary text and while reading the secondary sources in which the primary text is critiqued or interpreted. A second set of notecards may be used for your bibliography: the listing of all the publication information from each source you use in your paper.

Alternatively, you may wish to keep all notes and bibliographical material in your research notebook. Also in your research notebook, you should record your own impressions and comments on both the primary text and the secondary sources. It is crucial that, as you read, you not only report what the sources say, but you understand what they say. Putting that understanding into your own words in your research notebook will prove invaluable to you when you actually sit down to write the research paper. You may also write drafts of your research paper in your research notebook. How can you hope to explain to someone else the complexities of the subject if you have not adequately explained it to yourself? Keeping the notes from the sources and your own interpretations separate prevents you from confusing later on what you read in a source with what occurred to you on your own. Many students find it useful to reserve facing pages in their notebooks, one side for notes, the other for interpretive comments on those notes.

Preparation

You need to read the primary text carefully, taking notes from the text that record important comments by the author about the characters and incidents in the text. Notice and record as much as you can, whether direct quotes or paraphrases from the text. Label the notes with a key word or phrase for ease of identification: "Cathy as a child," or "Cathy's evil behavior as an adult." Each entry should also be identified as to its source, the primary text, which for convenience you should label (1). Each note from the primary text, then, will be identified with a (1) in the upper right-hand corner. Label and enter each note in your notebook, making sure to use quotation marks to indicate the author's exact words. Mark down at the end of the note the page number or numbers on which you found the information or idea.

In addition to the notes from the primary text, write your own comments in your research notebook. Jot down possible questions that occur to you as you read, particularly any that seem interesting or problematic: "What makes Cathy in *East of Eden* tick?" "Is she psychologically disturbed?" "Is there some medical disorder or mental disease that controls or would help explain her behavior?" and so on.

> **RESEARCH NOTEBOOK**
>
> My Comments
> I'm glad I picked this book. I think it's interesting to see how people think from the inside. I started out wondering what "disease" Cathy had. But I don't think she really had a mental problem. I just believe that Steinbeck wanted to show the reader how he would be as an individual if he let the bad within rule him. She was totally consumed by her evilness and there was no turning back.

✦ EXERCISE

Carefully read and take notes from your primary text. Make evaluative comments in your research notebook.

Developing a Search Strategy

You have now completed reading the primary text and taking notes on it. You should have formed some general impressions about the text and what it means. In our example, Sally shows that she is beginning to understand what Steinbeck was trying to say about Cathy, the most important character in *East of Eden*. Do not be concerned if you do not yet have a "topic" to write about. But do begin to formulate questions that occurred to you after your careful reading of the primary text: such questions may ask about characterization, themes, language devices, writing style, plot development, and so on. Remember in the inquiry process in general, the writer always needs a lot of time to prepare for an understanding of the subject before writing about it. Make a time schedule for your research, allowing enough time for ideas to incubate. Do not leave everything until the week before the project is due. To be effective, a research project must alternate times of conscious and subconscious activity.

Your library search will probably proceed from a look at general information about your primary text to specific works written about it. An outline of a search strategy is presented in the next paragraph. (Your particular search may differ somewhat from this outline.)

Sally's Search Strategy

1. Encyclopedias, dictionaries, biographies for general background information, including *Cassell's Encyclopedia of World Literature*.
2. Critical reviews and commentary on *East of Eden*, using *Book Review Index* and *Book Review Digest*.
3. Subject indexes for access to listings of specific secondary sources, particularly the *MLA Bibliography*.
4. Abstracts of particular secondary sources found in subject indexes, such as *Abstracts of English Studies*.
5. Library online catalog for location of sources and access to new material.

As you can see in this outline, your library search will probably begin in the reference area in the library. To illustrate the use of a library search strategy, we will follow the steps given in the previous paragraph, using Sally's research on *East of Eden* as a model for your own research.

✦ **EXERCISE**

Outline your own research strategy, beginning with general and working to specific sources. Draw up a time schedule for your research. Write down any questions you might want to pursue about your primary text.

General Sources

Reading general information on your primary text helps put the work in a context. Reading specialized encyclopedias, dictionaries, and bibliographies indicates to you what is considered common knowledge about the work and the author. Depending on your particular text, you will be reading general encyclopedias, such as *Academic American*, specialized encyclopedias, such as *Cassell's Encyclopedia of World Literature*, and biographies, such as *Twentieth Century Authors*. (Sources commonly used in the humanities are listed in this chapter on pp. 334–337). Sally used the following sources, which she listed in her research notebook, as the beginning of her working bibliography:

> <u>The World Book Encyclopedia</u>, 1979 ed.
>
> <u>Cassell's Encyclopedia of World Literature</u>. J.
>
>   Buchanan-Brown, ed. New York: Morrow, 1973.
>
> <u>American Writers, IV</u>. Leonard Unger, ed. New
>
>   York: Charles Scribner's, 1974.
>
> <u>Twentieth Century Authors</u>. Stanley Kunitz and
>
>   Howard Haycraft, eds. New York: Wilson,
>
>   1942.

Sally used the references listed at the end of each general source to continue to build her working bibliography. This is often an important way to locate key sources written about your primary text or author. For example, the major critical work by Peter Lisca, *The Wide World of John Steinbeck,* was listed in the bibliography of the Steinbeck article in *American Writers.* It is not necessary for you to look up each entry right away. Rather, it is sufficient for you to continue to list on your working bibliography any promising references you run across in your background reading.

✦ EXERCISE

Find and read background sources relevant to your topic to obtain general information (see the end of this chapter for a list of sources commonly used in the humanities).

Focusing Your Search

After you have read several general background sources about your primary text and author, you are ready to define a starting question that will help you focus your search. The question must be a realistic one that you are able to research given the information and time available to you. This question is critical to the success of your research paper. Take care that it is neither trivial nor overly ambitious but allows you sufficient scope for research. As you can imagine, with any primary text there are any number of questions that you could ask to guide your search. Generally, as with all research, the question is motivated by a problematic event or an incongruity you perceive in your text. As you were reading the primary text, you should have noted in your research notebook some of these important questions. Return to the primary text at this time with an eye to articulating such a question. Your starting question should be something that interests and intrigues you, and it should be supportable by evidence in the text and in secondary sources.

Good Questions (supportable by evidence in the text):
1. Are Cathy's immoral actions in *East of Eden* the result of a psychotic personality?
2. Did Steinbeck portray Cathy as a human or a demon?
3. Is Steinbeck's portrayal of Cathy believable and realistic?
4. Is Cathy's effect on those around her in the novel the result of her own nature or defects in the other characters?
5. How is this work related to others by Steinbeck?

Poor Questions:
1. What happens in the novel *East of Eden*? (too broad; reporting rather than researching)
2. How was the novel critically received and how have others interpreted it? (reporting rather than researching)
3. What poison did Cathy use to kill herself at the end of the novel? (too trivial)
4. What is Steinbeck trying to say about human nature in general in the novel? (too broad)

Once you have defined a starting question for yourself, it will be easier to decide which sources are relevant to your own particular search. Not every source will contain pertinent information. If you do not have a starting question, it is easy to wander aimlessly from one source to another, taking copious notes but getting nowhere. The question serves as a *focus* for your search and keeps you on a carefully delineated path.

✦ EXERCISE

Define a starting question for yourself to guide your research. Make sure that it is not too trivial or too broad.

Book Reviews

Since you are working with a primary text that has been generally received as an important work of literature, you may find that numerous book reviews have been written about it. These can be useful to you in your search, particularly if your research question is concerned with the work's critical reception at the time of its publication. The two most commonly used tools for finding book reviews are:

Book Review Digest, 1905–present
Book Review Index, 1965–present

Sally looked up Steinbeck's *East of Eden* in the *Book Review Digest* of 1952, the year the novel was published, to find listings of reviews. She added these references to her working bibliography. The following is an example of a review she found in the *Digest:*

> STEINBECK, JOHN. East of Eden. 602p $4.50 Viking "At the outset Steinbeck has a firm command of his materials, but the novel degenerates as it goes along. The improbabilities grow more flagrant, the sentimentality thicker, the intellectual naivete more exasperating." Charles Rolo Atlantic 190:94 0'52 350w

✦ EXERCISE

Locate and read reviews of your primary text (see Chapter 2, pp. 31–32, for a list of review sources).

Subject Indexes

There are other important indexes that can give you access to scholarly articles written about your primary text and author. These indexes are bibliographical listings of secondary sources. Some of the indexes may be available for computer searching, either online or on CD-ROM, as well as in print. If humanities indexes are available online in your library, you may want to begin there since searching by computer is generally both faster and more comprehensive. (For more information on searching online, see Chapter 2, pp. 34–43.)

The indexes may differ slightly in their organization, so it is important for you to get acquainted with the system of a particular index. When using an index for the first time, read the preface for instructions or consult the reference librarian for help. The following index was used by Sally in her search:

> *MLA International Bibliography of Books and Articles on Modern Language and Literature.* New York: Modern Language Association of America, 1921–present.

Sally began by looking up Steinbeck in the then most recent edition of the *MLA Bibliography.* She found a listing of books and articles written on Steinbeck in 1981 and discovered that a journal, the *Steinbeck Quarterly*, was devoted entirely to studies of Steinbeck's work. Again, she noted promising sources found in the index on her working bibliography so she could look them up later:

Cox, Martha Heasley. "Steinbeck's Family

Portraits: The Hamiltons." St Q. 1981; 14:

23-32.

McCarthy, Paul. John Steinbeck. New York: Ungar,

1980 (Mod. Lit. Monog.).

McDaniel, Barbara. "Alienation in East of Eden:

The 'Chart of the Soul.' " St Q. 1981; 14:

32-39. (Sources in Bible).

✦ EXERCISE

Use indexes to find titles of articles related to your primary text and topic (see pp. 336–337 in this chapter for a list of bibliographies and indexes commonly used in the humanities).

Abstracts and Guides to Periodicals

Next, begin to sort and narrow your list of possible sources on your working bibliography. Not every source you have listed will turn out to be relevant to your starting question. The books and articles are generally indexed by their titles, and these can be misleading. Sometimes you can use abstracts, short descriptive summaries of books and articles, as a method of initially sorting the relevant sources from the irrelevant sources. Sally used the following abstracts to eliminate some of the sources she had noted on her working bibliography and to add new sources she had not come upon before:

Abstracts of English Studies. Urbana, IL:

National Council of Teachers of English,

1958-present.

Bryer, Jackson, ed. Sixteen Modern American

Authors: A Survey of Research and Criticism.

New York: W. W. Norton, 1973.

Pownall, David E. Articles on Twentieth Century

Literature: An Annotated Bibliography, 1954

to 1970. New York: Kraus-Thomson, 1978.

As you can see, the process of searching in the library involves evaluating, eliminating, and adding sources as you refine your working bibliography to include only those actually relevant to your own starting question. As you evaluate the sources you have listed on your working bibliography, some useful tools can help you judge the relative merits of the sources, for example, Katz's *Magazines for Libraries* and Farber's *Classified List of Periodicals for the College Library.* You can look up journals and magazines on your working bibliography to find out whether they are respected, reputable sources. Sally looked up the *Steinbeck Quarterly* in Katz's guide and discovered the following information:

```
Steinbeck Quarterly, 1968. Tetsumaro

Hayashi, ed. "Many essays on any aspect of

Steinbeck, reviews, and bibliographies comprise

this small journal. Subscribers also receive the

annual Steinbeck monograph series."
```

According to Katz, the *Steinbeck Quarterly* is a useful journal for articles, reviews, and bibliographies on Steinbeck.

The Library Catalog

The last step of your search usually involves actually locating the sources listed in your working bibliography. Often the titles of the journals and magazines are listed in the indexes with abbreviations or initials. For example, if you have noted an article from the PMLA, you need to know that this abbreviation stands for *Publications of the Modern Language Association.* Look up the journal abbreviations in the front of the index and, if you have not already done so, write down the complete name of the journal on your working bibliography.

You can locate the books and articles listed on your working bibliography by looking them up in the library online catalog or your library's serials listing. You may also want to use the subject searching capabilities of the online catalog: by typing S=Steinbeck in the online catalog, you can locate all the books on Steinbeck in your library. These include critical, biographical, and bibliographical works. Sally found several important books in this way, including the following:

```
Hayashi, Tetsumaro. John Steinbeck: A Concise

    Bibliography. Metuchen, NJ: Scarecrow Press,

    1967.
```

Hayashi, Tetsumaro. <u>John Steinbeck: A Dictionary</u>

<u>of His Fictional Characters</u>. Metuchen, NJ:

Scarecrow Press, 1976.

Lisca, Peter. <u>John Steinbeck: Nature and Myth</u>.

New York: Crowell, 1978.

✦ EXERCISE

Use the online catalog's subject searching to locate sources and to find additional books and materials about your primary text. Use the LCSH list to find any other headings under which your topic might be listed in addition to the book's title and author.

Evaluation

Once you have found either a book or an article, evaluate it for its relevance or usefulness to your search. (For more information on source evaluation, see Chapter 3, pp. 67–68). You must continually evaluate your sources and discard any that are not immediately applicable to your search. If, after an initial screening, a book looks as though it could be useful, check it out at the circulation desk. Since articles are usually noncirculating and therefore cannot be checked out, you can either photocopy ones that interest you for later use or take notes from them while you are in the library. If a source is not available, check with the librarians about the possibility of an interlibrary loan.

✦ EXERCISE

In your research notebook, evaluate each article and book to be used in your research paper. Follow the source evaluation guidelines found in Chapter 3 on pp. 67–68.

Taking Notes

As you begin to take notes on the secondary sources, remember to keep complete information so you will not have to look up that particular book or article again. All notes (whether quoted or paraphrased) should be listed by the page number on which the information was found; all direct wording of the author must be designated by quotation marks. Taking care at this stage will benefit you when you actually begin to write your research paper.

Illumination

Since you are actively seeking the answer to the starting question you posed at the beginning of your search, you must continually "talk to yourself" while researching. Try to understand and interpret the source of information as you go, synthesizing data from numerous authors and sources, taking what is relevant and discarding what is not. This is where your research notebook can be of particular value. Take the time to write down your thoughts and comments as you go; mark for yourself those sources and ideas that you find particularly important or revealing. Gradually, you will arrive at a tentative answer to the question you posed, a thesis that will satisfactorily explain the answer to the question as you see it.

It is during this illumination stage of the inquiry process that you begin to "see the light" or the answer to your question. Perhaps your answer will be that there is no definitive answer; that would be perfectly acceptable. At any rate, present your understanding of your primary text, arrived at through your extensive preparation and research, in your thesis statement.

You will state your thesis, the proposition that explains your opinion of the primary text, as an opinion statement about what you believe based on the evidence you have gathered. For example, Sally first asked a question, then, through preparation and research, she came to a thesis that would guide the actual written presentation of the research:

1. Starting question: "Are Cathy's immoral actions the result of a psychotic personality?"
2. Thesis statement: "The character of Cathy in *East of Eden*, as seen in her behavior in childhood, young adult years, and adult life, reveals her totally evil nature and its effect on others."

✦ EXERCISE

Write a thesis statement that articulates your understanding of the primary text. Your thesis statement should be an opinion statement based on your own judgment as well as on the secondary criticism you have read.

Verification

Once you have defined your thesis statement, you will have a guide to use in organizing your actual written presentation of the research. As you write, however, you may find that the thesis statement needs to be revised in some way. The actual writing of the research findings will sometimes help you see things in new ways or discover new meanings. Actually writing down your ideas in a systematic fashion is an important way to verify the research you have done. As you try to articulate in writing your understanding of the topic, you may find that there are gaps in your knowledge that need further research, or you may find that your thesis really does not seem to explain the facts adequately. In the latter case, you will need to go back to both your primary and secondary sources for further information so you can re-state your thesis. However, you may find that your writing has clari-fied your ideas, thereby "verifying" them for you and your potential readers.

Organizing and Writing the Humanities Research Paper

Your thesis statement, together with your analysis of the rhetori-cal situation (see Chapter 5 pp. 137–140) may suggest an organizational plan to you. Sally's thesis sentence ("The character of Cathy in *East of Eden,* as seen in her behavior in childhood, young adult years, and adult life, reveals her totally evil nature and its effect on others") im-plies its own organizational plan. In this case, the paper will be a chronological account of Cathy's behaviors in her childhood, youth, and adult life showing how her evil nature affects others in the novel. Be aware, though, that such a chronological pattern should not take the place of a critical evaluation of the work and become a simple report-ing or summary of the plot.

Depending upon the writer's intentions and the needs of the au-dience, other theses might suggest other organizational plans, for ex-ample, cause and effect ("Cathy's evil nature caused catastrophes in the lives of those around her"), comparison and contrast ("Cathy is the most evil of Steinbeck's characters"), process ("The evil in Cathy's na-ture progressed from mild pranks to murder through the course of her life"), and example ("Steinbeck's preoccupation with the evil in human nature is evident in his novel *East of Eden*"). You as a writer will need to determine what approach to your subject matter makes the most sense given what you have learned in your research.

As you read back through your notes, it is a good idea to begin organizing your information by blocking related material together. First, ask yourself how many blocks of related material you seem to have. This might include a block of background material, a block of plot summary material, a block of related criticism in the secondary sources on a particular aspect of the primary text, and so on. Then consider what order the blocks of material would best be formed in to commu-nicate your ideas. How will each block of material be developed and how much space in the paper will each take to adequately discuss the ideas you want to present? Again, refer to your thesis statement as an organizational guide.

Outlining

Now you are ready to outline your research paper. Do not be overly concerned about formal outline structure. An outline should be a guide to writing, not a constraint that confines and limits your thinking. Many writers move back and forth between a sketchy outline and their written draft, changing both as they go along. Use your outline to help you write, but be open to the discoveries to be made about your topic while you are actually writing. Follow your teacher's instructions on your final outline form, since some teachers may prefer a formal sentence outline to a phrase outline. Sally constructed the following outline:

Sentence Outline

Thesis: The character of Cathy in <u>East of Eden</u>, as seen in her behavior in childhood, young adult years, and adult life, reveals her totally evil nature and its effect on others.

I. Cathy Ames is an evil child.

   A. Cathy is described as having the appearance of an angel and the mind of a devil.

      1. Cathy Ames is a beautiful, yet demonlike child.

      2. Despite Cathy's childlike appearance, her emotional mentality is that of a much older, vindictive person.

   B. Cathy's parents are unable to determine whether she is a normal child or whether there is something evil about her.

      1. Her father has contact with normal children and finds her somehow different and sinister.

      2. Cathy manipulates and finally murders her parents.

II. When Cathy becomes a young adult, she does not end her evil ways.

   A. Cathy's experiences with Mr. Edwards in Boston change her into a worldly woman who is suspicious of everyone.

   B. Cathy becomes increasingly more suspicious.

   C. She manipulates men, particularly the Trasks, who take her in after a severe beating that nearly kills her.

   D. Cathy's babies become the victims of her vicious and wicked schemes.

III. As an adult, Cathy spreads her evil influence to other people and finally causes her own death.

   A. As Cathy matures, her ability to overpower others becomes stronger, as in the case of Faye.

   B. Kate, as she calls herself, seems to reach a peak of destruction, and her evil force causes her own deterioration.

   C. It appears that Cathy's corruption has been transmitted to her son, Cal, even though she was not directly involved in his life.

   D. Cathy becomes physically and mentally old before her time and in her increasing bitterness, finally takes her own life.

✦ EXERCISE

Arrange and block your source material and notes, decide on an organizational plan, and construct an outline to guide your writing. Refer to Chapter 5 for help with organization (pp. 140–144).

Writing the First Draft

After you have completed your preliminary plan or outline, you are ready to write the first draft of your research paper. Remember, you are writing to present to your readers the answer that you have discovered to the starting question. Remind yourself of your starting question at this time. If you have prepared sufficiently, the actual writing of the paper will be an important way for you to verify the truth of your thesis. However, remain flexible as you write your first draft and be open to any fresh insights you may have along the way.

As you are writing the first draft, it is important to note which supporting material comes from which source. Do not be overly concerned at this point about the formal details of documentation, which you can deal with later, but do mark for yourself in the draft any ideas or words taken from your sources. Place any words you copy from a source, either the primary or secondary sources, in quotation marks, and follow them with the author's last name and the page number of the source in parentheses:

> East of Eden is "a symbolic story about the
> need for brotherhood" (Riddel 46).

Similarly, identify paraphrases and restatements of ideas taken from a source even though you have recast them in your own words:

> Cathy's parents are unable to determine
> whether she is a normal child, or if there is
> something evil about her. They really do not
> trust her, but are never sure why (Cooperman 80).

For general information on planning, writing, and revising your research paper, refer to Chapter 5. Use the following information on documentation in the humanities to create your citations. The sample research paper at the end of this chapter may also serve as a useful guide to you as you write.

DOCUMENTATION IN THE HUMANITIES: MLA STYLE

The MLA (Modern Language Association) documentation style, which uses in-text citation similar to that used in the social sciences, has been generally adopted by writers of research papers in language and literature. Other disciplines in the humanities and fine arts may use the footnote/bibliography system. I will first discuss the MLA style (as detailed in the *MLA Handbook for Writers of Research Papers,* 2d ed., Joseph Gibaldi and Walter S. Achtert, eds., New York: Modern Language Association, 1984) and then describe the footnote and bibliography styles commonly used in the humanities other than language and literature.

The MLA documentation style consists of parenthetical in-text citations and a list of works cited at the end of the paper. In the humanities, specific sources and page numbers are more important than the recency of the work. Thus, in-text citations show the author's name and the page number of the source rather than the author/year as in the sciences and social sciences.

Internal Citation

Both the author cited and the page number of the source are important for the internal citation. Observe the following principles in the text of your research paper:

1. Generally, introduce any paraphrase or direct quote with the name of the author. Then indicate the page number of the source in parentheses at the end of the material:

   ```
   French observes that one night Cal becomes
   angry with Aaron and takes him to visit "Kate's
   circus" (146).
   ```

2. When you do not use the author's name to introduce the paraphrased or quoted material, place the author's name along with the specific page number in parentheses at the end of the material:

   ```
   However, unlike his mother, Cal has
   "recognized the evil in himself, and is ready to
   act for good" (Cooperman 88).
   ```

   [Note: Do not separate author and page with a comma.]

3. Indicate every instance of borrowed material for the reader. You can indicate a paragraph taken from a single source by mentioning the author's name at the beginning of the paragraph and giving the parenthetical citation at the end:

   ```
   Judging from Steinbeck's description, Cathy
   Ames is a beautiful yet demonlike child. She has
   ```

an innocent heart-shaped face, golden hair, wide-
set hazel eyes, a delicate and thin nose and
high, wide cheekbones. She has a child's figure—
narrow hips, straight legs, delicate arms and
tiny hands. Her voice is "soft and husky—so sweet
as to become irresistible, fascinating, and
horrible" (Steinbeck 73).

4. When you have two works by the same author, identify them by
   the author, abbreviated title, and page number of the source:

According to Lisca, Samuel, who has been
working in the field all day, "associates the
buried meteorite (falling star, hence Lucifer),
which wrecks his well drill with Cathy . . ."
(<u>Wide World</u> 269). After her children's birth,
Cathy is once again compared with a serpent.
Lisca comments that "Cathy gives birth to the
twins as easily as a snake lays eggs" (<u>Nature and
Myth</u> 168).

5. When it is apparent that your citations refer to the same work, you
   need not repeat the author's name. The page number will suffice:

Steinbeck says it is "easy to say she was
bad, but there is little meaning unless we know
why" (184). The question of Cathy's wicked and
sinful existence "goes forever unanswered—just as
the 'reason' for the presence of evil itself goes
unanswered" (184).

6. For a primary source requiring frequent in-text citation, you can
   add a bibliographic footnote:

in-text

"irresistible, fascinating, and horrible."[1]

Footnote

¹John Steinbeck, <u>East of Eden</u> (New York: Viking, 1952) 32. Subsequent references are to this edition of the novel and are included parenthetically in the text.

[Note: Subsequent in-text references need only the page number.]

7. Other content footnotes may be included for the following:
A. Blanket citations

²For further information on this point, see Lisca (168), French (56), and Hayashi (29).

B. Related matters (not included in your paper)

³Although outside the scope of this paper, major themes in the novel are discussed by Hayashi and French.

C. Suggested sources (and related topics)

⁴For an additional study of Steinbeck's fictional characters, see Hayashi's <u>Dictionary of Fictional Characters</u>.

D. Comparisons with another source

⁵On this point, see also the article by Stanley Cooperman, in which he discusses symbolism in other Steinbeck novels.

[Note: If you have several content notes, you may type them on a separate endnote page, which immediately follows your text and is titled "Notes" or "Endnotes." Be sure any references listed in your footnotes or endnotes are also listed on your works-cited page.]

8. When your quote is lengthy (more than three lines of text) indent the quote ten spaces from the left-hand margin. Everything still remains double-spaced throughout the indented quote. Notice that the end punctuation for indented quotes differs from internal

citations that are run into the text: the period comes before the parenthetical citation for indented quotes.

```
Steinbeck explains it as follows:
```

> If she [Cathy] were simply a monster, that
> would not bring her in [the story]. But
> since she had the most powerful impact on
> Adam and transmitted her blood to her sons
> and influenced the generations—she cer-
> tainly belongs in this book. (<u>Journal</u> 42)

The Reference List

The reference list, at the end of the paper, contains all the sources actually cited in the paper (titled "Works Cited") or all the sources you used in writing your paper (titled "Bibliography"). The purpose of the reference list is to help readers find the materials you used in writing your paper, so you must provide complete, accurate information. These principles should be followed for your reference list:

1. Sources should be listed alphabetically by the last name of the author or (when there is no author given) by the first word of the title (excluding a, an, the). Type the first word of the entry at the left margin. Indent subsequent lines of the same entry five spaces. You should double space the entire reference page both between and within entries.
2. When you have more than one work by the same author, give the name for the first entry only. For subsequent works by the same author, substitute three hyphens and a period for the author's name and arrange the titles alphabetically:

```
Hayashi, Tetsumaro. John Steinbeck: A Concise
     Bibliography. Metuchen, NJ: Scarecrow Press,
     1967.

- - -. A Dictionary of His Fictional Characters.
     Metuchen, NJ: Scarecrow Press, 1976.
```

3. For books and monographs, give the author's name in full form as it appears on the title page, listed by the surname first followed by a comma, the given name, initial(s), and a period:

```
Steinbeck, John.
```

4. After the author's name, give the complete title of the work, underlined and followed by a period. Important words in the title should be capitalized:

```
Steinbeck, John. Journal of a Novel: The East of

    Eden Letters.
```

[Note: Do not underline a title within a title.]

5. Include the editor or translator, edition of the book, series, or number of volumes (if appropriate).
6. Indicate the city of publication (followed by a colon), publisher (followed by a comma), and date of publication (followed by a period):

```
Steinbeck, John. Journal of a Novel: The East of

    Eden Letters. New York: Viking, 1969.
```

7. For articles, follow a similar order: Author. Title of the article. Publication data. The title of the article is in quotation marks; the title of the journal is underlined. If a volume number is provided, it goes after the journal title, followed by the date in parentheses. A colon follows the parentheses. Then inclusive page numbers are provided for the entire article. For magazines that are published weekly, give only the date (not in parentheses) in order of day/month/year. A comma precedes the date. Then inclusive page numbers are provided for the whole article:

```
McDaniel, Barbara. "Alienation in East of Eden:

    The 'Chart of the Soul.'" Steinbeck

    Quarterly 14 (1981):32-39.

Greenfield, Meg. "Accepting the Unacceptable."

    Newsweek, 1 July 1985:64-65.
```

The model references that follow are based on the MLA documentation style as described in the *MLA Handbook*. The sample paper at the end of this chapter also uses MLA documentation.

MODEL REFERENCES: LANGUAGE AND LITERATURE (MLA)

Type of Reference

BOOKS

1. One author

   Frohock, William Merrill. <u>The Novel of Violence in America</u>. Dallas: Southern Methodist UP, 1958.

   [Note: UP is the abbreviation for University Press.]

2. Two or more authors

   Halliday, M. A. K., and Raquaia Hasan. <u>Cohesion in English</u>. London: Longmans, 1976.

3. Book with editor(s)

   Kunitz, Stanley J., and Howard Haycraft, eds. <u>Twentieth Century Authors</u>. New York: Wilson, 1942.

4. Book with editor and author

   Twain, Mark. <u>Letters from the Earth</u>. Ed. Bernard Devoton. New York: Harper & Row, 1962.

5. Essay, chapter, or section in edited work

   Gray, James. "John Steinbeck." <u>American Writers</u>, <u>IV</u>. Ed. Leonard Unger. New York: Scribner's, 1974. 47-65.

6. Encyclopedia entry

(signed)

Riddel, Joseph N. "John Steinbeck." <u>The World</u>
    <u>Book Encyclopedia</u>. 1983 ed.

(unsigned)

"John Steinbeck." <u>Encyclopedia Americana</u>. 1978 ed.

ARTICLES

1. Journal article (one author)

Cox, Martha Heasley. "Steinbeck's Family
    Portraits: The Hamiltons." <u>Steinbeck</u>
    <u>Quarterly</u> 14 (1981):23-32.

2. Journal article (two or more authors)

Flower, Linda, and John R. Hayes. "The Cognition
    of Discovery: Defining a Rhetorical
    Problem." <u>College Composition and</u>
    <u>Communication</u> 31 (1980):21-32.

3. Journal article that pages each issue separately (must include both
   volume and issue number)

Kail, Harvey, and John Trimbur. "The Politics of
    Peer Tutoring." <u>WPA: Writing Program</u>
    <u>Administration</u> 11.1-2 (1987):5-12.

4. Magazine article

(signed)

Will, George F. "Machiavelli from Minnesota?"
    <u>Newsweek</u> 16 July 1984:88.

(unsigned)

"It Started in a Garden." Time 22 Sept.
    1952:110-111.

[Note: For a monthly magazine, give only month and year.]

5. Newspapers

Engle, Paul. "A Review of John Steinbeck's East
    of Eden." Chicago Sunday Tribune 21 Sept.
    1952:A3.

[Note: A3 stands for section A, page 3.]

6. An abstract from Dissertation Abstracts International

Johnson, Nancy Kay. "Cultural and Psychosocial
    Determinants of Health and Illness." DAI 40
    (1980):4235B. U of Washington.

OTHER SOURCES

1. Film or movie

Indiana Jones and the Temple of Doom. Dir. Steven
    Spielberg. Paramount Pictures, 1984.

2. Dissertation, unpublished

Balkema, Sandra. "The Composing Activities of
    Computer Literate Writers." Diss. U of
    Michigan, 1984.

3. Interview

Johnson, James, President, A-1 Mobile Homes, Inc.
    Personal interview. 12 March 1984.

4. Personal letter

Reagan, Ronald. Letter to author. 8 Sept. 1983.

5. Unpublished paper or manuscript

```
Welter, William. "Word Processing in Freshman
     English: Does It Compute?" Unpublished
     essay, 1985.
```

6. Television program

```
"The Great Apes." National Geographic Special.
     Public Broadcasting Service. WGBH, Boston.
     12 July 1984.
```

7. Electronic Information
The MLA divides electronic publications into two types: portable databases (distributed on CD-ROMs) and online databases (accessible through computer networks).

Portable databases

```
Arms, Valerie M. "A Dyslexic Can Compose on a
     Computer." Educational Technology 24.1
     (1984):39-41. ERIC. CD-ROM. SilverPlatter.
     Sept. 1984.
```

```
Where in the World Is Carmen Sandiego? CD-ROM.
     Novato: Brederbund. 1992.
```

Materials found through online computer networks

```
Lawrence, Oliver J. "Pitfalls in Electronic
     Writing Land." English Education 16.2
     (1984):94-100. Online. Dialog. 14 Sept.
     1984.
```

```
Reid, Joy. "Computer-Assisted Text-Analysis for
     ESL Students." Calico Journal 1.3
     (1983):40-42. Online Abstract. Abstract
     from: Dialog file: ERIC Item: EJ298270.
```

Herz, John C. "Surfing on the Internet: A
     Nethead's Adventures Online." <u>Urban Desires</u>
     1.3 (March/April 1995): n. pag. Online.
     Internet. 15 Apr. 1995. Available:
     www/desires.com/ud.html.

Electronic Correspondence (such as e-mail messages and conversations via bulletin boards and electronic discussion groups)

Gardner, Susan. "Help with Citations." E-mail to
     Christine Hult. 20 Mar. 1995.

White, Edward. "Texts as Scholarship; Reply to
     Bob Schwegler." 11 Apr. 1995. Online
     posting. WPA discussion list. Bitnet.
     Available e-mail: WPA-L@ASUACAD.bitnet.

Shaumann, Thomas Michael. "Re: Technical German."
     5 Aug. 1994. Online posting. News group
     comp.edu.languages.natural. Usenet. 7 Sept.
     1994.

[Note: Include both the date of the posting and the date of access, if different.]

(See Li, Xia, and Nancy B. Crane. *Electronic Style: A Guide to Citing Electronic Information.* Westport: Meckler, 1993.)

FOOTNOTE AND BIBLIOGRAPHY STYLE

In the humanities and fine arts other than language and literature, a two-part documentation system is common. This system uses footnotes (or endnotes) plus a bibliography. The footnotes appear at the bottom of the page on which the source is cited; the endnotes are typed in consecutive order on a separate page at the end of the paper. The bibliography, like the bibliography in the MLA style, is a typed list of sources arranged alphabetically. Since the bibliography style is generally the same, I will discuss here only the footnote (and endnote) form. Please refer to the section on the reference list discussed previously for the style of the bibliography page. Principles to follow for notes are:

1. In the text, a note is indicated by a superscript number typed immediately after the source paraphrase or quotation:

   The <u>New York Times</u> called his work "a vital,

   sensitive, timely contribution which sheds light

   on mankind's spiritual heritage."[1]

2. For footnotes:
   A. Type single spaced at the bottom of the page on which they occur.
   B. Double space between notes if there is more than one note per page.
   C. Indent the note five spaces; use a superscript number followed by a space and the note itself.
   D. Number notes consecutively throughout the text.
   E. Separate footnotes from the text by typing a twelve-space bar line from the left margin.
3. For endnotes:
   A. Type endnotes on a separate page at the end of your paper, titled "Notes" or "Endnotes."
   B. List the notes as they occur in the text and number them consecutively, using a superscript number followed by a space.
   C. Double space the entire endnote page.
4. The format of both footnotes and endnotes is as follows:
   A. Indent the first line of the note five spaces, type the superscript note number, skip a space, and begin the note.
   B. The second line and each subsequent line of the same note should return to the left margin
   C. Begin notes with the author's name (given name first) followed by a comma:

   [7]Thomas Merton,

   D. Then provide the title of the book or article (underlined or in quotation marks):

BOOK

   [7]Thomas Merton, <u>Mystics and Zen Masters</u>

ARTICLE

   [9]Steven Brachlow, "John Robinson and the

   Lure of Separatism in Pre-Revolutionary England,"

E. Provide the publication information after the title. Include the place of publication, the publisher, the date of publication, and the page number of the source. The form differs slightly for books and articles:

BOOK

> [7]Thomas Merton, <u>Mystics and Zen Masters</u> (New York: Dell, 1967) 315.

ARTICLE

> [9]Steven Brachlow, "John Robinson and the Lure of Separatism in Pre-Revolutionary England," <u>Church History</u> 50 (1983): 288–301.

5. In subsequent references to the same text, you need not repeat all the information of the first note; use only author's last name and a page number:

> [9]Brachlow, 289.

6. Where there are two or more works by the same author, you must include a shortened version of the work's title:

> [12]Merton, <u>Mystics</u>, 68.
>
> [16]Merton, <u>Buddhism</u>, 18

MODEL NOTES: HUMANITIES

Type of Reference

BOOKS

1. One author

> [1]Francis A. Schaeffer, <u>How Should We Then Live? The Rise and Decline of Western Thought and Culture</u> (Old Tappan, NJ: Revell, 1976) 39.

2. Two or more authors

> [2]William Ebenstein, C. Herman Pritchett, Henry A. Turner, and Dean Man, <u>American Democracy</u>

<u>in World Perspective</u> (New York: Harper & Row, 1967) 365.

3. Book with editor(s)

   ³Louis Schneider, ed., <u>Religion, Culture, and Society</u> (New York: Wiley, 1964) 127.

4. Book with editor and author

   ⁴Albert Schweitzer, <u>An Anthology</u>, ed. Charles R. Joy (New York: Harper & Row, 1947) 107.

5. Essay, chapter, section in an edited work

   ⁵Morris R. Cohn, "Baseball as a National Religion," <u>Religion, Culture, and Society</u>, ed. Louis Schneider (New York: Wiley, 1964) 74.

6. Encyclopedia entry

   (signed)

   ⁶Frank E. Reynolds, "Buddhism," <u>The World Book Encyclopedia</u>, 1983 ed.

   (unsigned)

   ⁷"Buddhism," <u>Encyclopedia Americana</u>, 1976 ed. [Note: No page numbers are necessary in alphabetically arranged works.]

   ARTICLES

1. Magazine (signed) monthly

   ⁸Douglas H. Lamb and Glen D. Reeder, "Reliving Golden Days," <u>Psychology Today</u>, June 1986: 22.

   (unsigned) weekly

   ⁹"An Unmellowed Woman," <u>Newsweek</u>, 9 July 1984: 73.

2. Scholarly journal

> [10]Edward Voutiras, "Dedication of the
>
> Hebdomaiston to the Pythian Apollo," <u>American</u>
>
> <u>Journal of Archaeology</u> 86 (1982): 229.

3. Newspapers

> [11]P. Ray Baker, "The Diagonal Walk," <u>Ann</u>
>
> <u>Arbor News</u>, 16 June 1928: A2.

EXERCISES AND RESEARCH PROJECT

Follow the procedures outlined in this chapter to research a primary literary text and write a humanities research paper. The exercises that follow will give you additional practice with skills related to research projects.

1. Write an extended description of one major character in the primary text you have chosen to research. Describe the person's physical appearance, mental state, actions, and the like, so that your reader will be able to picture that person. Use direct evidence from the text to illustrate and support your description.

2. Discuss one major theme from your primary text. Trace the development of that theme through the text, using evidence to support your idea of how the author develops the theme.

3. For each entry on your bibliography, write a three- or four-sentence annotation describing the contents of that source.

4. Write a three- to four-page "review of the literature" report, summarizing the major ideas in your sources. Often a literature review, which lists and comments on the sources, is a component of a larger research project.

SAMPLE RESEARCH PAPER: HUMANITIES
FORMAT (MLA)

(optional title page)

Cathy, the "Eve" of Eden

Sally Batten

English 1302-011

Dr. Harvey

April 2, 1983

Sally Batten

Professor Harvey

English 1302-011

2 April 1983

Cathy, the "Eve" of Eden

John Steinbeck, one of America's
favorite authors, wrote the novel <u>East of
Eden</u> in 1952. The story takes place in
Salinas, California, where Steinbeck was
born and raised. His mother's family
name, Hamilton, is one of the names used
in his novel (Kunitz and Haycraft 1338).
According to Riddel, <u>East of Eden</u> is "a
symbolic story about the need for broth-
erhood." Joseph Fontenrose, one of
Steinbeck's critics, states,

> The design and magnitude of
> <u>East of Eden</u>, and Steinbeck's
> own remarks about it, indicate
> that it was meant to be a cli-
> mactic work, his greatest
> achievement, for which every
> earlier book was practice.
> (126)

Batten 3

Warren French notes that <u>East of Eden</u>'s "most conspicuous and provocative figure" (54) is Cathy Ames Trask. She is, he says,

> the wayward wife and successful
> brothelkeeper single-mindedly
> bent on exercising [her] will,
> ready to destroy anything that
> stands in [her] way, and will
> scruple nothing to achieve
> [her] end. [She is] also
> clever enough to manipulate
> other people in order to
> achieve [her] purpose, and is
> responsible for [her] own
> destruction. (56)

The character of Cathy, as seen in her behavior in childhood, young adult years, and adult life, reveals her totally evil nature and its effect on others.

Judging from Steinbeck's description, Cathy Ames is a beautiful yet demonlike child. She has an innocent heartshaped face, golden hair, wide-set hazel eyes, a delicate and thin nose and high wide cheekbones. She has a child's figure—narrow hips, straight legs, deli-

Batten 4

cate arms, and tiny hands. Her voice is
"soft and husky—so sweet as to become
irresistible, fascinating, and
horrible."[1] According to Lisca, her
beauty seems angelic in this sense, but
"Cathy is often described in the terms of
a serpent" (Wide World 268). She "has a
preference for dark dens and the colors
of a rattlesnake (rust and yellow)"
(Nature and Myth 168). Her angelic looks
are very deceiving. She is not an angel.
She is a devil.

Despite Cathy's childlike physical
appearance, her emotional mentality is
that of a much older, vindictive person.
Many of Steinbeck's critics go so far as
to compare her mental state to that of a
monster. Steinbeck himself says,

And just as there are physical
monsters, can there not be
mental or psychic monsters
born? The face and body may be

---

[1]John Steinbeck, East of Eden (New
York: Viking, 1952) 32. Subsequent references are to this edition of the novel and
are included parenthetically in the text.

> perfect, but if a twisted gene
> or a malformed egg can produce
> physical monsters, may not the
> same process produce a mal-
> formed soul? (<u>Eden</u> 72)

Cathy is "not like other people,
never was from birth" (<u>Eden</u> 72). She
seems to have no love or conscience.
Hayashi observes that she is "a consummate liar and learns to use selfishness,
lust, and fear to manipulate people"
(<u>Dictionary</u> 28). However, she never feels
as though she is different, even though
she wants to be:

> Cathy had some quality that
> made people look at her, then
> look away, then look back at
> her, troubled at something for-
> eign. Something looked out of
> her eyes, and was never there
> when one looked again. She
> moved quickly and talked lit-
> tle, but she could enter no
> room without causing everyone
> to turn toward her. (<u>Eden</u> 73)

But even though she makes people
uneasy, they want to stay by her and find

out the cause of this "disturbance she
gives out" (<u>Eden</u> 73). Cathy uses this
power to get the things she wants. Steinbeck says she has this power "because she
has simplified [people's] weaknesses and
has no feeling about their strengths and
goodnesses" (<u>Journal</u> 44). This might be
explained by the fact that "to a monster,
everyone else is a monster. . . . Once
you know Cathy is a monster then nothing
she does can be unusual" (<u>Journal</u> 44).
Because of her power, "Cathy is going to
worry a lot of children, and a lot of
parents about their children" (<u>Journal</u>
46). She tells so many lies that "you can
believe her lies, but when she tells the
truth, it is not credible" (<u>Journal</u> 60).
Steinbeck explains that Cathy's life is
"one of revenge on other people because
of a vague feeling of her own lack"
(<u>Journal</u> 124). He also justifies her monstrous actions by the fact that Cathy
feels rejected. Steinbeck puts it this
way:

> The greatest terror a child
> can have is that he is not
> loved and rejection is the

> hell he fears. I think every-
> one in the world to a large or
> small extent has felt rejec-
> tion. And with rejection comes
> anger, and with anger some
> kind of crime in revenge for
> the rejection, and with the
> crime, guilt. (<u>Journal</u> 57)

Maybe Cathy has a valid reason for her
vindictive acts, but perhaps she truly is
a psychic monster.

    Cathy's parents are unable to deter-
mine whether she is a normal child, or if
there is something evil about her. They
really do not trust her, but they are
never sure why (<u>Cooperman</u> 80). They are
unaware of her many lies. Cathy's lies
are "never innocent. Their purpose [is]
to escape punishment, or responsibility,
and they [are] used for profit" (<u>Eden</u>
74). She never forgets any of them, so
she is never caught telling a contradict-
ing story. Mrs. Ames, her mother, does
not believe Cathy is abnormal:

> Since Cathy was an only child,
> her mother had no close con-
> trast in the family. She

thought all children were like
her own. And since all parents
are worriers she was convinced
that all her friends had the
same problems. (<u>Eden</u> 74)

Mr. Ames, however, is "not so sure.
[He comes] in contact with other children
away from home, and he [feels] that Cathy
is not like other children" (<u>Eden</u> 75).
But he cannot put his finger on what
makes her seem different, sinister. When
Cathy discovers she is not fully trusted,
she learns to manipulate her parents. She
gains their full trust, and in their
eyes, she can do no wrong. But her parents are getting in the way of what Cathy
wants. She must rid herself of them. So
she sets a fire at three in the morning,
locks the door from the inside, takes the
key and leaves town. Her parents are now
out of the way and the entire community
believes that she, too, is dead. Possibly, Cathy's parents are the only people
who might have discovered her hidden
identity. Maybe Cathy knew this, and it
was the reason for their sudden deaths.

Batten 9

Cathy's experiences with Mr. Edwards, her pimp in Boston, will change Cathy from a naive child who believes she can handle anything to a worldly young woman who will become suspicious of everyone. She begins as a prostitute and does an excellent job of bringing in money. Mr. Edwards becomes fascinated by her charms, and she is able to camouflage her true self. Cathy is now "more than a shadowy 'Eve' figure, more than Woman who not only succumbs to the Serpent, but becomes the serpent itself. . . . Cathy triumphs over her victims—and consumes her own substance" (Cooperman 77). Cathy steals Mr. Edward's money, keeps men on the side, and uses every possible situation to get her way. However, her charade is over the day she drinks a little wine with Mr. Edwards. Although Cathy tries to disguise "her innate evil nature, it reveals itself at the slightest loss of control, such as from a little alcohol" (Gray 57). For the first time, Cathy shows a weakness. The warm alcohol loosens her tongue and lowers her defense, turning her into an irate animal who begins to reveal to Mr. Edwards everything. When he finds out that she has burned the house, killed her parents, stolen his money and used him, he begins to beat her mercilessly. He hits her on the forehead with a rock, and leaves her dead, or so he thinks. Steinbeck reveals that the scar left on her forehead becomes a symbol of evil—like Cain in the <u>Bible</u> when he was sent away by God because of his wickedness (<u>Journal</u> 63). Cathy is alone once more. But this time, she has learned an important lesson, one that she must never forget. She will now be very careful about the people she becomes personally involved with, and will never try to be vulnerable to a man, as she was to Mr. Edwards.

Cathy's new knowledge of men becomes evident when she appears on the front steps of Adam and Charles Trask's house. She uses her experience with Mr. Edwards as a lesson in manipulating the two unwitting brothers. She is close to death at this point; Adam, being the caring and

Batten 11

trusting nurse, brings her back to her
health. Charles never trusts her, maybe
because they are the same in many ways.
He also bears the evil scar upon his
forehead. He tries to warn Adam that
there is something sinister about Cathy,
but Adam has already fallen in love. He
is "bedazzled into marrying Cathy, an
embodiment of evil . . ." (French 144).
Steinbeck writes:

> Why Adam Trask should have
> fallen in love with her is
> anybody's guess but I think it
> was because he himself was
> trained to operate best under
> a harsh master and simply
> transferred that to a tough
> mistress. (Journal 39)

Cathy's feelings for Adam seem
almost genuine at first. However, there
is never any real love in Cathy. She
"really couldn't understand Adam's love
for her; but when he proposed, she
accepted because she knew she could control him" (Cooperman 80). Cathy does not
plan to stay married of their wedding,

Batten 12

Cathy tells Adam that she is not well enough to consummate the marriage. She gives him her sleeping medicine and climbs into bed with her drunken brother-in-law, Charles. That night, she conceives Charles's child and begins the first stages of destroying her faithful husband, Adam.

Cathy's babies also become the victims of her wicked and vicious schemes. She is very unhappy being pregnant. She even tries once to abort the babies, but is unsuccessful. Steinbeck describes Cathy at this time "sitting quietly waiting for her pregnancy to be over, living on a farm she did not like, with a man she did not love" (<u>Eden</u> 184). She tells Adam all along that she wants to leave and that she will after she gives birth; but he thinks that she is just nervous about becoming a mother. Adam's good friend, Samuel Hamilton, helps Cathy through labor. He thinks she is very strange because she demands total darkness and becomes like an animal with pain. She bites Samuel (who has fever for

Batten 13

three days afterward) and refuses to look
at the twins after they are born. According to Lisca, Samuel, who has been
working in the field all day,

> associates the buried meteorite
> (falling star, hence Lucifer)
> which wrecks his well drill
> with Cathy, who bites his hand
> while he is helping her give
> birth to her twin sons, on the
> same day he discovers the
> meteorite. (Wide World 269)

At her children's birth, Cathy is
once again compared to a serpent. Lisca
comments that Cathy "gives birth to the
twins as easily as a snake lays eggs"
(Nature and Myth 168). As soon as Cathy
recovers from giving birth, she once
again tells Adam that she is leaving him:

> Why doesn't Adam listen when
> Cathy says she will be going
> away. . . . Men don't listen to
> what they don't want to
> hear. . . . Adam has a picture
> of his life, and he will con-
> tinue to maintain his picture

Batten 14

against every influence until

his world comes down. (<u>Journal</u>

76)

Adam's only way of keeping Cathy at

home is locking her in. But she is able

to convince him that she has changed her

mind, and promises to stay. When he opens

the door, she shoots him with a .44 Colt

in the leg. Adam is so upset that he goes

into a state of emotional shock. He has

thought of Cathy as the perfect wife and

he cannot accept the fact that she is

anything less. He does not even name the

twins for almost a year. Once again,

Cathy has managed to destroy a part of

someone's life, and once again she

spreads her evil upon her closest

acquaintances.

As Cathy matures, her ability to

overpower others becomes stronger, as in

the case of Faye, Cathy's new madam. She

learns of Faye's brothel and goes there

to work. She changes her name to Kate and

dyes her hair black, but this conversion

will never cover up her evil. Steinbeck

says, "They [the readers] will forget I

said she [Kate] was bad. And they will

Batten 15

hate her because while she is a monster, she is a little piece of the monster in all of us" (Journal 97). Once again Kate is going to use the people she associates with to accomplish what she wants. Warren French reminds the reader that "Kate is a witch whose spell must be exorcised if her activities are not to continue to destroy innocent people" (57). Kate even manages to get Faye to leave the entire estate to her when Faye dies. Of course, it is in Kate's plan, not Faye's, that the death happen soon. Kate slowly poisons Faye. No one suspects the act—everyone believes that Faye has an illness that is making her weaker and pushing her closer to death. In the meantime, Kate is learning to be an expert prostitute:

> [She] knows the power of the
> sexual impulse, and that is
> her most profound weapon
> against the people she
> destroys. She knew, too, about
> the guilts that accompany sex-
> ual indulgence, and she turned
> these into a fine profit by

catering to the masochistic

wishes of the men of Salinas.

Whips and matches were tools

of her whorehouse trade, and

the need for them was devel-

oped by her deliberately,

making her house essential in

the community. (Cooperman 87)

Finally, Faye dies. Now Kate is in
charge. Kate has once again eliminated
the one who was getting to know her too
well and was in the way of her success.

Kate seems to have reached her peak
in destruction, but then, her evil begins
to deteriorate. The origin of this suici-
dal process occurs when Adam comes to the
brothelhouse to confront Kate. Only when
he confronts the reality of Cathy (Adam
never refers to her as Kate), only when
he sees the essential blasphemy of his
attempt to create an Eden morality
itself, can he redeem his own manhood
(Cooperman 77).

He discovers when he sees her again
that she means nothing to him. Cathy
hates him for being freed from her evil
grasp. Later, one of her partners, Joe,

Batten 17

begins to take monetary advantage of her—
at first without her knowledge. Kate
realizes that she is losing her ability
to overpower others. Even her beloved
pictures of the senators, congressmen,
and other important government officials
that had visited her business no longer
seem important to her. She has been sav-
ing them for years as blackmail if they
do not continue to come to her "house":

> [Kate] commits suicide when she
> supposes that, even if she can
> outwit Joe, she will eventually
> be outwitted by someone else
> of her own ilk. . . . Her
> death is not a catastrophe,
> but an unmixed blessing to the
> community. . . . Paranoia will
> destroy itself without disrupt-
> ing society. (French 155)

Lisca observes that toward the end
of the book, "the reader learns . . . that
the monster, Cathy, has become a religious penitent (Episcopal) and has
committed suicide because of moral lone-
liness" (<u>Wide</u> <u>World</u> 267). As Kate slowly
poisons herself, as she had Faye, alone

in the dark, Steinbeck seems almost sym-
pathetic; but he was "just putting it
down as it might have happened" (<u>Journal</u>
169). Lisca notes that "Cathy is too much
like Satan to be a credible human-being,
and too much like a weak, pitiful human-
being to be properly Satanic" (<u>Wide</u> <u>World</u>
273). Cathy is only thirty, but, as
Hayashi observes, "her cheeks (have)
become chubby, her stomach and shoulders
plump, and her legs and feet thick and
bulging. Her hands are crippled with
arthritis" (<u>Dictionary</u> 28). Even though
Kate is physically gone, her malevolence
lives on in those she has emotionally
destroyed.

It appears that Cathy's corruption
has been transmitted to her son, Cal,
even though she is not involved with him
in any way. Steinbeck explains it as
follows:

> If she [Cathy] were simply a
> monster, that would not bring
> her in [the story]. But since
> she had the most powerful
> impact on Adam and transmitted
> her blood to her sons and

Batten 19

influenced the generations—she

certainly belongs in this book.

(<u>Journal</u> 42)

Cal has dark moods like his natural

father, Charles. He is lonely because the

people who are afraid of him ignore him.

He is also jealous of his brother, Aaron.

However, unlike his mother, Cal has "rec-

ognized the evil in himself, [and] is

ready to act for good" (Cooperman 88).

When Cal finds out who his mother is, he

is convinced that he is evil like her.

But Lee, the Chinese housekeeper, points

out that "all men have evil in their

ancestry, but the final choice of good or

evil is solely the individual's" (Cooper-

man 83). Before Cathy commits suicide,

Cal visits her. He does not tell his

brother Aaron, who is studying to be a

priest, that his mother is still alive,

because Cal always protects him. But one

night he becomes angry with Aaron and

takes him to "Kate's circus" (French

146). Aaron is so upset that he runs away

and joins the army, where he is killed in

action. When Adam learns that his beloved

Aaron has died, he has a stroke. The fam-

ily also learns at this point that Cathy
has committed suicide. Cal takes full
blame for everything that has gone wrong.
However, with Lee's help, Adam forgives
Cal and Cal is released from his guilt.
Cal now realizes that he does not have
Cathy's evil in him and that if he is
evil, it's the evil within his own
nature, an evil that he can control
(French 146). Finally, Cathy's evil has
ended. Even though she has almost killed
Adam and destroyed Cal's emotional state,
her monstrous effects have been snuffed
out. Adam and Cal are free.

Cathy Ames Trask's continuous evil
effect on her family and acquaintances is
clearly shown in this novel. Frohock
states that it may be easy to believe
women like Cathy exist:

> [and] that they burn home and
> parents, commit adultery with
> their brothers-in-law, and
> retire from family life to
> resume the oldest of profes-
> sions; but it is extremely
> difficult to make a woman like
> Cathy take on the kind of

Batten 21

actual existence which could
make her believable as a central character in a
novel—especially when, as in
the case of <u>East of Eden,</u> such
a woman is seen entirely from
the outside and the reader has
no clear notion of the reason
for her behaving as she does.
(Frohock 141)

But Steinbeck's character, Cathy, is
still a mystery. The readers can never
know if she is really a monster, because
they do not know what she wanted out of
life or if she got it. It is "easy to say
she was bad, but there is little meaning
unless we know why" (<u>Eden</u> 184) Steinbeck
says the question of Cathy's wicked and
sinful "existence goes forever unanswered—just as the 'reason' for the
presence of evil itself goes unanswered"
(<u>Eden</u> 184).

Bibliography

Cooperman, Stanley. <u>The Major Works of</u>
<u>John Steinbeck: Notes</u>. New York:
Monarch, 1964.

Cox, Martha Heasley. "Steinbeck's Family
Portraits: The Hamiltons." <u>Steinbeck</u>
<u>Quarterly</u> 14 (1981): 23-32.

Fontenrose, Joseph. <u>John Steinbeck: An</u>
<u>Introduction and Interpretation</u>. New
York: Holt, Rinehart-Winston, 1963.

French, Warren. <u>John Steinbeck</u>. Boston:
Twayne, 1975.

Frohock, Wilbur Merrill. <u>The Novel of</u>
<u>Violence in America</u>. Dallas: South-
ern Methodist UP, 1958.

Gray, James. "John Steinbeck." <u>American</u>
<u>Writers, IV</u>. Ed. Leonard Unger. New
York: Scribner's, 1974. 47-65.

Hayashi, Tetsumaro. <u>John Steinbeck: A</u>
<u>Concise Bibliography</u>. Metuchen, NJ:
Scarecrow Press, 1967.

- - -. <u>John Steinbeck: A Dictionary of</u>
<u>His Fictional Characters</u>. Metuchen,
NJ: Scarecrow Press, 1976.

Kunitz, Stanley J., and Howard Haycraft,
eds. <u>Twentieth Century Authors</u>. New
York: Wilson, 1942.

Lisca Peter. <u>The Wide World of John
     Steinbeck</u>. New Brunswick, NJ: Rut-
     gers UP, 1958.

- - -. <u>John Steinbeck: Nature and Myth</u>.
     New York: Crowell, 1978.

McCarthy, Paul. <u>John Steinbeck</u>. New York:
     Ungar, 1980.

McDaniel, Barbara. "Alienation in <u>East of
     Eden</u>: The 'Chart of the Soul.' "
     <u>Steinbeck Quarterly</u> 14 (1981):
     32-39.

Riddel, Joseph N. "John Steinbeck." <u>The
     World Book Encyclopedia</u>. 1983 ed.

Steinbeck, John. <u>East of Eden</u>. New York:
     Viking, 1952.

- - -. <u>Journal of a Novel</u>: The East of
     Eden <u>Letters</u>. New York: Viking,
     1969.

DISCIPLINE-SPECIFIC RESOURCES
FOR HUMANITIES

General Sources and Guides to Literature

Art Research Methods and Resources: A Guide to Finding Art Information. L. Jones. Dubuque, IA: Kendall Hunt, 1985. A guide to sources in art.

Field Guide to the Study of American Literature. H. Kolb. Charlottesville, VA.: University of Virginia Press, 1976. A guide to selected sources in American literature.

Guide to Dance in Films: A Guide to Information Sources. D. L. Parker and E. Siegel. Detroit: Gale, 1978. A general guide to sources.

Guide to Historical Literature. American Historical Association. New York: Macmillan, 1961. A guide to sources in American history.

Harvard Guide to American History. Rev. ed. F. Freidel, ed. Cambridge, MA: Harvard University Press, 1974. A guide to sources in American history; contains an introduction to the discipline.

Information Sources in Architecture. V. J. Bradfield. Stoneham, MA: Butterworth, 1983. A general guide to sources.

Literary History of the United States. 4th ed. R. E. Spiller et al. New York: Macmillan, 1974. A history of U.S. literature from colonial times to 1960s.

New Cambridge Modern History. Cambridge, England: Cambridge University Press, 1957–70. An introduction to history from the Renaissance through the modern period.

Oxford History of English Literature. F. P. Wilson and B. Dobree, eds. Oxford, England: Oxford University Press, 1969–77. An introduction to English literature from early to modern times. Includes extensive bibliographies.

Oxford History of Music. W. H. Hadow, ed. Oxford, England: Oxford University Press, 1990. A comprehensive, historical overview.

Philosopher's Guide to Sources, Research Tools, Professional Life and Related Fields. R. DeGeorge, ed. Lawrence: Regents Press of Kansas, 1980. A guide to sources in philosophy, religion, social science, fine arts, literature, and other related fields.

Reader's Guide to the Great Religions. C. J. Adams, ed. New York: Free Press, 1977. Introduces major religions and discusses sources.

Reference Sources in English and American Literature: An Annotated Bibliography. 4th ed. J. Lang and D. Masters. Chicago: American Library Association, 1977. A good starting source.

Dictionaries

Dictionary of American Philosophy. S. Elmo, Jr. New York: Philosophical Library, 1974. General information and definitions.

Dictionary of Architecture. 3 vols. New York: Gordon Press, 1980. General information.

Dictionary of Comparative Religions. S. G. Brandon, ed. New York: Scribner's, 1978. Provides information on the world religions.

Dictionary of Composers and Their Music. E. Gilder. New York: Holt, 1986. Useful background information.

Dictionary of Contemporary American Artists. P. Cummings. New York: St. Martin's, 1988. Provides concise information on living American artists.

Dictionary of Literature in the English Language. 2 vols. R. Meyers. New York: Pergamon, 1979. Useful background information on classical English literary works.

Encyclopedic Dictionary of Religions. 3 vols. P. K. Meagher, ed. Washington, D.C.: Catholic University Press, 1979. Provides complete background information on the world's great religions.

Funk & Wagnalls' Standard Dictionary of Folklore, Mythology, and Legend. M. Leach, ed. New York: Funk & Wagnalls, 1984. Provides concise information on myths and legends.

Harvard Dictionary of Music. 2nd ed. W. Apel. Cambridge, MA: Harvard University Press, 1969. Contains valuable information on all aspects of music, including musical terminology.

McGraw-Hill Dictionary of Art. B. Myers, ed. New York: McGraw-Hill, 1969. Provides information on all aspects of art: artists' lives and careers, styles, periods, buildings, museums, terms.

The New Grove Dictionary of Music and Musicians. 20 vols. S. Sadie, ed. London: Macmillan, 1980. Provides information on musical topics from ancient to modern times.

Encyclopedias

Britannica Encyclopedia of American Art. Chicago: Encyclopaedia Britannica, 1973. Provides concise information on all facets of American art. Contains many illustrations.

Cassell's Encyclopaedia of World Literature. Rev. ed. J. Buchanan-Brown, ed. New York: Morrow, 1973. Provides concise background information on the world's great literature and authors.

Encyclopedia of American History. R. B. Morris. New York: Harper & Row, 1982. Valuable overview of American history; contains brief biographies of famous Americans.

Encyclopedia of Bioethics. W. T. Reich, ed. New York: Macmillan, 1982. Provides information on philosophy and religion.

Encyclopedia of Philosophy. P. Edwards, ed. New York: Free Press, 1973. Complete reference work on philosophical thought, both Eastern and Western.

Encyclopedia of Religion. 16 vols. New York: Macmillan, 1986. Concise articles on world religions.

Encyclopedia of Science Fiction and Fantasy. D. Tuck. Berkeley, CA: Adventure Press, 1983. Concise articles on works of science fiction.

Encyclopedia of World Art. New York: McGraw-Hill, 1958–68. Provides information on the world's art and artists.

An Encyclopedia of World History: Ancient, Medieval, and Modern. W. L. Langer, ed. Boston: Houghton Mifflin, 1973. Lists major world events from earliest times to 1970. (*The New Illustrated Encyclopedia of World History* is essentially the same work with illustrations.)

The New College Encyclopedia of Music. J. A. Westrop and F. L. Harrison. New York: Norton, 1981. Provides concise information on all aspects of music.

Princeton Encyclopedia of Poetry and Poetics. A. Preminger, ed. Princeton, NJ: Princeton University Press, 1974. Provides concise information on poetry and poetics through time, covering history, theory, technique, and criticism of poetry.

Biographies

American Novelists Since WWII. J. Helterman and R. Layman, eds. Dictionary of Literary Biography Series, vol 2. Detroit: Gale, 1978. Provides illustrated biographical entries on recent American novelists.

American Poets Since WWII. D. Greiner, ed. Dictionary of Literary Biography Series, vol 5. Detroit: Gale, 1980. Provides illustrated biographical entries on recent American poets.

Contemporary American Composers: A Biographical Dictionary. R. Anderson. Boston: G. K. Hall, 1976. Provides information on American composers born since 1870.

Contemporary Authors: A Biographical Guide to Current Authors and Their Works. Detroit: Gale, 1962–present. Provides information on current American Authors.

Directory of American Scholars. 8th ed. New York: Bowker, 1982. A biographical directory that includes information on notable scholars still active in their fields.

(See also Biographies, pp. 30–31, and Encyclopedias, p. 30.)

Indexes, Bibliographies, and Abstracts

ART AND ARCHITECTURE

Architectural Index
*Art Index
Ceramics Abstracts

ENGLISH AND LANGUAGE STUDIES

Abstracts of English Studies
American Literature Abstracts
Annual Bibliography of English Language and Literature
Articles on American Literature
Cambridge Bibliography of English Literature
Essay and General Literature Index
Granger's Index to Poetry
International Guide to Classical Studies

Language and Language Behavior Abstracts
*MLA (Modern Language Association) International Bibliography
Short Story Index
Year's Work in English Studies

FOLKLORE

Abstracts of Folklore Studies
Index to Fairytales, Myths and Legends

HISTORY

*America: History and Life
Combined Retrospective Index to Journals in History
*Historical Abstracts

* = Computer searching available

Writings on American History

HUMANITIES GENERAL
*Arts and Humanities Citation Index
*Humanities Index
 Index to Book Reviews in the
        Humanities
 Social Science and Humanities Index

JOURNALISM
Journalism Abstracts

MOTION PICTURES AND FILM
Film Literature Index
International Index of Film
        Periodicals
Landers Film Reviews
New York Times Film Reviews
*New York Times Index

MUSIC
 Music Article Guide
 Music Index
*RILM Abstracts

PHILOSOPHY
Philosopher's Index

RELIGION
Religion One Index
Religious and Theological Abstracts

THEATER
New York Times Theater Reviews
Play Index

WOMEN'S STUDIES
Women's Studies Abstract

9

✦ ✦ ✦

Writing a Research Report in Business

INTRODUCTION

In business, writers often produce research reports in which they seek to become "experts" on particular topics in order to communicate that expertise to other concerned individuals. The businessman or woman must have knowledge of the business world in general and should be familiar with library tools used by those in business to gain access to current information in the field.

In the business report, your task is to summarize for your readers the present situation in a particular field or market. Your contribution, then, is to interpret and organize the information you find, thus making it easily accessible to your readers. Generally, in the business report, through paraphrase and summary, you are reporting on the information you discovered in your research as objectively as you can.

Some business research reports use primary research, such as marketing reviews, surveys, technical studies, or computer data. For many business research projects, library research is also involved. Several library research principles and skills will be important for you as you investigate your chosen topic. These skills include the following:

1. Familiarity with library resources, including bibliographies and indexes used in business.
2. The ability to understand and evaluate data from a variety of sources.
3. The ability to paraphrase and summarize information in your own words.

4. The ability to synthesize the information gathered into an organized presentation of the data.

5. The ability to employ the formal conventions of business reports.

A GUIDE TO THE BUSINESS
RESEARCH PROCESS

To begin your report, first determine a research topic. If you are
taking a business course now, look in your textbook for research ideas,
checking its table of contents as well as any references that may be
listed. Another source of ideas is current business journals. Greg Hartman, whose research will serve as a model for this chapter, became interested in the subject of computer-aided design and drafting (CADD)
in the business world, since he was studying engineering as well as
business. He conducted his research as an assignment in a business
course called Business Information Systems. You should select a topic
that will hold your interest and attention, preferably one that you already know something about, so that you will be an informed and objective reporter.

Preparation

Gather the materials you need for your research project, including a research notebook or notecards; then make a schedule that will
give you enough time to conduct your library research and to write a
draft and final copy of your report. If your research project involves any
primary research, be sure to allow yourself enough time to gather and
analyze the data. Careful planning at the outset of such a major project
will ensure that you have time to carry out the research necessary to
write an informed report.

Developing a Search Strategy

Greg had formulated some general impressions about CADD
through his own reading. He wanted to find out the current thinking
in the business world about how CADD could be applied and what its
impact was on industry. He began his library search, then, with a look
at general background sources in an effort to define what CADD is and
how it is used. Next, he looked more closely at articles specifically
about the use of CADD with microcomputers. An outline of his search
strategy is presented here (your particular search may differ somewhat
from this outline):

Greg's Search Strategy

1. Encyclopedias and dictionaries (general and specialized), for background information, including the *Academic American Encyclopedia* and the *McGraw-Hill Encyclopedia of Science and Technology.*
2. Reviews of research, using the *Index to Scientific Reviews.*
3. Indexes, abstracts, and databases for access to source articles, including the ABI-INFORM database and the *Applied Science and Technology Index.*
4. Online card catalog, for access to books and other sources, using the LCSH for correct terminology ("computer-aided design"; "computer graphics," and so on).
5. Primary research, such as marketing reviews, computer data, or technical studies, if appropriate.

When you are writing a business report, you are often looking for very recent information. You will find recent information primarily in journals related to the specific field. Your library search will probably begin in your library's reference area, since it contains the tools that give you access to journal articles. To illustrate the use of a library search strategy in business, we will follow the steps listed previously, using Greg's research as a model.

✦ EXERCISE

Outline your own search strategy, beginning with general and working to specific sources. Include any primary research needed for your project. Draw up a time schedule to guide your research.

General Sources

To begin your research, read general information about your topic to put it into a context and to help you focus by narrowing your topic to a manageable size. Also, reading general and specialized encyclopedias and dictionaries helps you define what is considered common knowledge on the topic. Depending on your particular topic, you will be reading general encyclopedias, such as the *World Book,* and specialized encyclopedias, such as the *Encyclopedia of Management.* (The sources commonly used in business are listed on pages 369–371.) Greg used the following background sources, which he listed in his notebook as the beginning of his working bibliography:

Academic American Encyclopedia. "Computer-Aided

  Design and Computer-Aided Manufacturing."

George Zinsmeister. Danbury, Conn.: Grolier,

1987 ed.

<u>McGraw-Hill Encyclopedia of Science and</u>

<u>Technology</u>. "Computer-Aided Design and

Manufacturing." Herbert W. Yankee. 5th

ed. 1982.

At the end of each general source, such as the encyclopedias mentioned above, you will usually find a list of references that may lead you to other related sources on your topic. List any promising references on your working bibliography, but do not necessarily look up each entry at this time.

✦ EXERCISE

Find and read background sources relevant to your topic to obtain general information (see pp. 369–371 for a list of sources often used in business).

Focusing Your Search

After reading several background sources about your topic, you are ready to narrow the focus of your report. Greg, for example, began his search by looking for information on computer-aided design and drafting in general. His starting questions included the following: "What exactly is CADD and what is it used for? What are some of its advantages? What impact is it having on business?" As he began reading background sources, he discovered that the newest development in CADD technology was the use of microcomputers, called microCADD, to aid designers and drafters in industry. He discovered that the future of CADD seemed to be with microcomputers, so he decided to focus his search on microCADD rather than discussing CADD in general. Without such a focus, he could have wandered aimlessly through the material with no clear idea of what he was looking for. Take care to define carefully for yourself just what topic you are trying to research for your report.

✦ EXERCISE

Define clearly for yourself what topic you wish to report on. Narrow the focus of that topic to a manageable size.

Reviews and Reports

For many business topics, reviews and reports may be important. Greg used the *Index to Scientific Reviews* to locate any reviews done on CADD. He found one recent reference; however, it turned out to be too technical for use in his research report:

```
Deman H. Evolution of CADD Tools. Rev Phys
    Ap. 22(1): 31-45 '87.
```

Indexes and Abstracts

The main resources for anyone investigating a current topic in business will be the online and print indexes and abstracts. Find out which business indexes and abstracts your library contains access to via computer searching, since searching online is generally both faster and more comprehensive than searching manually through print indexes.

Many business indexes are now searchable by microcomputer, including CompuServe and ABI-INFORM. Greg found these databases to be very useful in his research. Using the ABI-INFORM database on CD-ROM, Greg typed in key terminology such as "computer graphics" and "computer-aided design." The screen listed several recent sources, which Greg printed out to include in his working bibliography:

```
Kalb, B. "PC-based CAD Sprouts Unusual Benefits."
    Chilton's Automotive Industries 167 (May
    1987): 104-108.
Milburn, K. "CAD: Designs on Business." Personal
    Computing 21 (April 1988): 108-124.
Teicholz, E.; Smith, D. "State of the Art."
    Planning 53 (January 1987): 25-28.
```

The print indexes, such as *Business Periodicals Index* and *Business Index,* list articles published in a given year by subject and/or author. By using these indexes, you can search for titles of journal articles written on your topic. Unless you are doing a historical study, you should start with the most recent volume of the index and work your way back, looking up your topic in several volumes of the index. For example, using the Applied Science and Technology Index, Greg looked up "computer graphics" to find several recent articles on the subject of CADD, including the following sources, which he listed on his working bibliography:

```
CAD/CAM The feast is yet to come. B. Darrow.

    Design News 43:74-80; 1987.

The use of CAD in ship design. W. W. VanDevender.

    Marine Technology 25:36-43; 1988.

Fast CAD 1.10. P. Robinson. Byte 12:178-80; 1987.
```

Another type of reference tool you may use is the abstract. An abstract provides a brief summary of the important works in a field. For example, the *Economic Titles/Abstracts* provides access to books, reports, and journal articles in economics. Depending on your topic, you may find such a source useful.

✦ EXERCISE

Use databases, indexes or abstracts to find titles of articles related to your topic (see pp. 370–371 for a list of indexes used in business).

The Library Catalog

At this point in your search, you may wish to use the online library catalog to locate additional book titles and/or journal titles on the same or related topics. Greg looked up "computer graphics" and "computer-aided design," using the online book catalog of the library. In this way he found a recent book that was exactly on his topic:

```
Goetsch. D. L. MicroCADD: Computer-Aided Design

    and Drafting on Microcomputers. Englewood

    Cliffs, NJ: Prentice-Hall, 1988.
```

✦ EXERCISE

Use the catalog to locate sources and to find additional source material on your topic. Use the LCSH list to find the heading(s) under which materials on your topic are cataloged.

Evaluation

Once you have located either a book or an article, evaluate it for its relevance or usefulness in your search. If, after an initial screening, a book looks as though it can be useful to you, check it out at the circulation desk. In the case of articles, either photocopy them for later use or take notes from them in the library, since they are generally noncirculating materials and cannot be checked out.

✦ **EXERCISE**

In your research notebook, evaluate each article and book to be used in your research. Follow the source evaluation guidelines in Chapter 3 found on pages 80–81.

Taking Notes

As you begin to take notes from your sources, remember to keep complete information for each source you read, so you will not have to look up a particular source again. Be certain to put into quotation marks any information you take directly from the source and to mark down the exact page number on which you found the note at the end of the note itself. Also specify whether you paraphrased the author's words or quoted directly. Taking care at this stage will benefit you when you get to the actual writing stage of your report.

Primary Research

If your business report project includes any primary research, such as marketing reviews, computer data, or technical studies, you will need to design and conduct that research and analyze your data.

✦ **EXERCISE**

Conduct any primary research connected to your project. Analyze your data and determine the best way to display your results, whether in a graph, table, or discussion.

ORGANIZING AND WRITING THE BUSINESS REPORT

A major task in writing a business report is organizing the material you have gathered. It is your job to make sense of the information you have found and to present it logically for the reader in an objective, comprehensive manner. When Greg narrowed his topic to micro-CADD, he decided to report on the state of the art in microCADD for a novice reader: defining what it is and what it can do; describing some applications of microCADD in business and industry; and indicating the future of computer-aided design. He outlined a preliminary plan that would cover these major sections as follows:

Tell what microCADD is
Cover briefly the development of microCADD
Advantages of microCADD over commercial CADD systems
Advantages of microCADD over manual drafting
Cover briefly how microCADD works
Give some applications in business and industry
Suggest the future of microCADD

Once he had decided on the organizational plan, he blocked information in his notebook into the appropriate sections to fit the subtopics of the plan. He set aside any information that did not seem to fit in the paper. To have a unified, coherent presentation of your research, you must also discard any information that is irrelevant to your particular focus.

Planning and Outlining

Your preliminary plan will give you the skeleton for an outline of your paper, which will guide you when you write but not constrain or limit your thinking. Your outline may change several times as you make new discoveries while writing:

Informal Outline
Title: MicroCADD for All
Thesis: Computer-aided design and drafting (CADD) on microcomputers is a new and rapidly growing field.
Introduction
    Tell what microCADD is
History
    Development of microCADD up to its standing today
Advantages of microCADD
    MicroCADD vs. commercial CADD systems
    MicroCADD vs. manual drafting
How microCADD works
    Examples of relevant commands and functions
Applications of microCADD
    Who uses it?
    What do they use it for?
Future of microCADD

✦ EXERCISE

Organize your source material, decide on an organizational plan, and construct an outline to guide your writing of the first draft of your research report. Refer to Chapter 5 for help with organization (pp. 140–144).

Writing the First Draft: Verification

After you have completed your outline, you are ready to write the first draft of your report. Remember, you are writing to report to your readers the current status of a particular issue or topic. Remind yourself at this time of your general understanding of your topic. When writing your first draft, use concrete and simple language to explain as objectively as you can your understanding of the topic. Your outline will guide the writing of this first draft.

As you write the first draft, it is important to note down which material comes from which sources. Do not be overly concerned at this point about the formal details of documentation, which can be dealt with later, but do mark for yourself in the draft any ideas or words you take from your sources. You should place any word or sentence you copy from a source in quotation marks, followed by the last name, the date of publication, and the page number of the source (in parentheses):

```
"The drafter can produce finished drawings

in much less time" (Stanton 1985, 3).
```

Similarly, document paraphrases and restatements of ideas taken from a source even though you have recast them in your own words:

```
Reasons for the low cost include ease of

setup and less user training (Teicholz and Smith

1987, 25).
```

When referring generally to a source, it is not necessary to provide a page reference:

```
Zinsmeister (1987) reports that microCADD is

used to test designs instead of building a costly

prototype.
```

For general information on planning, writing, and revising your business report, refer to Chapter 5. Use the following information on documentation in business and economics for the correct form for citations. The sample research report at the end of this chapter can serve as a model for a business report.

DOCUMENTATION IN BUSINESS AND ECONOMICS

In business and economics, it is common to use the same general author/year system used in the sciences and social sciences. This system includes (1) in-text citations giving the author's name and the publication year of the source, and (2) an alphabetized list of references at the end of the paper.

Internal Citations

In business and economics, the citations within the text provide enough information to refer the reader to the complete list of references on the references page. The following principles should be observed:

1. When an author's work in general is cited, you list the author's name and the year of publication in parentheses at the end of the information or use the author's name to introduce the information:

   ```
   Today there are nearly 200 microCADD vendors
   (Goetsch 1988).
   ```

   ```
   Goetsch (1988) states that today there are
   nearly 200 microCADD vendors.
   ```

2. When an author's words or ideas are directly quoted or directly paraphrased, a page number should be included (without p.):

   ```
   User training takes "less than a month to
   learn" (Teicholz and Smith 1987, 25).
   ```

3. When a work has more than three authors, use *et al.* (and others) for the in-text citation. Thus a work by Schulz, Chote, Horn, and VanDevener would be listed as follows:

   ```
   (Schulz et al. 1988)
   ```

4. When two or more references are given together, they are separated by semicolons:

   (Kalb 1987; Woodcock and Binsacca 1987)

5. When no known author is given for a work, use the title of the sponsoring group or organization, such as (Federal Reserve Bank of Boston 1976); or in the case of magazines and newspapers, use an abbreviated form of the title ("Applications Still Flood In" 1983).

The Reference List

The reference list in business and economics (similar to that used in the social sciences) is an alphabetized list of all the sources actually cited in the paper. It is titled "References." The actual format of the entries differs somewhat from that in the sciences or social sciences. The following principles are generally accepted in business and economics journals:

1. Authors are listed by complete name (when known) or by surname and initials.
2. Capital letters are used for all important words in the title of an article, and the title is enclosed by quotation marks.
3. Names of books and journals are underlined. Names of journals are not abbreviated.
4. For books, the title is followed by the place of publication, the publisher, and the date:

   Melman, Seymour. <u>Our Depleted Society</u>. New York:

   Del Publishers, 1965.

5. For articles, the date, volume number, and the inclusive page numbers follow the name of the journal:

   Powell, Gary N. "Sexual Harassment: Confronting

   the Issue of Definition." <u>Business Horizons</u>

   9 (July-August 1983):24-28.

6. The first word of the entry is typed at the left margin. Subsequent lines of the same entry are indented five spaces. The entire reference page is double spaced.

If you are writing a research paper for a class in business or economics, it is important for you to ask your instructor which documentation form he or she prefers. A style manual frequently used in business and industry is *The Chicago Manual of Style,* 14th ed., published by the University of Chicago Press (1993). You may wish to refer to this manual for your papers in business courses. The model references and sample paper below use the style (and a few of the models) outlined in the *Chicago Manual.*

MODEL REFERENCES: BUSINESS AND ECONOMICS (CHICAGO)

Type of Reference

BOOKS

1. One author

Cole, Robert H. <u>Consumer and Commercial Credit

Management</u>, 5th ed. Homewood, IL: Irwin,

1976.

2. Two or more authors

Weston, J. Fred, and Eugene F. Brightman.

<u>Managerial Finance</u>, 5th ed. New York: Dryden

Press, 1975.

[Note: Include the names of all authors listed on the title page. Use et al. only with in-text citations.]

3. Book with editor

Rathe, Alex W., ed. <u>Gantt on Management</u>. New

York: American Management Association, 1961.

4. Essay, chapter, or section of edited work

Ogilvy, David. "The Creative Chef." In The

<u>Creative Organization</u>, edited by Gary

Steiner, 199-213. Chicago: University of

Chicago Press, 1965.

5. Corporate author

> International Monetary Fund. <u>Survey of African</u>
>   <u>Economies</u>. Vol. 7, <u>Algeria, Mali, Morocco,</u>
>   <u>and Tunisia</u>. Washington, D.C., 1977.

6. Encyclopedia entry

> "Sexual Harassment." <u>Encyclopedia of Management</u>,
>   3rd ed., edited by Carl Heyel. New York: Van
>   Nostrand Reinhold, 1982.

ARTICLES

1. Journal article (one author)

> Boyer, Ernest. "The Recovery Is Shaping the
>   Economy." <u>Fortune</u> 108 (October 1983):60-65.

2. Journal article (two or more authors)

> Lear, Ronald, and C. Groneman. "The Corporate
>   Ph.D.—Humanities Scholars Bring New
>   Perspective to Business Problems." <u>Man-</u>
>   <u>agement Review</u> 72 (September 1983):32-33.

3. Journal, magazine, or newspaper article (no known author)

> "The Applications Still Flood in, but Slight Rise
>   in Vacancies Cheers Graduate Recruiters."
>   <u>Personnel Management</u> 15 (August 1983):12-13.

4. Newspaper article

> Schickel, Richard. "Far Beyond Reality: The New
>   Technology of Hollywood's Special Effects."
>   <u>New York Times Magazine</u>, 18 May 1980, p. 8

[Note: When an article skips to the back of the newspaper, provide the first page number only.]

OTHER SOURCES

1. Dissertation or thesis

King, Andrew J. "Law and Land Use in Chicago: A
    Pre-History of Modern Zoning." Ph.D. diss.,
    University of Wisconsin, 1976.

2. Paper presented at conference

Saunders, Robert. "Today's Manager." Paper
    presented at the annual meeting of the
    American Institute of Industrial Engineers,
    New York, 1983.

3. Personal communication (letters and interviews)

Ewing, Nancy. Letter to author. 24 January 1985.

Hughes, Howard. Interview with author. Las Vegas,
    Nevada, 15 July 1970.

4. Public documents

U.S. Department of Justice Law Enforcement
    Assistance Administration, 1970. <u>Criminal</u>
    <u>Justice Agencies in Pennsylvania</u>. Wash-
    ington, D.C.: Government Printing Office.

5. Electronic Information
   Electronic publications can be divided into two major types:
   portable databases (distributed on CD-ROMs) and online databases (accessible through computer networks).
   Portable databases

Arms, Valerie M. "A Dyslexic Can Compose on
a Computer." <u>Educational Technology</u> 24.1 (1984):
39–41. <u>ERIC</u>. CD-ROM. SilverPlatter. Sept. 1984.

<u>Where in the World Is Carmen Sandiego</u>? CD-
ROM. Novato: Brederbund. 1992.

Materials found through online computer networks

Lawrence, Oliver J. "Pitfalls in Electronic
Writing Land." <u>English Education</u> 16.2
(1984):94-100. Online. Dialog. 14 Sept.
1984.

Reid, Joy. "Computer-Assisted Text-Analysis for
ESL Students." <u>Calico Journal</u> 1.3 (1983):
40-42. Online Abstract. Abstract from:
Dialog file: ERIC Item: EJ298270.

Herz, John C. "Surfing on the Internet: A
Nethead's Adventures Online." <u>Urban Desires</u>
1.3 (March/April 1995): n. pag. Online.
Internet. 15 Apr. 1995. Available:
www/desires.com/ud.html.

Electronic Correspondence (such as e-mail messages and conversations via bulletin boards and electronic discussion groups)

Gardner, Susan. "Help with Citations." E-mail to
Christine Hult. 20 Mar. 1995.

White, Edward. "Texts as Scholarship: Reply to
Bob Schwegler." 11 Apr. 1995. Online
posting. WPA discussion list. Bitnet.
Available e-mail: WPA-L@ASUACAD.bitnet.

Shaumann, Thomas Michael. "Re: Technical German."
5 Aug. 1994. Online posting. Newsgroup
comp.edu.languages.natural. Usenet. 7 Sept.
1994.

[Note: Include both the date of the posting and the date of access, if different.]

(See Xia Li and Nancy B. Crane. <u>Electronic Style: A Guide to Citing Electronic Information.</u> Westport: Meckler, 1993.)

EXERCISES AND RESEARCH PROJECT

Complete the exercises in this chapter as you research and report on a carefully defined business topic. The exercises provided give you additional practice with skills associated with business reports.

1. For each entry on your bibliography, write a three- or four-sentence annotation describing the contents of that source.

2. Write a "review of the literature" report that summarizes in three to four pages the major ideas found in your sources. Often, a literature review, which lists and comments on the works done to date in a particular area, is a component of a larger paper. The review of the literature proceeds in chronological order based on the publication date of the source and thus will differ from the report itself, which may be organized around concepts or other categories.

3. When you have finished writing your report, write a synopsis fifty to one hundred words in length in which you summarize the main points of your paper. A synopsis is a brief, general condensation of the report. See the sample synopsis included with the model paper in this chapter; also see the discussion of abstracts in Chapter 5.

4. When you have finished writing your report, write a table of contents for your report. See the table for the model paper in this chapter.

SAMPLE RESEARCH REPORT: BUSINESS AND ECONOMICS FORMAT (CHICAGO)

MicroCADD for All

Presented To:

Professor Susan Larsen

Business Information Systems 255

Presented By:

Greg Hartman

2 June 1988

Contents

Title: MicroCADD for All

2

MicroCADD for All

MicroCADD means design and drafting
accomplished using microcomputers. Computer-aided design and drafting (CADD)
joins the power of the computer with the
creativity and skills of the engineer,
architect, designer, and drafter. The
microcomputers used in CADD have high-
resolution monitors and dual-disk-drive
configurations consisting of a hard disk
and one floppy drive (Goetsch 1988). A
simple way to describe the use of CADD is
as follows:

> The drafter, working from an
> engineer's or architect's rough
> sketch, creates drawings on a
> computer screen. The pens,
> inks, compasses, and other
> tools used by drafters for
> generations are replaced by a
> keyboard, graphics tablet, dig-
> itizer, and light pen. Instead
> of a line of ink on paper, a
> line of glowing phosphorus
> appears on a video console.
> Through a series of programmed

3

        commands, the drafter can pro-
duce finished drawings in much
less time and of a higher
quality than those produced
manually. (Stanton 1985, 3)

Computer-aided design and drafting
has been going through a continuous
development since its beginnings in the
early 1960s. These early commercial CADD
systems came about in the late 1970s,
along with the development of the microcomputer. This dual development created
problems for the microCADD systems in
that more memory, better processing
speeds, and better graphics capabilities
needed to be made available to make CADD
more than just a "toy." By the early
1980s, these developments had been made.
Along with the advances in computer technology came the interest of many large
firms in creating a new CADD market.
These numerous companies, which develop
and sell microCADD equipment (vendors),
numbered 100 in the mid-1980s. Today
there are nearly 200 such vendors
(Goetsch 1988). Some big-name vendors
include AutoCAD, AutoSketch, Drafix 1

4

Plus, FastCAD, Generic CADD, and VersaCAD
Design, to name just a few (Milburn
1988). This increase of 100 vendors
within the past couple of years would
seem to show that computer-aided design
and drafting on microcomputers is a sudden and rapidly growing phenomenon.

MicroCADD vs. Commercial CADD Systems. When comparing microCADD with
traditional CADD systems, the overall low
cost of microCADD is usually the greatest
advantage. A good CADD system can cost
anywhere from $50,000 to $250,000 and
higher, while microCADD systems average
around $10,000 for the entire setup. Rea-
sons for this low cost are the given low
initial costs, lower maintenance costs,
ease in setting up the system, and
finally, less user training—it takes
"less than a month to learn" (Teicholz
and Smith 1987, 25).

Another big advantage microCADD has
over CADD is convenience. Whereas CADD
systems need to be purchased directly
from a vendor and require special equipment to set up, microCADD can be
purchased through computer stores and can

5

be run on an already existing office
microcomputer. MicroCADD systems are also
portable and easily moved and accommo-
dated.

A final comparison that may not be
realized is that the time it takes to
execute a command can be faster than on
CADD systems, even though CADDs use
larger, more powerful mainframe computers. This holds true because a number of
terminals are usually tied into the mainframe and all terminals are working at
the same time, thus slowing down the
response time to each terminal. In contrast, since only one user is tied to the
microcomputer on a microCADD system,
response time is much quicker.

MicroCADD vs. Manual Drafting. When
comparing microCADD to manual design and
drafting techniques, it is clear that the
increase in productivity is the biggest
advantage of microCADD. Drawings created
by hand are time-consuming and, even
worse, a problem to store. Pencil drawings are used repeatedly in making
blueprint copies, causing them to fade,
smear, and stain the more they are used.

6

MicroCADD, on the other hand, is more
productive in that you have faster drawing creation and manipulation, more
convenient data storage, and faster data
output.

Two of the most time-consuming manual drafting faults are correcting and
revising designs. The editing capabilities of a microCADD system make
corrections and revisions quick and easy,
also increasing productivity. Calling up
a drawing file is also much easier than
locating a drawing in a group of files
without damaging the files.

Creativity is another advantage
microCADD has over manual design and
drafting. A person who wants to change a
design manually may be a bit reluctant
because of all the work that would be
involved in doing so, whereas by using a
microCADD system, the design can be
altered easily.

How MicroCADD Works. MicroCADD systems perform operations through various
commands and respond to user prompts in
the software. Commands are issued through
the combined use of the keyboard and menu

7

items found on the display screen. These
commands are always available and easily
accessed. (The commands are described in
several articles, including Milburn 1988,
and Teicholz and Smith 1987.)

Some common data creation commands
are as follows: Point (which allows the
user to pick a specific point), Line
(which allows the user to draw lines of
various types and thickness), Circle
(which asks for a center point and then
the radius or diameter), Polygon (which
asks for the point of placement and the
number of sides), Arc (which can ask for
a variety of methods to create the arc,
identify the points, identify the end-
points and radius, and so on), and Text
(which contains a variety of fonts or
styles and can be typed in any angle or
shape).

Common data editing commands are as
follows: Delete (which acts as a type of
eraser to delete lines or whole groups of
objects), Break (used to break out a
piece of line or circle), Move (which
allows the proper placement of a point or

8

object), Copy (which allows the user to
create multiple copies of a part of a
drawing, eliminating the need to redraw
the part), Zoom (which magnifies a user-
specified area to allow for greater
detailing), and Pan (which lets the user
stay on a specified magnetism and move to
other parts of the drawing).

All of these commands and many more
can be used to create or modify any type
of drawing, no matter how complex or
detailed.

Applications of MicroCADD. When discussing the applications of microCADD,
there are two levels of applications to
be concerned with. One is the design and
drafting level, in which fields such as
architecture, civil engineering, mechanical engineering, and so on are
considered. The other level looks at some
of the fields in which microCADD has
applications: architectural design and
drafting, construction design and drafting, survey drafting, electrical design
and drafting, mechanical design and
drafting, heating and cooling design and

9

drafting, and many more that may also be
in a subfield of these. Within these various fields, there are a variety of ways
in which microCADD is used: performing
calculations, collecting statistics,
developing models, storing reports, producing two- and three-dimensional
documentation, developing short- and
long-range planning models, making growth
projections, space analysis, cost analysis, and developing project management
documents.

MicroCADD is used in a variety of
different obvious areas that anyone could
think of and some areas that may not be
so obvious. Bethlehem Steel in Johnstown,
Pennsylvania, used an AutoCAD system to
design the huge rollers that turn steel
ingots into various structural shapes.
Johnson Wax Co. in Sturtevant, Wisconsin,
used a VersaCAD package to draft and lay
out designs for its plant. Hussy Seating
Co. of North Berwick, Maine, uses AutoCAD
in designing its popular folding bleach-
ers and let-down backboards found in
high-school gyms (Kalb 1987). McKinney

10

Homes in Houston, Texas, uses an AutoCAD
system in its home-building design and as
a managerial tool for estimating, cus-
tomizing, and marketing (Woodcock and
Binsacca 1987). MicroCADD is also used in
creating models that represent objects to
test the design on computer instead of
physically building a costly prototype
(Zinsmeister 1987). The police use micro-
CADD to create a crime scene, to find
crime patterns, and to create composite
drawings to identify crime suspects. As a
final example, dentists use microCADD to
plan oral surgery and to show patients
before-and-after pictures of how the
surgery will affect them.

  Future of MicroCADD   The future of
microCADD is thought to be limitless.
Prospects are being looked at to teach
microCADD to students with disabilities
or serious handicaps. The increase in the
use of microCADD systems will generate
new occupations for CADD operators to run
the equipment. Solid modeling and better
three-dimensional packages will be developed, allowing for a better represen-

11

tation of the solid nature of objects and more realistic shading of the object.

The rapid growth of microCADD has been so sudden that its applications have not fully been realized. Its continued growth will only better the development of the systems produced. Along with work being done with microcomputers (increase in speed and memory), the work in micro-CADD seems unlimited.

12

References

Goetsch, David L. MicroCADD: Computer-
    Aided Design and Drafting on
    Microcomputers. Englewood Cliffs,
    NJ: Prentice-Hall, 1988. Complete
    book on the development of micro-
    CADD. Tells a little bit of
    everything included in a microCADD
    system. A good book for those inter-
    ested in an overview of microCADD.

Kalb, Bill. "PC-Based CAD Sprouts Unusual
    Benefits." Chilton's Automotive
    Industries 167 (May 1987):104-108.
    Gives examples of companies that use
    CADD, how they use it, and how they
    feel it has helped, including price
    range for different setups.

Milburn, Ken. "CAD: Designs on Business."
    Personal Computing 21 (April 1988):
    108-124. Tells how microCADD works
    (commands). Describes and evaluates
    various microCADD software packages.

Stanton, Michael. "Computer Aided
    Design." Occupational Outlook Quar-
    terly 19 (Spring 1985):2-8. Future
    outlook of CADD and CADD operators
    for employment opportunities. States

13

that more education and training are
needed.

Teicholz, Eric, and Dan Smith. "State of
the Art." <u>Planning</u> 53 (Jan. 1987):
25-28. Tells of advantages of micro-
CADD over CADD. Describes the
contents of microCADD systems.

Woodcock, Deborah, and Richard Binsacca.
"Are Builders Ready for CADD?"
<u>Builder</u> 10 (Sept. 1987):54-55.
Describes CADD being used in architecture, what it's used for, and why
some still aren't using it.

Zinsmeister, George. "Computer-Aided
Design and Computer-Aided Manufacturing." <u>Academic American</u>
<u>Encyclopedia</u>, 2d ed. Danbury, Conn.:
Grolier, 1987. General description
of CADD and its various uses.

DISCIPLINE-SPECIFIC RESOURCES FOR BUSINESS AND ECONOMICS

General Sources and Guides to Literature

Business Information Sources. L. M. Daniells, Berkeley, CA: University of California Press, 1985. A guide to sources in business.

Economics and Foreign Policy: A Guide to Information Sources. M. R. Amstutz. Detroit: Gale, 1977. A bibliography of books and articles—annotated.

Guide to Library Research in Public Administration. A. E. Simpson. Washington, D.C.: National Center Public Products, 1976. Useful guide to the field of public administration.

Information Sources in Economics. 2nd ed. J. Fletcher. Stoneham, MA: Butterworth, 1984. Good starting place for recognized sources in economics.

Research Guide in Economics. C. E. Helppie, J. R. Gibbons, and D. W. Pearson. Morristown, NY: General Learning Press, 1974. A guide to research in economics for undergraduates.

Standard and Poor's Industry Surveys. New York: Standard and Poor's, 1959-present. A useful source for investment research. Detailed information on American industry.

Dictionaries

American Dictionary of Economics. D. Auld and G. Bannock. New York: Facts on File, 1983. Short, factual information on economics.

Dictionary of Accounting. R. Estes. Cambridge, MA: MIT Press, 1985. Defines key terms and concepts in accounting.

Dictionary of Advertising. S. R. Smith. New York: Fairchild, 1991. Defines key terms and concepts in advertising.

Dictionary of Business and Economics. C. Ammer and D. S. Ammer. New York: Free Press, 1984. Defines key terms and explains major economic theories.

McGraw-Hill Dictionary of Modern Economics: A Handbook of Terms and Organizations. 3rd. ed. New York: McGraw-Hill, 1983. Provides concise definitions of key terms and concepts in economics.

Mathematical Dictionary for Economics and Business Administration. W. Skrapek et al., eds. Boston: Allyn & Bacon, 1976. Defines mathematical terms and concepts important for business and economics.

New Palgrave: A Dictionary of Economics. 4 vols. J. Eatwell et al., eds. New York: Macmillan, 1987. A comprehensive dictionary of terms in economics.

VNR Concise Dictionary of Business and Finance. D. Brownstone et al. New York: Van Nostrand Reinhold, 1980.

Encyclopedias

Encyclopedia of Accounting Systems. Englewood Cliffs, NJ: Prentice-Hall, 1975. Provides concise analyses of accounting systems for various types of industry.

Encyclopedia of Banking and Finance. 9th ed. M. Glenn and F. Garcia. Boston: Bankers, 1990. Provides concise information on all aspects of banking and finance.

Encyclopedia of Business Information Sources. 10th ed. Detroit: Gale, 1994. Provides concise information and access to sources in business.

Encyclopedia of Management. 3rd ed. C. Heyel, ed. New York: Van Nostrand Reinhold, 1982. Concise information on many current business topics.

Biographies

Who's Who in Finance and Industry. 25th ed. Wilmette, IL: Marquis, 1988 plus annual updates. Biographical information.

(See also Biographies, pp. 30–31)

Almanacs, Yearbooks, Atlases, Handbooks

CBS News Almanac. New York: CBS News, annual. Contains newsworthy information from the previous year, as seen by CBS news correspondents.

Commodity YearBook. 1939–present (annual). Walter Emergy. New York: Commodity Research. Covers basic commodities and analyzes commodity trends.

Demographic Yearbook. 1948–present (annual). Washington, D.C.: Department of Economic and Social Affairs, United Nations Organization. Annual issues focus on a special topic, such as rates of population increase, life expectancy, birth and mortality rates, and so on.

Economic Handbook of the World. 1981 with updates to 1983. A. S. Banks et al., eds. New York: McGraw-Hill. Covers information on business, labor, and government.

The Municipal Year Book: An Authoritative Resume of Activities and Statistical Data of American Cities. 1934–present (annual). Washington, D.C.: International City Management Association. Provides information on questions and issues associated with local government and city management.

National Geographic Atlas of the World. 6th ed. Washington, D.C.: National Geographic Society, 1990. Provides detailed information about all countries on large-scale maps.

Statistical Abstract of the United States. 1879–present (annual). Washington, D.C.: U.S. Bureau of Census. Provides statistics on various industrial, social, political, economic, and cultural activities of the United States. This work includes information on every subject of public interest to Americans.

Indexes and Abstracts

ACCOUNTING

Accountants' Index
Commerce Clearinghouse of Accounting Articles

ADVERTISING AND MASS COMMUNICATIONS

Communication Abstracts

Topicator

BUSINESS—GENERAL

*ABI-INFORM
Business Education Index
Business Index
Business Periodicals Index
*Compact Disclosure

* = Computer searching available

Current Packaging Abstracts
*F & S Index of Corporations and
      Industries
*Public Affairs Information Services
      (PAIS)
Wall Street Journal Index
Work Related Abstracts

ECONOMIC—GENERAL

*Economic Titles/Abstracts
 Housing and Planning Reference
*Index of Economic Articles
 Journal of Economic Literature
*World Agricultural Economics and
      Rural Sociology Abstracts

PERSONNEL MANAGEMENT

Personnel Literature
Personnel Management Abstracts

Index

✦ ✦ ✦

The abbreviation f stands for figure